Traditionally, human cognition has been seen as existing solely "inside" a person's head, and studies on cognition have by and large disregarded the social, physical, and artifactual surroundings in which cognition takes place. Recently, however, research in cognition and in such fields as anthropology and cultural psychology has compelled us to reexamine our preconceptions. The essays in this volume propose that a clearer understanding of human cognition would be achieved if studies were based on the concept that cognition is *distributed* among individuals, that knowledge is socially constructed through collaborative efforts to achieve shared objectives in cultural surroundings, and that information is processed between individuals and the tools and artifacts provided by culture.

Although the phenomenon of distributed cognitions is a wide-ranging one with provocative consequences for theories of the mind, learning, and education, it has not yet been thoroughly examined. When "distributed cognitions" are the units of analysis for research and theory construction about reasoning and learning, several questions arise: What exactly is distributed and how does it become distributed? Are all cognitions always distributed? How do the distributed qualities of the mind relate to the ones that are still "inside" it? What constraints govern the dynamics of such distribution? In addressing these questions, this volume reveals their importance for such educational issues as the cultivation of mental skills, the acquisition of knowledge, and the role of social interaction and intelligent tools in the learning process.

# Distributed cognitions

# Learning in doing: Social, cognitive, and computational perspectives

GENERAL EDITORS: ROY PEA
JOHN SEELY BROWN

# Distributed cognitions

## Psychological and educational considerations

*Edited by*

GAVRIEL SALOMON
*University of Haifa, Israel*

CAMBRIDGE
UNIVERSITY PRESS

PUBLISHED BY THE PRESS SYNDICATE OF THE UNIVERSITY OF CAMBRIDGE
The Pitt Building, Trumpington Street, Cambridge, United Kingdom

CAMBRIDGE UNIVERSITY PRESS
The Edinburgh Building, Cambridge CB2 2RU, UK
40 West 20th Street, New York, NY 10011-4211, USA
10 Stamford Road, Oakleigh, VIC 3166, Australia
Ruiz de Alarcón 13, 28014 Madrid, Spain
Dock House, The Waterfront, Cape Town 8001, South Africa

http://www.cambridge.org

First published 1993
First paperback edition 1997
Reprinted 2001

Typeset in Ehrhardt

*A catalog record for this book is available from the British Library*

*Library of Congress Cataloging in Publication Data is available*

ISBN 0 521 41406 7 hardback
ISBN 0 521 57423 4 paperback

Transferred to digital printing 2003

# Contents

# Contributors

Doris Ash
University of California,
  Berkeley
School of Education
Berkeley, California

Ann L. Brown
University of California,
  Berkeley
School of Education
Berkeley, California

Joseph C. Campione
University of California,
  Berkeley
School of Education
Berkeley, California

Michael Cole
University of California, San
  Diego
Laboratory of Comparative
  Human Cognition
La Jolla, California

Yrjö Engeström
University of California, San
  Diego
Laboratory of Comparative
  Human Cognition
La Jolla, California

Howard Gardner
Harvard University
Graduate School of
  Education / Project Zero
Cambridge, Massachusetts

Ann Gordon
University of California,
  Berkeley
School of Education
Berkeley, California

Thomas Hatch
Harvard University
Graduate School of
  Education / Project Zero
Cambridge, Massachusetts

Louis C. Moll
University of Arizona
College of Education
Tucson, Arizona

Kathryn Nakagawa
University of California,
   Berkeley
School of Education
Berkeley, California

Raymond S. Nickerson
5 Gleason Rd.
Bedford, Massachusetts

Roy D. Pea
Northwestern University
Institute for the Learning
   Sciences
Evanston, Illinois

D. N. Perkins
Harvard University
Graduate School of
   Education / Project Zero
Cambridge, Massachusetts

Martha Rutherford
University of California
   Berkeley
School of Education
Berkeley, California

Gavriel Salomon
University of Haifa
School of Education
Haifa, Israel

Javier Tapia
University of Arizona
College of Education
Tucson, Arizona

Kathryn F. Whitmore
University of Arizona
College of Education
Tucson, Arizona

# Series foreword

This series for Cambridge University Press is becoming widely known as an international forum for studies of situated learning and cognition.

Innovative contributions are being made by anthropology, by cognitive, developmental, and cultural psychology, by computer science, by education, and by social theory. These contributions are providing the basis for new ways of understanding the social, historical, and contextual nature of the learning, thinking, and practice emerging from human activity. The empirical settings of these research inquiries range from the classroom, to the workplace, to the high-technology office, to learning in the streets and in other communities of practice.

The situated nature of learning and remembering through activity is a central fact. It may appear obvious that human minds develop in social situations, and that they come to appropriate the tools that culture provides to support and extend their sphere of activity and communicative competencies. But cognitive theories of knowledge representation and learning alone have not provided sufficient insight into these relationships.

This series was born of the conviction that new and exciting interdisciplinary syntheses are under way, as scholars and practitioners from diverse fields seek to develop theory and empirical investigations adequate for characterizing the complex relations of social and mental life, and for understanding successful learning wherever it occurs. The series invites contributions that advance our understanding of these seminal issues.

Roy Pea
John Seely Brown

# Editor's introduction

The idea for this book was born in stages. It all began on the beach of Tortola, the British Virgin Islands, in the summer of 1989, where three of us – David Perkins, Roy Pea, and myself – participated in a small conference about computers and learning convened by the Social Science Research Council. Perkins spoke there of representations for mathematics and science learning, I spoke of intellectual partnerships with computers, and Pea introduced the idea of distributed cognitions. It became immediately evident that the three of us, while sharing similar concerns, had different views about distributed cognitions and the purposes of education. We thought of this diversity of views as providing a potentially unique opportunity for stimulating debate and raising new questions. We created such an opportunity by planning a symposium at the 1990 American Educational Research Association conference in Boston. The participants in this symposium – Ann Brown, Jerome Bruner, Roy Pea, David Perkins, and myself – decided then that the ideas formulated and presented there, together with the ideas of other scholars in the field, would constitute an interesting, thought-provoking book. This is the book you are holding in your hands, a fine product of distributed cognitions.

A scholarly community often settles on an agreed-upon way to view a phenomenon and a unit of analysis to match, and then studies the phenomenon in ways that are congruent with that consensually held conception. The more such research is done, the more the initial conception appears valid and "correct," supporting the prevailing view of that phenomenon. Karl Weick (1979) has commented that, as consensus grows, the views become "refractory to disproof" and appear to be so self-evident that alternatives are rarely discussed. But then, for whatever reason, the phenomenon suddenly becomes examined in a new context, which, quite disturbingly, requires new units of analysis, leading in turn to the formulation of new perceptions and definitions of that phenomenon. The result is the birth of a new phenomenon.

Consider, for example, the current state of memory research. In a recently published debate about the validity and scientific merits of research on memory in real-life situations, Banaji and Crowder (1989) argued that "the more complex a phenomenon, the greater the need to study it under controlled conditions, and the less it ought to be studied in its natural complexity" (p. 1192). This position assumes, of course, that the phenomenon studied under tightly controlled conditions is the *same* as the one encountered in real-life circumstances. Unfortunately for that approach, memory (like other psychological phenomena) changes profoundly in nature, appearance, and function when studied in its natural complexity, as contrasted with its study under highly controlled conditions. The laboratory-based study of episodic memory, as Conway (1991) points out, although ostensibly examining the same phenomenon as the study of autobiographical memory, is *in fact* a study of something quite different: Everyday, autobiographical memory deals with memory infused with prior knowledge and personal meanings, which the memory-in-the-lab arrangement tries to "control for." This contrast, then, raises a principled issue that transcends the specific boundaries of memory research: Changing the unit of analysis or changing the context in which a phenomenon is studied may reveal a qualitatively different phenomenon (e.g., Ceci & Bronfenbrenner, 1991).

There is a striking parallel between the study of memory in the two contexts and the study of cognition in the laboratory versus its study in daily-life settings. Traditionally, the study of cognitive processes, cognitive development, and the cultivation of educationally desirable skills and competencies has treated everything cognitive as being *possessed* and residing *in the heads* of individuals; social, cultural, and technological factors have been relegated to the role of backdrops or external sources of stimulation. This perception is fine as far as it goes, allowing us to examine in great detail some specific mechanisms of information processing, problem solving, and learning. But once human behavior is examined in real-life problem-solving situations and in other encounters with the social and technological surrounds, a rather different phenomenon emerges: People appear *to think in conjunction or partnership* with others and with the help of culturally provided tools and implements. Cognitions, it would seem, are not content-free tools that are brought to bear on this or that problem; rather, they emerge in a situation tackled by teams of people and the tools available to them (e.g., Lave & Wenger, 1991). Consider a team that works cooperatively to plan a political campaign, an economic planner who does her thinking with a powerful computerized spreadsheet, or a student who studies history while filling out note cards, marking the margins of the textbook, and constructing on paper "networks" of facts to remember. The thinking of these individuals might be considered to entail not just "solo" cognitive activities but *distributed* ones. As Perkins points out in Chapter 3 of this volume, what characterizes such daily events of thinking is that the social and artifactual surrounds, alleged to be "outside" the individuals' heads, not only are sources of stimulation and guidance but are actually *vehicles of thought.* Moreover, the arrangements, functions, and structures of these surrounds change in the process to become genuine *parts of the learning* that results from the cognitive partnership with them. In other words, it is not just the "person-solo" who learns, but the "person-plus," the whole system of interrelated factors.

The idea of distributed cognitions is not necessarily new. As Cole and Engeström show in Chapter 1, one could find its origins in the writings of turn-of-the-century psychologists and philosophers (see also Phillips, 1976). For example, Dewey wrote more than a century ago: "The idea of environment is a necessity to the idea of organism, and with the conception of environment comes the impossibility of considering psychical life as an individual, isolated thing developing in a vacuum" (1884, p. 285).

There is an interesting affinity between the consideration of cognitions as socially and culturally distributed and the study of human behavior as part of a wider system entailing cultural, social, situational, and technological elements. Such functionally oriented study would treat individual *and* environment, social, cultural, or physical, as integrated units, such that the activities of the individual would be seen as "processes of the full situation of organism-environment"

(Dewey & Bentley, 1946, p. 256). But this approach was often associated with "holistic," "soft," and qualitative modes of inquiry, closer to anthropology than to "hard-core" scientific psychology. No wonder therefore that it was (and to some extent continues to be) in the shadow of mainstream psychological and educational research, which emphasizes individuals' behaviors and cognitions while largely disregarding their distributed nature.

Perceptions are changing. With a growing acceptance of a constructivist view of human cognitions comes a serious examination of the possibility that cognitions are situated and distributed rather than decontextualized tools and products of mind. Accompanying this possibility is the acknowledgment not only that social and other situational factors have a strong impact on "in-the-head" cognitions but that social processes should be treated *as* cognitions (Resnick, 1991).

Such conceptual changes do not emerge out of nowhere. A cursory examination of recent developments in cognitive and mainly educational-cognitive thought suggests at least three sources for the surge of interest in distributed cognitions. One is the increasingly important role that activities with computer tools have come to play in handling intellectual tasks. It becomes observable, if not patently evident, that the collaboration of individuals and computers is often characterized by intellectually superior performance that cannot easily be accounted for by individuals' cognitions alone (Salomon, Perkins, & Globerson, 1991). A second source appears to be the growing interest in Vygotsky's cultural-historical theory, a theory that situates individuals' cognitions *within*, rather than just interacting with, social and cultural contexts of interaction and activity (e.g., Moll, 1991). A third source appears to be the growing dissatisfaction with cognitions as in-the-head tools, shifting focus to their situated, context-dependent, and thus potentially distributed nature (Brown, Collins, & Duguid, 1989; Lave & Wenger, 1991).

If social and possibly other "external" processes are to be taken as integral parts of the cognitive process, maybe the whole concept of cognitions ought to be reexamined. Are they perhaps distributed rather than located in the head? And if intellectual processes and products can be seen as being distributed among individuals or between individuals and culturally provided implements, may it not also be the case that intelligence is an emerging quality rather than a "possession"?

Serious consideration of the notion of distributed cognitions opens up a whole range of questions and suggests a long list of provocative implications for education. This book is an attempt to explicate, illustrate, and critically examine the idea of distributed cognitions in its general and educational manifestations. If cognitions and cognitive abilities are not to be seen as "wired" possessions but as situationally, socially emerging qualities, what exactly are they? How do cognitions become distributed? What is distributed about them? What compels us to acknowledge that cognitions are (sometimes?) distributed? How are cognitions distributed in different situations and in different activities? Given the distribution of cognitions, what role, if any, do we want to ascribe to individuals' "solo" cognitions? How does the distribution of cognitions differ from "division of labor," "sharing of ideas," or "mutual stimulation"? How can we identify distributed cognitions, and where would it be most interesting and useful to look for them? Educationally, what of the cultivation of cognitive abilities and proclivities if these are not to be seen as the developing possessions of the individual? If cognitive performance is a distributed quality, what should education's goals be? How should the learning environment be designed? What should be examined and studied? What roles should teachers play and what role students?

The contributors to this volume are not of the same mind, nor do they necessarily share the exact meaning of the term "distributed cognitions." In this sense, this book is an attempt to raise questions and start a debate rather than present a unified view with worked-out implications. The authors have different opinions as to how individuals' cognitions should be dealt with once the reality of distributed cognitions is partly or fully acknowledged. In fact, the authors present two somewhat different conceptions of distributed cognitions. One such conception, perhaps the more radical, is presented by Cole and Engeström, Pea, and Moll, Tapia, and Whitmore. According to their view, while individuals' cognitions are not to be dismissed, cognition *in general* should be reexamined and conceived as principally distributed. As pointed out elsewhere by Cole (1991), the proper unit of psychological analysis should be the *joint* (often, but not necessarily) *socially mediated activity* in a cultural context. This might be taken as the strong version of distributed cognition, since it proposes a deviation from the common view that cognitions are possessed by individuals and serve as tools ready for application in daily situations.

The second, less radical conception is presented by Perkins, Salomon, Hatch and Gardner, and Brown et al. According to them, "solo" and distributed cognitions are still distinguished from each other and are taken to be in an interdependent dynamic interaction.

The eight chapters of this book are of two kinds. The first four are mainly theoretical. The next three are partly theoretical as well, but their main focus is on specific educational case studies of distributed cognition. The book ends with a critical examination of the concept and its potential contribution to the study of cognition and to education.

Leading the theoretical part of the book is Chapter 1, by Cole and Engeström. The authors examine the origins of the distributed-cognitions idea, tracing it back to the writings of Wundt and Münsterberg. In the light of these roots and the cultural-historical theories of such scholars as Vygotsky and Luria, Cole and Engeström present the argument that cognitions are to be seen as culturally mediated, part of whole activity systems that include culture, community, tools, and their self-regulatory counterparts – symbols. Inspired by recent anthropological work, Cole and Engeström extend the cultural-historical view by noting that cognitions are distributed in the medium of culture, whereby "the combination of goals, tools, and setting . . . constitute simultaneously the context of behavior and the ways in which cognition can be said to be distributed in that context." Cole and Engeström also point out how cognitions are distributed neuropsychologically – different parts of the brain process different kinds of experiences and stimuli, socially and temporally. The presentation of two detailed examples, the acquisition of reading (in which cognitions are distributed among teacher, learner, other learners, and cultural artifacts) and the reorganization of medical work in a Finnish clinic (working through a new division of labor among the health-care providers so that the distributed cognitive resources of the system will be better exploited), allows the authors to show that once the idea of mediation through artifacts and other individuals is seen as a central distinctive characteristic of humans, the adoption of the distributed view of cognitions is inescapable.

Chapter 2, by Pea, is intended to provoke new inquiries. Pea disagrees with the widespread, indeed dominant, conception of intelligence as the property of the mind. Rather, he argues, intelligence is to be seen as *accomplished* rather than *possessed*. Distributed intelligence, as Pea sees it, is ever present in the tools, modes of representation, and other artifacts we create to off-load what would otherwise be a heavy and error-prone cognitive burden. According to Pea, the phenomenon of distributed cognitions makes apparent how external resources change the nature and functional system from which activities emerge, profoundly affecting our conception of what, how, and why one needs to know. The goal of having everyone possess the knowledge of, say, long division or the multiplication table gives way to the goal of estimation and problem solving – activities of reasoning with tools rather than independently of them. It follows that one would wish to place greater emphasis on access to tools to think with than on solo understanding without tools, on partnership rather than on the cultivation of in-the-head cognitions. Clearly, computer tools and programs designed to cater to distributed cognitions, emphasizing partnership and access, will be very different from tools aimed at the cultivation of solo abilities. This, then, is likely to change the conception of educational goals from mastery to jointly accomplished performance.

Perkins (Chapter 3) generally accepts the notion of distributed cognitions as a system that entails both person and surround, a new unit of analysis that jointly participates in thinking as well as learning. To this conception he applies the *equivalent access hypothesis*, according to which what is important is the kind of *knowledge* present, the way it is *represented*, how readily it is *retrieved*, and how it is *constructed*, rather than where all this takes place. To the extent that a joint system, the "person-plus," entails the four access characteristics, it does not much matter where the knowledge, the representation, or the construction resides. Using this framework, Perkins examines the way the executive functions, on the one hand, and higher-order knowledge of a field, on the other, are distributed. While the former can and often are socially distributed (they are ceded to teachers and textbooks), higher-order knowledge, in the form of heuristics, patterns of explanation, and modes of inquiry, is represented nowhere and cannot become distributed; it does not meet the four access criteria except *within* the person-solo. It follows that while many cognitions are often distributed, particularly during inquiry activities, not all cognitions can be so distributed. Higher-order knowledge, a crucial element in mastering a field and in the operations of the executive functions, is a matter of the person-solo.

In Chapter 4, the last theoretical chapter, I go one step further in raising critical questions about the radical version of distributed cognitions. I argue that not all cognitions are *constantly* distributed, not all of them *can* be distributed, and no cognitive theory, particularly one that attempts to account for *developments and changes* over time, can do without reference to individuals' mental representations (or their equivalents). These, after all, are the "substance" that enter into situations of distributed cognitions. Having arrived at this conclusion, I offer an interactive, spiral-like dynamic view of how "solo" and distributed cognitions interact over time, affecting each other and developing from each other. In this way, I overcome the situational determinism I see in the radical view of distributed cognitions and the intrapersonal determinism in radical solo views of cognition. Elaboration of this interactive approach, in turn, suggests implications for the selection of educational goals – the cultivation of partnership together with the cultivation of solo capabilities – as well as for educational design.

In the first of the three case-study chapters (Chapter 5), Moll, Tapia, and Whitmore employ the prism of (mainly socially) distributed cognitions to examine qualitatively two activity settings that offer distributed "funds of knowledge": a household of a Mexican-American family close to the Mexican border and a whole-language classroom in which socially mediated learning activities are an organizing principle. The purpose of the chapter's ethnographic studies is to translate the conceptual notions of distributed cognitions into specific dynamics of distributed cognitive resources. Examination of the family household reveals how active it is in coping and how interconnected it is with other households with which it shares and exchanges knowledge, skills, and other resources needed for their daily functioning. The story of the classroom reflects a similar distribution of intellectually shared resources. Social processes and cultural resources mediate learning activities, thereby manifesting the socially shared nature of learning.

Another case is provided by Hatch and Gardner in Chapter 6. Unlike the anthropologically oriented work of Moll and associates, the case that Hatch and Gardner present is aligned with a child-development tradition. Hatch and Gardner challenge the prevailing view of intelligence as a unitary, in-the-head, and stable possession of the individual. They suggest that three interdependent forces contribute to cognitions in the classroom: personal, local, and cultural. The three are seen as concentrically arranged, such that the personal forces are at the core and the cultural ones serve as the outer circle. Intelligence, enmeshed as it is in all of a person's activities, reflects the influences of the local affordances and constraints, the cultural values and expectations, and the personal proclivities and accumulated experiences. This concentric model is examined in a child-centered kindergarten in which four children are observed for a number of months during free play at the sand table and the art table. The authors draw two important conclusions from their detailed observations. First, although personal, solo forces play an important role in the authors' scheme, they are seen to reflect the cultural and local forces at work in the settings and activities in which the children are engaged. Changes and variations in the cultural and local forces are thus reflected in changed and diverse manifestations of intelligence, which thus explains the variability in human performance. Second, the way the personal forces become manifested and possibly developed is greatly dependent on the local and cultural forces, thus highlighting the extent to which such intelligence can be said to be locally and culturally determined.

Chapter 7 by Brown and her associates complements the anthropologically and more developmentally oriented case studies with an instructional intervention study. The authors describe how a classroom learning environment can be designed and implemented to foster a community of learners who engage in guided appropriation of meanings through mutual negotiations, thus gradually creating a *distributed network of expertise.* Such environments are places where students learn to learn, becoming "intelligent novices" who – in their interactions with teachers, peers, materials, and computer tools – create overlapping zones of proximal development. The question of distributed cognitions thus shifts from where cognitions reside to how the classroom can be so designed as to foster the development of a community of discourse in which expertise becomes distributed in ways that provide the seeding ground for mutual appropriation. The authors provide a detailed description of such classroom design, anchored in theoretical constructs that support its psychologic.

The book ends with Nickerson's discussion in Chapter 8 of each of the chapters and a critical examination of the concept of distributed cognitions and its implications. Nickerson asks what is new about the concept of cognition and intelligence as distributed, what new theoretical and practical mileage it affords, and where it leads us. He then offers some middle ground on which both individuals' and distributed cognitions could be jointly considered.

So heated conversations initially held on the Tortola beach have gradually matured into formulated positions that can be accompanied by real-life examples and appropriate manifestations in medical clinics, households, kindergartens, and classrooms. I hope that the assortment of theoretical positions and case studies presented here will stimulate further debate and exchange of ideas. If nothing else, I hope that this volume will shake the dust off old notions and long-cherished conceptions, thereby contributing new and exciting ideas to the domain of cognition and intelligence as they pertain to educational matters.

### References

Banaji, M. R., & Crowder, R. G. (1989). The bankruptcy of everyday memory. *American Psychologist, 44,* 1185–93.

Brown, J. S., Collins, A., & Duguid, P. (1989). Situated cognitions and the culture of learning. *Educational Researcher, 18,* 32–42.

Ceci, S. J., & Bronfenbrenner, U. (1991). On the demise of everyday memory: "The rumors of my death are much exaggerated" (Mark Twain). *American Psychologist, 46,* 27–31.

Cole, M. (1991). On socially shared cognitions. In L. Resnick, J. Levine, & S. Behrend (Eds.), *Socially shared cognitions* (pp. 398–417). Hillsdale, NJ: Erlbaum.

Conway, M. A. (1991). In defense of everyday memory. *American Psychologist, 46,* 19–26.

Dewey, J. (1884). The new psychology. *Andover Review, 2.*

Dewey, J., & Bentley, A. F. (1946). Interaction and transaction. *Journal of Philosophy, 43,* 505–17.

Lave, J., & Wenger, E. (1991). *Situated learning.* Cambridge University Press.

Moll, L. C. (1991). Introduction. In L. C. Moll (Ed.), *Vygotsky and education.* Cambridge University Press.

Phillips, D. C. (1976). *Holistic thought in social science.* Stanford, CA: Stanford University Press.

Resnick, L. B. (1991). Shared cognition: Thinking as social practice. In L. Resnick, J. Levine, & S. Behrend (Eds.), *Socially shared cognitions* (pp. 1–19). Hillsdale, NJ: Erlbaum.

Salomon, G., Perkins, D. N., & Globerson, T. (1991). Partners in cognition: Extending human intelligence with intelligent technologies. *Educational Researcher, 20,* 10–16.

Weick, K. E. (1979). *The social psychology of organizing.* Reading, MA: Addison-Wesley.

# 1    A cultural-historical approach to distributed cognition

*Michael Cole and Yrjö Engeström*

It was supposedly Goethe who observed that everything has been thought of before; the task is to think of it again in ways that are appropriate to one's current circumstances. Whoever made the remark, we have thought of it often in relation to the current wave of discovery that both the content and process of thinking (however those slippery terms are interpreted) are distributed as much among individuals as they are packed within them.

Our own rediscovery of the distributed nature of mind has grown from our acquaintance with the cultural-historical school of psychology. Consequently, we have decided to explore approaches to distributed cognition by tracing this line of thinking back to the origins of psychology as a distinct discipline, by relating how it was developed by the cultural-historical school of psychology earlier in this century, and by suggesting the advantages of working within the cultural-historical framework (informed by modern cognitive psychology, anthropology, and sociology) when studying cognition as a distributed phenomenon.

## Wundt's version of distributed cognition

Around the time that psychology was celebrating its centennial as a scientific discipline, there was a good deal of discussion about the work of Wilhelm Wundt – according to the discipline's folklore, the "father" of scientific psychology (Blumenthal, 1980; Farr, 1987; Toulmin, 1981). Among the many issues raised in this reevaluation was the failure of modern psychologists to realize that virtually half of Wundt's writings were devoted not to the study of elementary sensations using brass instruments and the method

1

of trained introspection, but to the study of historically accumulated, culturally organized knowledge as revealed in the written accounts of explorers and early anthropologists as well as the analyses provided by philologists and historians (Wundt, 1921).

The better known half of Wundt's dual system was called "physiological psychology," the study of immediate experience based on the experimental method. The goal of this half of the discipline was to determine how elementary sensations arise in consciousness and the universal laws by which the elements of consciousness combine. The label "physiological" for this half of Wundt's enterprise is somewhat misleading, because experiments carried out in its name rarely involved physiological measurement. Rather, it was believed that the verbal reports of subjects who were presented carefully controlled stimuli would yield results that could eventually be traced to physiological processes. Experiments conducted with this goal in mind concentrated on the qualities of sensory experience and the decomposition of simple reactions into their components. The psychological processes corresponding to external stimulation were presumed to take place inside of individual people's heads.

The other half of Wundt's system involved the study of "higher psychological functions," including processes of reasoning and the products of human language. Wundt claimed that this second branch of psychology, which he called *Völkerpsychologie*, could not be studied using laboratory methods focused on the contents of consciousness, because the phenomena being studied extend beyond individual human consciousness. He argued, for example:

A language can never be created by an individual. True, individuals have invented Esperanto and other artificial languages. Unless, however, language had already existed, these inventions would have been impossible. Moreover, none of these has been able to maintain itself, and most of them owe their existence solely to elements borrowed from natural languages. (Wundt, 1921, p. 3)

According to Wundt's view, higher psychological functions had to be studied by the methods of the descriptive sciences, such as ethnography, folklore, and linguistics. The results were to be formulated in terms of historically contingent phenomena that could be described but not explained according to the canons of experimental science. Wundt believed that the two enterprises must supplement each other; only through a synthesis of their respective insights could a full psychology be achieved. To those who would claim that *Völk-erpsychologie* could be entirely subsumed under experimental psychology, Wundt replied that "individual consciousness is wholly incapable of giving us a history of the development of human thought, for it is conditioned by an earlier history concerning which it cannot of itself give us any knowledge" (Wundt, 1921, p. 3). In modern terms, Wundt was arguing that while elementary psychological functions may be considered to occur "in the head," higher psychological functions require additional cognitive resources that are to be found in the sociocultural milieu.

The same folklore that tells us that Wundt was the founding father of the discipline also holds that within a few decades Wundt's influence dwindled to insignificance; his methodology was rejected and his distinction between physiological/experimental and cultural/descriptive approaches was ignored. However, there is no mistaking the fact that those currently interested in distributed cognition have rediscovered some of Wundt's ideas, especially his ideas about *Völkerpsychologie*, the methods for its study, and the difficulty of reconciling data obtained from the two ways of knowing about minds.

### Hugo Münsterberg

In view of the fact that many of the people who study distributed cognition gather their data from socially valued, practical activities, such as those that occur in schools, hospitals, and the workplace, it is interesting that Hugo Münsterberg, the "father of applied psychology," fully adhered to Wundt's dual-psychology distinction and provided one of the earliest systematic statements of the distributed nature of cognition. Münsterberg (1914, p. 16) referred to the experimental half of Wundt's program as "causal" psychology and the descriptive half as "purposive" psychology, warning that it was "extremely important to keep them cleanly separated and to recognize distinctly the principles which control them."

In connection with his discussion of the purposive half of psychology, Münsterberg (1914) argued that cognition occurs not only "in the head," where millions of brain cells interact outside the range of consciousness to "remember for us," "to think for us," "to will for us," but in the objective elements of communication among individuals:

A letter, a newspaper, a book, exists outside of the individuals themselves, and yet it intermediates between two or between millions of persons in the social group. . . . The book remembers for the social group, and the experiences of the group, objectively recorded in it, shape the social action and the social thought. The letter can connect any distant social neurons; the paper may distribute the excitement from one point of a social group to millions of others. Every objectified expression becomes a social short cut. (pp. 267–8)

Although there is a renewed interest in the ideas of these pioneer psychologists (see, e.g., Cahan & White, 1992; Farr, 1987; Toulmin, 1981), the overall programs they espoused did not give rise to any recognizable, modern approach to human cognition.[1] History (thus far) has been kinder to the originators of the cultural-historical approach associated with the names of Alexei Leont'ev, Alexander Luria, and Lev Vygotsky.

## The cultural-historical approach

The basic ideas of cultural-historical psychology are contained in a series of articles and monographs written in the late 1920s and early 1930s (Leont'ev, 1932; Luria, 1928, 1932; Vygotsky, 1929, 1960). While remaining firmly committed to a Darwinian theory of human phylogeny, one of the central tenets of the cultural-historical school is that "the process of the historical development of human behavior and the process of biological evolution do not coincide; one is not a continuation of the other. Rather, each of these processes is governed by its own laws" (Vygotsky, 1960, p. 71).

The presumed qualitative discontinuity between human and animal development is characterized in a variety of interlocking ways by the initiators of the cultural-historical school. In the first article about

[1] A possible exception to this generalization is John Dewey. Although Dewey cannot be considered a major influence in contemporary cognitive psychology, his ideas about education and development continue to be influential among social scientists. In a small book summarizing his ideas about education and experience, Dewey (1938/1963) wrote the following: "Experience does not go on simply inside a person. . . . In a word, we live from birth to death in a world of persons and things which is in large measure what it is because of what has been done and transmitted from previous human activities. When this fact is ignored, experience is treated as if it were something which goes on exclusively inside an individual's body and mind. It ought not to be necessary to say that experience does not occur in a vacuum. There are sources outside an individual which give rise to experience" (p. 39).

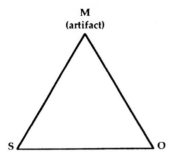

Figure 1.1. The basic mediational triangle with subject (S), object (O), and medium (M) at its vertices indicating the basic constraints on mind.

the school's ideas to appear in English, Alexander Luria opens with the well-known assertion that "man differs from animals in that he can make and use tools." These tools, he writes, "not only radically change his conditions of existence, they even react on him in that they effect a change in him and his psychic condition" (Luria, 1928, p. 493).

The structural change that arises pari passu with tool mediation is that "instead of applying directly its natural function to the solution of a particular task, the child puts between that function and the task a certain auxiliary means . . . by the medium of which the child manages to perform the task" (Luria, 1928, p. 495). The basic structure of human cognition that results from tool mediation has traditionally been pictured as a triangle, as in Figure 1.1.

Simplifying for purposes of explication, "natural" ("unmediated") functions are those along the base of the triangle; "cultural" ("mediated") functions are those where interactions between subject and object are mediated by an auxiliary means, at the vertex of the triangle. While Luria's initial statement seems to imply that the cultural route totally replaces the natural route, in many places in his writings and those of his colleagues it is made clear that both routes exist simultaneously. Such a conclusion is necessary because human beings do not cease being phylogenetically evolved creatures by virtue of their ability to create, transmit, and acquire culture.

The way in which Luria writes about tool mediation may incline one to think that he had in mind such tools as hoes and plates. However, he and his colleagues considered language to be an integral part of the overall process of cultural mediation, the "tool of tools," and they had a decidedly two-sided notion of tool mediation. As Vygotsky explains in his monograph "Tool and Symbol" (1978), what we conventionally call tools and what we conventionally call symbols are two aspects of the same phenomenon: Mediation through tools was said to be more outwardly oriented, mediation through signs was more inwardly oriented, toward "the self," but both aspects adhered in every cultural artifact.

Many years later, Luria (1981) summarized the psychological consequences of culturally mediated behavior, referring in particular to human language, as follows:

> The enormous advantage is that their world doubles. In the absence of words, human beings would have to deal only with those things which they could perceive and manipulate directly. With the help of language, they can deal with things that they have not perceived even indirectly and with things which were part of the experience of earlier generations. Thus, the world adds another dimension to the world of humans. . . . Animals have only one world, the world of objects and situations. Humans have a double world. (p. 35)

Here we see clearly that the classical mediational triangle is a description of the basic structural constraints on individual human cognition. But such a static description leaves out the dynamic, double world of which Luria writes. Consequently, we have to add another dimension to this structural picture – time – in the course of which the two worlds (the directly given and the culturally mediated) are constantly synthesized to provide the mental foundations of people's real-time actions in the world. This expanded version of the basic mediational triangle is shown in Figure 1.2, which emphasizes the fact that cognition requires analysis and synthesis of (at least) two sources of information in real time.

An important implication of these remarks is the assumption that other human beings, both those present to the senses and those of prior generations, play a crucial role in the formation of human cognitive capacities. This point is summed up in what Vygotsky (1934/1987) called the "general law of cultural development":

> The history of the development of signs brings us, however, to a far more general law that directs the development of behavior. Janet calls it the fundamental law in psychology. The essence of the law is that the child in the process of development begins to apply to himself the very same forms of behavior which others applied to him prior

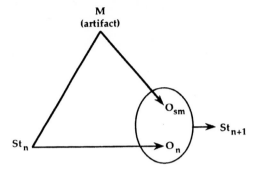

Figure 1.2. The basic mediational triangle with time included in the unit of analysis. This figure symbolizes the fact that new states of the subject arise from coordination of information from both the mediated (cultural) and direct (phylogentic) connections between subject and object. M, Medium; $St_n$, subject's state of knowledge at time $n$; $O_{sm}$, object as represented via the medium; $O_n$, object at time $n$; $St_{n+1}$, emergent new state of subject's knowledge at time $n + 1$.

to that. The child himself acquires social forms of behavior and transposes those on to himself. . . . The sign originally is always a means of social contact, a means of influence upon others, and only subsequently does it find itself in the role of a means for influencing oneself. (Vygotsky, 1960, p. 192)

Although useful as schematic "minimal structures" of human cognitive functions, the mediational triangles in Figures 1.1 and 1.2 fail to account for the collective nature of human activities, or activity systems as Leont'ev (1978, 1981) called them. In Figure 1.3 we have added certain crucial elements to the abstract, individual model depicted in Figures 1.1 and 1.2. First, the fact that individuals ("subject") are constituted in communities is indicated by the point labeled "community." As indicated in Figure 1.3, the relations between subject and community are mediated, on the one hand, by the group's full collection of "mediating artifacts" and, on the other hand, by "rules" (the norms and sanctions that specify and regulate the expected correct procedures and acceptable interactions among the participants). Communities, in turn, imply a "division of labor," the continuously negotiated distribution of tasks, powers, and responsibilities among the participants of the activity system.

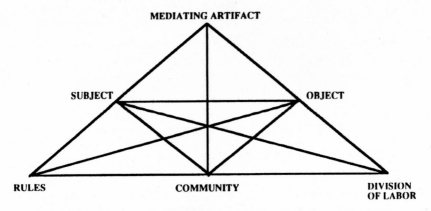

Figure 1.3. The basic mediational triangle expanded (after Engeström, 1987) to include other people (community), social rules (rules), and the division of labor between the subject and others.

Using Figure 1.3 to represent the idea that activity systems are a basic unit of analysis leads to certain important insights. First, it provides a conceptual map to the major loci among which human cognition is distributed. Second, it includes other people who must somehow be taken into account simultaneously with the subject as constituents of human activity systems.

Another important feature of activity as a basic unit of analysis of human behavior is that when activities become institutionalized, they are rather robust and enduring. Once they gain the status of cultural practices, they often have radically longer half-lives than an individual goal-directed action. In fact, activity systems such as those that take place in schools and doctors' offices, for example, appear to reproduce similar actions and outcomes over and over again in a seemingly monotonous and repetitive manner that gives cultural constraints on action a seemingly overpowering quality. However, closer analysis of apparently unchanging activity systems reveals that transitions and reorganizations are constantly going on within and between activity systems as a fundamental part of the dynamics of human evolution.

Consequently, activity systems are best viewed as complex formations in which equilibrium is an exception and tensions, disturbances, and local innovations are the rule and the engine of change. When an activity system is followed through time, qualitative overall transformations may also be found. Institutionalized activity systems seem to move through developmental cycles that typically last years (Engeström, 1987).

We can summarize the cultural-historical conception of the basic structure of human activity as follows:

1.  The psychological functions shared with our prehuman cousins, so-called natural functions, develop according to principles that are different from psychological functions that are mediated through tools and rules – for example, "cultural" functions.
2.  Cultural mediation creates a species-specific, universal structure of human mind and associated morphology of action.
3.  Cultural mediation has a recursive, bidirectional effect; mediated activity simultaneously modifies both the environment and the subject.
4.  Cultural artifacts are both material and symbolic; they regulate interaction with one's environment and oneself. In this respect, they are "tools" broadly conceived, and the master tool is language.
5.  The cultural environment into which children are born contains the accumulated knowledge of prior generations. In mediating their behavior through these objects, human beings benefit not only from their own experience, but from that of their forebears.
6.  Cultural mediation implies a species-specific mode of developmental change in which the accomplishments of prior generations are cumulated in the present as the specifically human part of the environment; culture is, in this sense, history in the present.
7.  Cultural mediation implies a special importance of the social world in human development since only other human beings can create the special conditions needed for that development to occur.
8.  A natural unit of analysis for the study of human behavior is activity systems, historically conditioned systems of relations among individuals and their proximal, culturally organized environments.

Although accepting activity systems as a unit of analysis in principle, Russian cultural-historical research based on the ideas summarized here was restricted primarily to the level of individual actions using the "method of dual stimulation." The basic idea of this method (see Valsiner, 1988, for an excellent, extended discussion) is to put a person in a problem-solving situation where direct action proves ineffective, so that the individual must find or create auxiliary means to reach the goal. In the hands of Vygotsky, Luria, and Leont'ev, experiments using this method were also considered a specific version of a microgenetic experiment, which provoked the process of psychological change under controlled laboratory conditions.[2]

A wide variety of studies carried out by Russian cultural-historical psychologists made use of this method. For example, in studies of the development of voluntary behavior in young children, Alexander Luria demonstrated that the acquisition of self-control in simple situations where children were asked to squeeze a rubber bulb or refrain from squeezing was intimately related to the children's ability to mediate their activity through language. Such results substantiated his belief that "voluntary behavior is the ability to create stimuli and to subordinate [oneself] to them; or in other words, to bring into being stimuli of a special order, directed at the organization of behavior (Luria, 1932, p. 401).

Just as studies with children could lay bare the way in which the acquisition of mediational means was crucial to the ontogeny of behavior, so such studies of the mediational means crucial to the remediation of behavior in cases of injury or disease could permit analysis of the microgenetic processes of everyday thinking. In a well-known early example of this principle, Luria and Vygotsky carried out pilot work with a patient suffering from Parkinsonism. So severe was this condition that the patient could not walk across the floor. Paradoxically, however, the patient could climb stairs. Vygotsky and Luria (reported in Luria, 1979) hypothesized that, when the patient was climbing stairs, each stair represented a signal to which the patient had to respond in a conscious way. When Vygotsky placed pieces of paper on a level floor and asked the patient to walk across the room stepping over them, the formerly immobile patient was able to walk across the room unaided. In a series of studies, Luria and Vygotsky showed that a variety of techniques that induced subjects to regulate

---

[2] Vygotsky (1978, p. 61) referred to this form of experimentation as "experimental-developmental," an idea taken from Kurt Lewin. Borrowing from Heinz Werner, he declared: "Any psychological process, whether the development of thought or voluntary behavior, is a process undergoing changes right before one's eyes. The development in question can be limited to only a few seconds, or even fractions of seconds (as in the case of normal perception). It can also (as in the case of complex mental processes) last many days or even weeks. Under certain conditions, it becomes possible to trace this development.

their behavior indirectly through language and artificial signs produced the same kinds of remedial effects.

Subsequently this "remediation" strategy was used in a wide variety of studies of the development of higher psychological functions both in children and in adults who were injured in some way. For example, Luria (1929/1978)studied the development of writing as a way of overcoming heavy demands on memory, Leont'ev (1981) studied the development of the use of mnemonic devices in normal and retarded children, Maniulenko (1948/1975) studied the way in which play can reorganize memory and motor functions, while many investigators including Leont'ev, Luria, and Zaporozhets developed remediational techniques to deal with injury cases in which speech, memory, and motor functions had been destroyed.

Summing up this early theorizing, we can see that the Russians took seriously Wundt's distinction between two kinds of psychology and accepted the notion that the study of higher psychological functions must be approached by a distinct methodology. However, unlike Wundt, who claimed that the two psychologies were necessarily distinct, they aspired to create a unified psychology with cultural mediation, and hence the assumption that cognition is a distributed phenomenon, at its core.

## Using cultural-historical psychology to think about distribution of mind

After the 1950s, a number of publications of the cultural-historical school began to appear in English, German, and other languages. There were, naturally enough, varied, selective interpretations of these ideas when they were taken out of the Russian context (for better or for worse – see Valsiner, 1988, for both an accessible summary of main lines of research and a trenchant critique of U.S. versions of cultural-historical scholarship). Consequently, all we can offer is "a" cultural-historical approach to the problem at hand.

Our own view is that several productive expansions of cultural-historical psychology have grown out of the U.S. and European hybrids of Russian approaches. We will explore these expansion in two ways. First, using the representation of mediated activity in Figures 1.1 through 1.3 as a heuristic device, we will sketch various ways in which cognition can be said to be distributed in different fundamental loci of an activity system. Then we will provide two examples from our own research that exploit these ideas.

### Distribution of cognition "in" the person

One must keep in mind that knowledge and forms of thought are not uniformly distributed in the brain, as Luria never tired of saying. Luria's remediational procedures were based on methods that deliberately redistributed cognition depending on the particular brain deficit afflicting a patient (Luria, 1973).

In a passage that clearly indicates his acceptance of Wundt's dual psychology, Luria makes explicit his belief in an extrasomatic distribution of cognition:

The chasm between natural scientific explanations of elementary processes and mentalist descriptions of complex processes could not be bridged until we could discover the way natural processes such as physical maturation and sensory mechanisms become intertwined with culturally determined processes to produce the psychological functions of adults. We needed, as it were, to step outside the organism to discover the specifically human forms of psychological activity. (Luria, 1979, p. 43)

His point has been made quite markedly by contemporary neuroscientists (e.g., Edelman, 1987) who urge on us the recognition that which parts of the brain are engaged in what way in getting through a particular event depends critically on the cultural constitution of that event. Experiencing a Chopin scherzo and experiencing a Chagall painting give rise to very different patterns of brain activity, and both differ crucially from an experience like giving birth to a child. The heterogeneity of activity within the brain is conditioned in part by the structure of the events, in both their sensual and symbolic aspects, in which the person is participating.

### Distribution "in" the medium culture

Not surprisingly, since culture is their foundational concept, anthropologists have made a major contribution to our understanding of both the universal process of culturally mediated cognition and the various ways in which the heterogeneity of culture supports and requires the distribution of cognition.

The basic sense in which cultural mediation implies the distribution of cognition was emphasized by Gregory Bateson, who proposed the following thought experiment:

Suppose I am a blind man, and I use a stick. I go tap, tap, tap. Where do I start? Is my mental system bounded at the hand of the stick? Is it bounded by my skin? Does it start halfway up the stick? Does it start at the tip of the stick? (1972, p. 459)

Bateson goes on to argue that the answer to the question changes depending on how the event is conceived. Analysis of mind's focus must include not only the man and his stick, but his purposes and the environment in which he finds himself. When the man sits down to eat his lunch, the stick's relation to mind totally changes, and it is forks and knives, not sticks, that become relevant. In short, the ways in which mind is distributed depend crucially on the tools through which one interacts with the world, and these in turn depend on one's goals. The combination of goals, tools, and setting (or perhaps "arena," in Lave's, 1988, terminology) constitutes simultaneously the context of behavior and the ways in which cognition can be said to be distributed in that context.

The notion that mediation of activity through artifacts implies a distribution of cognition among individual, mediator, and environment, as well as the fundamental change wrought by artifact-mediated activity, is eloquently expressed by two otherwise very different anthropologists, Leslie White and Clifford Geertz. Writing about the nature of the discontinuity between *Homo sapiens* and its near phylogenetic neighbors, White (1942) wrote:

Man differs from the apes, and indeed all other living creatures so far as we know, in that he is capable of symbolic behavior. With words man creates a new world, a world of ideas and philosophies. In this world man lives just as truly as in the physical world of his senses. . . . This world comes to have a continuity and a permanence that the external world of the senses can never have. It is not made up of present only but of a past and a future as well. Temporally, it is not a succession of disconnected episodes, but a continuum extending to infinity in both directions, from eternity to eternity. (p. 372)

Among other properties White here attributes to culture, his emphasis on the way it creates an (artificial) continuity between past and future merits special attention, as we will attempt to show a little later. It is also significant that both White and the Russian

cultural-historical psychologists (e.g., Vygotsky, 1934/1987) emphasize that, as mediators of human action, all artifacts can be considered tools and symbols. As White (1959) expressed the relationship:

> An axe has a subjective component; it would be meaningless without a concept and
> an attitude. On the other hand, a concept or attitude would be meaningless without
> overt expression, in behavior or speech (which is a form of behavior). Every cultural
> element, every cultural trait, therefore, has a subjective and an objective aspect.
> (p. 236)

What White refers to as the "subjective aspect" of artifacts should be
thought of in the context of this discussion as the cognitive residue of
prior actions crystallized in the object.

It is to Clifford Geertz that we owe some of the most explicit statements of both the distributed nature of mind and the interpenetration
of the cultural-historical and phylogenetic aspects of human cognition. He argued, on the basis of the archaeological and paleolithic evidence, that "culture, rather than being added on, so to speak, to a
finished or virtually finished animal, was ingredient, and centrally ingredient, in the production of that animal itself" (Geertz, 1973, p.
47). In words that echo strongly the ideas of the founders of the
cultural-historical school in Russia, Geertz went on to write:

> By submitting himself to governance by symbolically mediated programs for produc-
> ing artifacts, organizing social life, or expressing emotions, man determined, if un-
> wittingly, the culminating states of his own biological destiny. Quite literally, although
> quite inadvertently, he created himself. (p. 48)

> Such symbols are thus not mere expressions, instrumentalities, or correlates of our
> biological, psychological, and social existence; they are prerequisites of it. Without
> men, no culture, certainly; but equally, and more significantly, without culture, no
> men. (p. 49)

### Patterning of culturally distributed cognition

There is a tendency in some anthropological circles to think
of culture as a uniform, patterned ensemble of beliefs, values, symbols, tools, and so on that people share. This "configurational" approach is greatly influenced by the work of Franz Boas and his
students in anthropology (see Bock, 1988, or Stocking, 1968, for an
excellent summary of Boas's work) as well as by the cross-cultural
psychologists who study "cognitive style" (Berry, 1976).

There is no doubt that culture is patterned, but there is also no doubt that it is far from uniform, because it is experienced in local, face-to-face interactions that are locally constrained and, hence, heterogeneous with respect to both "culture as a whole" and the parts of the entire cultural toolkit experienced by any given individual. This point has been emphasized by Ted Schwartz (1978, 1990), who explores the way in which knowledge is distributed differentially across persons, generations, occupations, classes, religions, institutions, and so on. Schwartz argues that culture is necessarily a distributed phenomenon insofar as it is brought to bear, and acquired, in everyday interactions among people, no two of whom share all of the culture of the group to which they belong. (Note that even the notion of group must be left underspecified, because it could refer to a group of children who have gone to the same summer camp, or to all of the people living in a particular place at a particular time speaking the same language, or to all of the residents of a large, modern, multiethnic, national state.)

This distributed view of culture, like the distributed view of brain processing espoused by the early Russian cultural-historical psychologists, also requires us to "step outside" a category boundary (in this case, culture rather than the brain) in order to specify how culture/cognition is distributed. For example, some of the commonality to be found in the schema/word meanings of a culture arises because of shared phylogenetic structure of human brains evolved under common environmental circumstances, while some of it arises from joint activity subordinated to phylogenetically underspecified, but historically accumulated cultural constraints (Boster, 1991). A distributed notion of culture also requires one to think about how cognition is distributed among people by virtue of their social roles (which, again, are both phylogenetically and culturally constrained). As Fussell and Krauss (1989) clearly demonstrate, part of one's cultural knowledge is knowledge about the extent to which others are likely to share one's knowledge and cognitive perspective. Hence, the social distribution of cognition both adds to, and subtracts from, the degree of common culture mediating any particular interaction.

While it may readily be agreed that culture is not a seamless configuration and that knowledge is distributed among people within a cultural group, it is still important to specify the units in terms of which cultural structuration operates. In one well-known formulation, Geertz (1973) proposed that "culture is best seen not as complexes of concrete behavior patterns – customs, usages, traditions, habit clusters – ... but as a set of control mechanisms – plans, recipes, rules, instructions (what computer engineers call 'programs') – for governing behavior" (p. 44). Significantly (since these mechanisms might seem to be located entirely inside people's heads and therefore entirely ideal) Geertz goes on to write in a manner that links up neatly with the notion of artifact mediation central to the cultural-historical approach:

> The "control mechanism" view of culture begins with the assumption that human thought is basically both social and public – that its natural habitat is the house yard, the marketplace, and the town square. Thinking consists not of "happenings in the head" (though happenings there and elsewhere are necessary for it to occur) but of traffic in what have been called, by G. H. Mead and others, significant symbols – words for the most part but also gestures, drawings, musical sounds, mechanical devices like clocks. (p. 45)

A complementary notion of structured ensembles within the overall medium of culture is offered by Roy D'Andrade, another anthropologist, who suggests the term "cultural schemas" to refer to units that organize entire sets of conceptual/material artifacts. In D'Andrade's (1984) terms:

> Typically such schemas portray simplified worlds, making the appropriateness of the terms that are based on them dependent on the degree to which these schemas fit the actual worlds of the objects being categorized. Such schemas portray not only the world of physical objects and events, but also more abstract worlds of social interaction, discourse, and even word meaning. (p. 93, original in italics)

D'Andrade's approach, like Geertz's, might be read as locating culture (and cognition) inside the head. However, D'Andrade (1986, p. 22), like Geertz, makes it quite clear that objects should be considered "reified ideas in a solid medium"; that is, objects are suffused with conceptual content.

D'Andrade refers to physically realized cultural models as mediating structures, using as an example Hutchins's (1986) discussion of checklists as tools to accomplish complex cognitive tasks involving people who work together. His points out that when using such mediator-cum-cultural models the user does not coordinate his or her behavior directly with the task environment, but rather coordinates with a mediating object that has a structure that is like the task environment in some important way. (p. 107)

After describing in detail all of the subroutines that must be mastered and executed in order for the checklist/script/model to be effective, D'Andrade concludes that "what might at first look like a simple device in fact turns out to be a complex of mediations – that is, of coordinations between structures" (p. 107). In the case of the checklist it is essential that the model and the reality it represents be identical. A highly experienced expert, on the other hand, may directly recall the actions and operations to be taken and their effects on the environment.

### *The distribution of cognition in the social world*

These descriptions of the units of organization of human activity within a cultural medium, like Bateson's example of the blind man with a stick, help us to think about the distribution of cognition between an individual, a mediating artifact, and the environment. At the same time, they invite us to locate those actions in a wider system of activity. For example, we might assume that Batesons' blind man is just stopping off at a café to have a beer and chat with friends before going down the block to participate in a local dramatic circle. This larger perspective makes us attend to the fact that short-lived actions of walking and sitting down are actually embedded in something collective and relatively enduring. Not only are the blind man's thoughts focused on the technical procedure of moving from place to place. When he sits down at the table he is part of one activity system with its standing rules, community, and division of labor. Should his companions at the café also be actors, they may be inhabiting one setting physically, but their mental activity may be organized (collectively) around a quite different one that they will participate in shortly. In short, constituents of the blind man's cognitive processing are to be located both in the immediate setting (distributed to each of the nodes in the expanded triangle in Figure 1.3) and in the upcoming activity, which is presupposed in all of his actions. Within each local setting, such "cognitive actions" as remembering and decision making are distributed not only among the artifacts (the menu, the arrangement of chairs and tables, the sign pointing to the restrooms) but among the rules (one pays before leaving the premises; sitting down at a table with strangers requires one to ask permission) and among people according to the division of labor (waiters fulfill different parts of the activity at the café than the customers or the dishwasher; the janitor must remember to put away the mop and bucket; the owner is responsible for paying the janitor and waiter). It is such considerations that motivated Douglas (1987) to write a book about "how institutions think" and Connerton (1989) a book about "how societies remember."

### The distribution of mind in time

The final way in which we suggest that cognition is distributed is in time. We can best illustrate the properties of temporal distribution that we have in mind with an example drawn from a real-life event, the birth of a baby. Our example comes from the work of pediatrician Aiden Macfarlane (1977), who published several transcripts of the reactions of parents when they first caught sight of their newborn child and discovered its sex. Typical comments include "We shall be worried to death when she's eighteen" and "It can't play rugby" (said of another girl). Aside from their interest as indicators of sexism in Anglo-Saxon cultures in the 1960s, these remarks and the phenomena associated with them illustrate the kinds of distribution of cognition in time that are highlighted by a cultural-historical theory of mind.

In each of these examples, the adults interpret the biological characteristics of the child in terms of their own past (cultural) experience. In the experience of English men and women living in the mid-twentieth century, it could be considered "common knowledge" that girls do not play rugby and that when they enter adolescence they will be the object of boys' sexual attention, putting them at various kinds of risk. Using this information derived from their cultural past and assuming that the world will be very much for their daughter as it has been for them, the parents project a probable future for the child. (She will be sought after by males as a sexual partner, causing the parents anxiety. She will not participate in a form of activity [rugby] requiring strength and agility that is the special preserve of males.)

The different ways in which temporality enters into the distribution of cognition in time illustrated by Macfarlane's example are represented in Figure 1.4. Figure 1.4a presents five time lines, the bottom four of which correspond to the four "developmental domains" (Wertsch, 1985) that, according to the cultural-historical framework espoused here, simultaneously serve as major constraints on, and resources for, human development. At the top of Figure 1.4a is what might be called "physical time," or the history of the physical universe that long precedes the appearance of life on earth. The second line represents phylogenetic time, the history of life on earth. The third represents cultural-historical time, which has co-evolved with phylogenetic time. The fourth line represents ontogeny, the history of a single human being, and the fifth line represents microgenesis, the moment-to-moment time of lived human experience. The ellipse running vertically through the figure is the event under analysis, the birth of a baby girl. The four horizontal lines correspond to four kinds of genesis, four temporal scales: phylogenesis, culturogenesis, ontogenesis, and microgenesis, each "lower" level embedded in the level "above it."

To begin with, Macfarlane's example forces on us the need to keep in mind that not one but *two* ontogenic time scales are interacting here. This added time dimension is included in Figure 1.4b. That is, at a minimum one needs a mother and a child in a single social context for the process of birth to occur and for human development to continue. These two ontogenies are coordinated in time by the simultaneous structuration provided by phylogeny, culture, and microgenetic processes of interaction. Following the arrow from the "thought" of the mother, one can see that it traces this thought process from the present into the cultural-historical past and then into the imagined future of the child, and finally back to the present in the form of patterned interactions with the child. In short, cognition is distributed both "vertically" in the different time dimensions occupied by each of the participants and "horizontally" with respect to past, present, and future.

This example also helps us to illustrate another feature attributed to culturally mediated thought: the process by which the "ideational" side of all cultural artifacts is transformed into its "material" side. If one traces the temporal course of the mother's thought from the

**(a)**

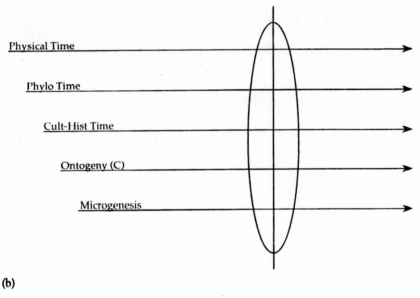

**(b)**

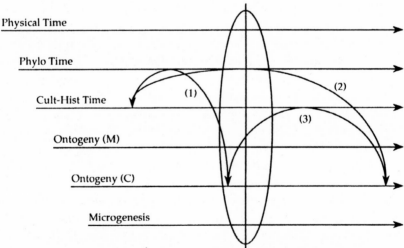

Figure 1.4. (a) The successive horizontal lines represent separate time scales corresponding to the history of the physical universe, the history of life on earth (phylogeny), the history of human beings on earth (cultural-historical time), the life of the individual (ontogeny), and the history of

present into the cultural past (taking note of the phylogenetic structure of the child), one sees that the parents' (purely ideal/cultural) projection of their child's future becomes a fundamentally important (material/cultural) constraint organizing the child's life experiences in the present. As copious research has demonstrated, even adults totally ignorant of the real gender of a newborn will treat the baby quite differently depending on its symbolic/cultural "gender." Adults literally create different material forms of interaction based on conceptions of the world provided by their cultural experience when, for example, they bounce "boy" infants (those wearing blue diapers) and attribute "manly" virtues to them, while they treat "girl" infants (those wearing pink diapers) in a gentle manner and attribute beauty and sweet temperaments to them (Rubin, Provezano, & Luria, 1974). Macfarlane's example also motivates the special emphasis placed on the social origins of higher psychological functions by cultural-historical psychologists. As his transcripts clearly demonstrate, human nature is social in a sense that is different from the sociability of other species because only a culture-using human being can "reach into" the cultural past, project it into the future, and then "carry" that (purely conceptual) future "back" into the present in the shape of beliefs that then constrain and organize the present sociocultural environment of the newcomer. It is worth recalling in this context White's telling image, that temporally the culturally constituted mind "is not a succession of disconnected episodes, but a continuum extending to infinity in both directions, from eternity to eternity." The assumption that the cultural future will be more or less like the cultural past, or (which may amount to the same thing) that we can only project a future based on past, culturally mediated experience, provides one essential basis of continuity in human mental life.

Figure 1.4. (*cont.*) moment-to-moment lived experience (microgenesis). The vertical ellipse represents the event of a child being born. (b) Another line, the ontogeny of the child, has been added to that of the individual. The distribution of cognition in time is traced sequentially into (1) the past of the mother, (2) the mother's imagination of the future of the child, and (3) the subsequent behavior of the mother. In this same sequence, the ideal aspect of culture is transformed into its material form as the mother and other adults structure the child's experience consistent with their (imagined) future identity.

### Two research programs: applying cultural-historical ideas in practice

Having laid out in a general way how a cultural-historical, activity-based approach to cognition leads one to think about the distribution of cognition among people, cultural artifacts, and time, we now provide two examples drawn from our own research that employ these ideas in addressing research issues of general interest to students of human cognition. Each example highlights a somewhat different mix of the distributive properties we have summarized.

#### Reading acquisition

There is broad agreement that reading is a "complex skill requiring the coordination of a number of interrelated sources of information" (Anderson, Hiebert, Scott, & Wilkinson, 1985), and a great deal is known about how those who have acquired some degree of skill behave. But despite intensive research efforts throughout this century, and especially over the past two decades, the process of acquisition remains disputed (see Foorman & Siegel, 1986, for a juxtaposition of conflicting views). Especially troublesome has been the problem of accounting for "reading with comprehension" and the sequence of interactions through which this process develops. We believe that part of the problem in contemporary research on reading is that the psychological models of reading acquisition fail to take account of the distributed properties of cognition. In particular, they are especially weak in their conception of learning to read as joint, mediated, meaning-making activity between teachers and students in which the distribution of cognitive work must be systematically transformed.

Despite important differences among them, modern cognitive science approaches to reading share certain properties. First, they distinguish a series of "levels" in the constitution of written language that begin at the lowest level with features and proceed "upward" to letters, which make up words, which make up sentences, and so on. In principle, theories of reading posit the existence of both "bottom-up" decoding processes that assemble larger and larger units of text and "top-down," comprehension-driven processes that constrain the bottom-up processes to permit interpretation of the decoded texts.

When cognitive scientists present such models, the "bottom-up" parts of the process tend to be well specified up to the level of a word and, perhaps, to the level of a sentence or even a paragraph. But the "ultimate" top-down constraint appears only as an arrow descending from the top of the diagram, descending, as it were, from the bow of Zeus (McClelland & Rumelhart, 1981). Implicitly, this sort of model assumes reading to be a solitary activity occurring inside the head of the learner; the fact that learning is part of a larger, joint activity, called instruction, is not acknowledged. In reality, with very few exceptions, acquiring the ability to read is most decidedly *not* an individual process, and we have a pretty good idea of where Zeus's arrow is coming from – the teacher, the bearer of the cultural past, the bearer of authority concerning the correct interpretation of the text, the organizer of the teaching/learning process.

When we apply ideas about the distribution of cognition that flow from a cultural-historical, activity approach to the problem of reading acquisition, two principles present themselves as relevant:

1.  The cognitive processing involved in learning to read is not an individual matter; the requisite cognitive processes are distributed among teacher, pupil, other students, and the cultural artifacts around which they coordinate in the activity called "teaching/ learning" to read.
2.  The expected future state, mature reading, must somehow be present at the beginning of instruction as constraints enabling the development of the to-be-acquired new system of mediation, mature reading.

*Bringing the endpoint "forward" to the beginning.* We begin by examining, in terms of the basic mediational triangle, the necessary structural properties of the interactions that should organize the activity setting we create at the "student–teacher" level of description. Figure 1.5 displays in graphic form the fact that at the beginning of instruction there are two preexisting mediational systems that can create the constraints necessary to permit the development of reading in the child. At the far left of the figure we represent the commonsense fact that children enter reading instruction with years

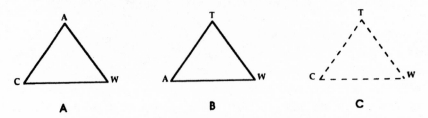

Figure 1.5. The to-be-coordinated systems of mediation that exist when a novice begins to learn to read from an expert. (A) The child C can mediate interactions with the world W via an adult A. (B) The adult can mediate interactions with the world via text. (C) The child–text–adult relationship is the goal of instruction.

of experience at mediating their interactions with the world via adults. In the center we represent the equally commonsense fact that literate adults routinely mediate their interactions through text. Finally, on the far right we represent the to-be-developed system of mediation that is our target.

Figure 1.6 shows the next stage in the analytic/instructional strategy: The given and to-be-developed systems of child mediations must be juxtaposed and the preexisting adult system superimposed on them, to create the skeletal structure of an "interpsychological" system of reading. As depicted in Figure 1.6, this mediational system establishes a dual system of mediation for the child, which permits the coordination of text-based and prior-world-knowledge-based information of the kind involved in the whole act of reading. The instructional/developmental task is now better specified: We must somehow create a system of interpersonal interaction such that the combined child–adult system at the right of Figure 1.6 can coordinate the child's act of reading before the child can accomplish this activity for him- or herself.

*Creating the activity.*    Having identified the skeletal structural relations that must be coordinated at the level of teacher–student–test relations, we now need to figure out the system of activity that will achieve the needed coordinations. Our strategy for accomplishing this goal was to create an artificial activity system including a script, props, and roles. This system, understood as a distinctive form of ac-

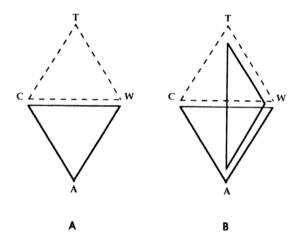

Figure 1.6. The juxtaposition of existing and to-be-formed systems of mediation that have to be coordinated. (A) The two existing systems. (B) The two existing systems plus the to-be-formed system.

tivity, deliberately distributes cognition through a system of artifacts so as to maximize both the teacher's ability to diagnose the state of the child's understanding and the chances that the child will learn to read. The specific procedure is a modification of the reciprocal teaching procedure of Palincsar and Brown (1984), in which teacher and student silently read a passage of text and then engage in a dialogue about it that includes summarizing the text, clarifying comprehension problems that arise, asking a question about the main idea, and predicting the next part of the text. For a number of reasons (see King, 1988; Laboratory of Comparative Human Cognition, 1982, for additional details), our modification of reciprocal teaching was instantiated as a small-group reading activity with third- to sixth-grade children identified by their teachers as experiencing extraordinary difficulties learning to read.

The key mediational tools of the procedure are a text, a publicly visible script for the joint activity written on a blackboard, a set of roles (each corresponding to a different hypothetical part of the whole act of reading reified in a set of role cards printed on 3-in. × 5-in. index cards), and rules for conducting the activity we called "Question-Asking-Reading."

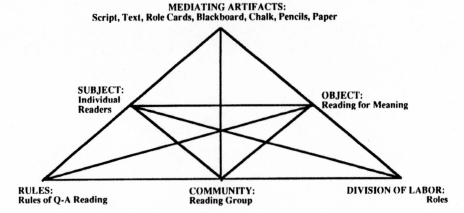

Figure 1.7. Question-Asking-Reading represented in terms of the expanded activity system model.

To connect the resulting procedure to the preceding and following discussion, Figure 1.7 represents the triangular structure of activity presented earlier in Figure 1.3 with the specific tools, object, community, division of labor, and social rules appropriate to the activity under construction. Figure 1.7 also specifies how we conceive of the distribution of cognition in the Question-Asking-Reading activity.

Question-Asking-Reading activity unfolded as shown in Figure 1.8. Each session began with "goal talk" about the children's reasons for wanting to learn to read. These included such poorly understood reasons (from the children's point of view) as the need to obtain an attractive job (e.g., as an astronaut), intermediate-level goals (graduating from Question-Asking-Reading to assist adults with computer-based instruction), and quite proximate goals (the desirability of getting correct answers on the quiz that came at the end of each reading session).

Next the group leader produced the text to be read and various paraphernalia important to the activity – role cards, pencils, paper, and a timer – and then turned attention from the script outline of the activity on the board to the text, simultaneously passing around the paraphernalia used in Question-Asking-Reading. This preparatory sequence ended with the choice of role cards. These cards specified the following roles:

1. The person who asks about words that are hard to say
2. The person who asks about the words that are hard to understand
3. The person who asks a question about the main idea
4. The person who picks the person to answer questions asked by others
5. The person who asks about what is going to happen next

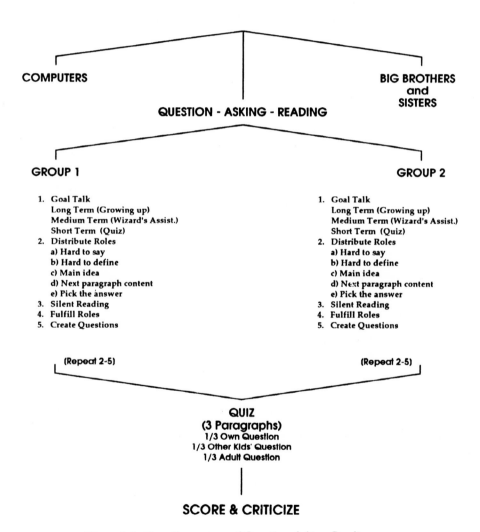

Figure 1.8. Overall structure of Question-Asking-Reading.

A good deal of discussion usually ensued about who had gotten what roles; picking the answerer was an obvious favorite, while the card implicating the main idea was avoided like the plague.

Once the role cards were distributed, the text for the day (usually taken from local newspapers with content of potential interest to the children) was distributed, one paragraph at a time. The participants (including the instructor and one competent reader, usually an undergraduate at the University of California, San Diego, and the children), then bent over their passages to engage in silent reading.

These and other procedural arrangements constituted our attempt to create a medium that would repeatedly create moments when the three mediational triangles depicted in Figure 1.5 would be coordinated to create the conditions for children to experience, and then perhaps acquire, the full act of reading.

Our evidence for the way in which this procedure worked is derived from several sources: videotaped recordings of the instructional sessions, the children's written work on the quizzes that completed each session, and various test results (see Griffin, King, Diaz, & Cole, 1989, for more details). Of greatest interest in the present context is the way in which this system allowed us to trace the microgenesis of reading acquisition.

For the first few sessions, the children were uncertain of the rules, roles, and tools for this strange form of reading. But the two competent readers present kept the activity going, and mutual help was encouraged. Within a few sessions, Question-Asking-Reading was a well-known routine. The children began to develop strategies for getting their favorite role cards. Various aspects of the procedure that provoked discoordination and repairs in the early sessions began to be presumed, not even acted out, by the children and the adults.

Once a relatively steady state of coordination around the artifacts and goals of Question-Asking-Reading was achieved, it became apparent that different children discoordinated with the routine in systematically different patterns. For example, one child experienced great difficulty in coming "unglued" from the letter–sound correspondences when he attempted to arrive at the main idea. When asked about the main idea, he repeatedly returned to the text and sought a "copy match" in which some word from the question appeared in the text, read the relevant sentence aloud, and then puzzled over it. A second child's problem was of a quite different order: he continually lost track of the relevant context, importing information from his classroom activities that day or previous reading passages, although they had no relevance to the text being read.

Over the course of the sessions, the ability of all of the children to carry out parts of Question-Asking-Reading increased; that is, they could fulfill more roles more often without engendering any discoordination in the joint activity of reading with comprehension. Many of them displayed improved performance in their classrooms, and some showed improvement on state-mandated reading tests.

With respect to the in situ data, our ability to detect selective discoordinations in a joint, mediated activity served as powerful testimony to the efficacy of our approach to reading acquisition. But with respect to criteria external to the activity, such as grades and test scores, we had nothing principled to say because we had no proper control group. Having focused on the *process* of our system of reading instruction, we failed to address adequately the relative quality of the *product*. In order to address the issue of relative efficacy, King (1988) replicated the small-group reading procedures in a follow-up experiment that included appropriate control conditions and more stringently quantified pre- and posttest measures.

In addition to testing the effectiveness of Question-Asking-Reading against a no-treatment control group, King included a group of children who were provided the kind of structured intervention that Scardamalia and Bereiter (1985) call "procedural facilitation" to assess whether the dynamic, dialogic characteristics of Question-Asking-Reading were any more effective than workbook exercises that required children to complete each of the tasks corresponding to the role cards individually in written form. Once again children with difficulties in learning to read were selected from the upper elementary grades.

King found that both Question-Asking-Reading and her version of the procedural facilitation technique boosted the children's reading performance. However, children in the Question-Asking-Reading group retained significantly more material from the training passages than did the students in the procedural facilitation group. The students in the Question-Asking-Reading group also spent more total time actively engaged with the task and demonstrated a greater interest in the content of the readings, indicating an intimate link between the motivational, social-interactional, and cognitive aspects of activity-in-context.


### Expertise in transition

Although education has traditionally been a primary area of human practice studied by cultural-historical researchers, a number of interesting studies illustrating the dynamics of cognition as a distributed phenomenon have been carried out in the domain of work. Our second example is taken from a longitudinal research project studying the reorganization of medical work in a Finnish health center that provides primary health-care services to the population of a middle-sized city (see Engeström, 1990, in press).

Work activity in a complex organization is an obvious case of distributed, artifact-mediated cognition. As an object of study it differs from reading acquisition in some important ways. The organization of an ongoing work activity cannot be designed from scratch by the researcher. Experimentation through design and implementation of a new model system of activity can nonetheless be built into the study of work. In what is called "developmental work research," researchers provide data and conceptual tools for the practitioners, who analyze the contradictions of their own work and design a new model for it in order to master and solve those contradictions. Such transformation is essentially an expansive learning process (Engeström, 1987) in which the practitioners acquire a new way of working while designing and implementing the new practices themselves.

A workplace is not a homogeneous activity system. Jay Katz (1984) points this out with regard to physicians:

> The public, and professionals as well, need to become more aware of the fact that many disparate groups now live under medicine's tent. Contemporary medicine is not a unitary profession but a federation of professions with differing ideologies and senses of mission. This diversification has changed medical practices. (p. 189)

There is also a historical dimension to be observed. Competing schools of thought and practice originate in different historical periods and conditions. Old traditions persist and are modified. In this sense, alternative frames of reference may be analyzed as if they are historical layers of expertise, to be identified by an "archaeology of expert knowledge." Competing and contradictory historical layers of expertise can regularly be discovered within one and the same organization, and often within the actions and thoughts of one and the same practitioner.

To begin with, we conducted an extensive interview with each of the 16 physicians of two health stations in a single health center. The interview contained, among other themes, a cluster of questions concerning the physician's conception of the object of his or her work. These questions required the physicians to describe and justify their reactions in hypothetical difficult situations (e.g., a patient visit the physician considers medically unnecessary; a patient with unclear or incomprehensible symptoms; a patient with mental symptoms; a patient with a self-made diagnosis; a patient with multiple problems).

The analysis of the interview protocols resulted in a classification of the physicians' frames of reference concerning the object of their work (Table 1.1). The five frames of reference found among the physicians of this organization correspond to five historically distinct and culturally deep-seated theoretical patterns of thinking about illness (see, e.g., Arney & Bergen, 1984; Shorter, 1985). These frames of reference cannot be conceived of in terms of stages along a one-dimensional path from novice to expert: The 16 subjects were a quite homogeneous group in terms of age and years of professional experience.

In addition to conducting interviews, we videotaped five or six randomly chosen patient consultations with each of the doctors. Analyses of the videotapes support the conclusion that these distinct frames of reference are in fact connected to different practical procedures or "scripts" for dealing with patients in practice (Engeström, 1989).

This kind of diversity or multivoicedness is an important feature of the distribution of cognition in expert work. Potentially it is a rich source of resources, making the activity system capable of combining different viewpoints and skills in the handling of complex problems.

However, in this particular organization, as in so many modern organizations, the potential advantages of multivoicedness were all but impossible to tap. The health centers in Finland provide primary-care services free of charge. In the center we studied, there were a

Table 1.1. *Physicians' conceptions of the object of their work*

| Object of work | Number of subjects | Corresponding theory of illness | Key expressions in the transcripts |
|---|---|---|---|
| Somatic diseases | 4 | Ontological-biomedical | Old-fashioned diseases; small problems medically unnecessary; clear-cut causes; psychic problems difficult; self-made diagnosis aggravating; care is under control; patient is honest and compliant |
| Consumers of health-care services | 4 | Administrative-economic | Types of visits and patients; misuse; referrals; self-made diagnosis aggravating; relationship between patient and institution; patient should observe the agreed-upon appointment |
| Patient as a psychosomatic whole | 1 | Psychiatric | Mental health problems; no unnecessary visits; deepest psychic reasons revealed through interviewing; patient must be made to talk; give patient time |
| Patient's social life situation | 2 | Sociomedical | Social problems and multiple illnesses; no unnecessary visits; psychic problems have social origins; patient's own diagnosis important |
| Patient as collaborator | 5 | Systemic-interactive | Active thinking patients; unnecessary visits caused by lack of knowledge and bureaucracy; make patient reflect on his or her own situation and alternative action; make patient take health into his or her own hands; patients more critical and informed than they used to be; equal collaboration |

large number of patients who used the services excessively and changed doctors constantly (either willingly or unwillingly). These patients usually seemed to have multiple problems, often with psychosocial implications. These were important features of the substantial complexity of physicians' work in the health center. The physicians were compartmentalized in their work, both organizationally and in terms of their approaches. Organizationally, any patient could see any doctor, depending on who happened to be on duty or have available time slots. A doctor was not assigned any population list or geographic area for which he or she would be permanently responsible. Doctor–patient relationships were dominated by anonymity and discontinuity. These facts, together with strong production pressures, created an atmosphere of deepening crisis in the activity system.

The physicians had little time or incentive to stop and reflect on the problem of complex patients, let alone to discuss them jointly. The immediately available communicative tool, the computerized medical records system, in no efficient way helped or prompted the physicians to analyze and plan the care of these patients collaboratively. Health center assistants, trained as assistant nurses, were effectively reduced to gatekeepers allotting appointment times to patients.

The compartmentalized organization of expertise led to recurrent open and latent disturbances and discoordinations in the functioning of the activity system. The following is a rather commonplace example of such occurrences (for more details, see Engeström, Engeström, & Saarelma, 1988).

A male patient in his early 20s comes as an acute case to see a female doctor whom he has not seen before. The patient complains of a cold and cough. The doctor examines the patient and gives him a sick leave for two days. She then suggests that the current symptoms might have something to do with the patient's previous chest pains and hyperventilation problems, of which she learned from the patient's computerized medical record. The patient denies the connection. In a postconsultation interview the doctor explains that from the patient's multiple previously recorded visits she got an impression of a "young man who may react sensitively with his body."

This doctor is unusual in that she takes a very careful look at the past record of a patient with a common cold, even if the patient makes it clear that the symptoms have only emerged the previous day. The doctor hypothesizes a link between the cold and the patient's frequent visits and his history of frequent colds, chest pains, and hyperventilation, for which he has been treated in a hospital. Considering the fact that the doctor has never seen the patient before and that she hasn't had a chance to discuss the patient with her colleagues, the computerized record functions here in a remarkable manner as a diagnostic aid, providing a bridge between the past recorded by others and the present faced by the first-timer.

The same patient returns to the health center about three months later. He comes to another female doctor whom he has not seen before, again as an acute case without an appointment. Again, the complaint is rather commonplace: "When I breathe out or cough or laugh, it hurts here kind of like in the lung." The doctor examines the patient. She then asks whether the patient has ever before had "anything in his lungs." The patient says no. The doctor gives the patient a two-day sick leave. She then sends the patient to the X-ray department to make sure that there is no organic abnormality in the lungs. She enters the referral to that department into the computer.

All in all, this doctor takes an approach that is very different from the previous one. Instead of studying the record to make a hypothesis based on the patient's history, the doctor acts on the basis of the patient's explicit statements and physical examination. In the postconsultation interview, she justifies her approach by referring to the acute nature of the case. She states that had the patient had a similar problem previously, she would have suspected anxiety or related mental reasons. But since the patient denied having similar lung or chest problems before, she went ahead on a purely biomedical basis.

In other words, the first doctor's hypothesis about a connection between the patient's repeated colds, previous chest pains, hyperventilation, and possible underlying psychic problems was not followed up by the second doctor. The two consultations happened as if with two different patients. Ostensibly this break occurred because the second doctor did not check the patient's previous records.

In his postconsultation interview, the patient expressed no dissatisfaction with such discontinuity and compartmentalization. Rather, it seemed to fit and reinforce his own way of drifting through the events of life – and from one doctor to another.

It might be tempting to dismiss this patient's case as too vague and confused to be taken seriously. However, the patient used many health-care services by drifting from one doctor to another and from one variation of symptoms to another. He thus contributed to the production pressure felt by practitioners in the activity system.

The communicative rupture between the two consultations remained latent and unnoticed. It did not surface as an open disturbance – although such situations often do. It would be easy to blame the second doctor for the rupture. But that would in no way help us understand the recurrent features of the activity system that make such ruptures commonplace. Actually the second doctor acted according to the rules of the system. It was the first doctor who violated the rule requiring that in acute cases attention to be paid only to the current, acute symptoms.

In this activity system, deep-seated contradictions were a better explanation for such breaks than were mere technical shortcomings of the medical record system or so-called psychological resistance of the doctors to computers and communication. The first contradiction was that between the complexity of the patient's problems and the arbitrary distribution of patients to physicians, each compartmentalized and effectively separated from the others. The second contradiction was that between the demand for quality care for complex problems and the rule requiring speedy consultations, especially in the category of acute consultations without an appointment. The ensuing production pressure reinforced a compartmentalized approach on the doctor's part. The third contradiction was that between complex patient problems and rather traditional tools of biomedical diagnosis. In such conditions, the medical record easily served as only a minimal administrative device.

In Figure 1.9, the three contradictions are placed in appropriate locations within our general model of an activity system. The compartmentalized and alienated approach to health care, reinforced by drifting on the patients' part, eventually contributed to increased production pressure. A vicious circle was thus established.

The researcher's task was to provide data (such as the videotapes and interview transcripts of the case discussed earlier) and conceptual

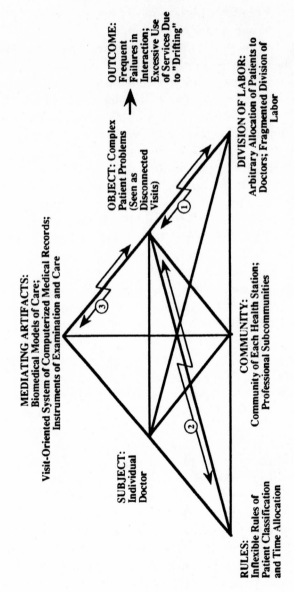

**MEDIATING ARTIFACTS:**
Biomedical Models of Care;
Visit-Oriented System of Computerized Medical Records;
Instruments of Examination and Care

**OBJECT:** Complex Patient Problems (Seen as Disconnected Visits)

**OUTCOME:**
Frequent Failures in Interaction; Excessive Use of Services Due to "Drifting"

**SUBJECT:**
Individual Doctor

**RULES:**
Inflexible Rules of Patient Classification and Time Allocation

**COMMUNITY:**
Community of Each Health Station; Professional Subcommunities

**DIVISION OF LABOR:**
Arbitrary Allocation of Patients to Doctors; Fragmented Division of Labor

Figure 1.9. A representation of the health-care workers' activity system with major contradictions indicated.

tools (such as the models in Figures 1.3 and 1.9) that enabled the practitioners to break the vicious circle by realizing how their division of labor reinforced and perpetuated the production pressure and alienation they felt. The identification and conceptualization of such contradictions by the practitioners were a crucial precondition for their focused effort to design a new model for their work.

The key feature of this new model is a new division of labor that radically alters the conditions for exploiting the distributed cognitive resources of the system. Each physician is assigned a geographic area with a population of 2,000 to 2,500 inhabitants for whose primary health services the physician is responsible. Four physicians and two health center assistants responsible for adjoining areas constitute a team. Team members help one another; for example if a doctor is ill, others in the team make sure that an excessive patient backlog will not be generated for that doctor. Each team has its own designated physical space and reception within a health station. In that way, the large health stations are effectively decentralized. The inhabitants receive a letter telling them who their designated physician and team are to be. The teams meet regularly to organize, plan, and evaluate their work. Teams are responsible for analyzing the health-related needs of their target populations (community diagnosis). Health center assistants are drawn into direct interaction with patients, giving guidance and participating in actual care. As full-fledged team members, they also take responsibility for the overall functioning of the team. The key features of the new model are summarized in Figure 1.10.

The implementation of the new model produced some dramatic outcomes. In 1987 and 1988, the crisis of the health center began to manifest itself in the form of an increasing number of vacant positions for physicians. Several doctors left the activity system, often moving to the private health care sector. It was extremely difficult to recruit new doctors.

The new model required that for each carefully composed population area there was a designated doctor. In the fall of 1988, the two health stations where the project was carried out were anxious to start implementing the new model, but the lack of doctors threatened to postpone the implementation. It was feared that the postponement

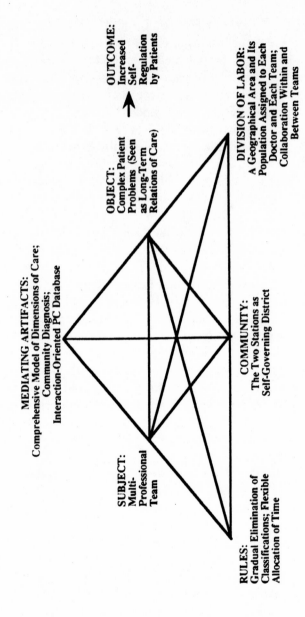

MEDIATING ARTIFACTS:
Comprehensive Model of Dimensions of Care;
Community Diagnosis;
Interaction-Oriented PC Database

OBJECT:
Complex Patient
Problems (Seen
as Long-Term
Relations of Care)

OUTCOME:
Increased
Self-
Regulation
by Patients

DIVISION OF LABOR:
A Geographical Area and its
Population Assigned to Each
Doctor and Each Team;
Collaboration Within and
Between Teams

SUBJECT:
Multi-
Professional
Team

COMMUNITY:
The Two Stations as
Self-Governing District

RULES:
Gradual Elimination of
Classifications; Flexible
Allocation of Time

Figure 1.10. A representation of the created system of activity following resolution of the crisis of change.

would allow the crisis to deepen, thus making the implementation even more improbable. In other words, an aggravated form of a vicious circle was emerging. After an initial two-month postponement, a series of crisis meetings were held among the personnel of the stations. The personnel of the smaller station came up with a solution. They proposed lending some of their doctors temporarily to the bigger station, so that the implementation could proceed in the population areas of that station. The smaller station would operate with minimal personnel resources, as if on an emergency basis, until the new model's beneficial impact in the bigger station could attract a sufficient number of new physicians to the system. This proposal was accepted.

The implementation was in fact so successful that, by the summer of 1989, all the vacancies were filled and the two stations started to operate jointly on the basis of the new model. The new model dramatically changed the availability and accessibility of care. Long waiting times and queues have all but disappeared, and there is no longer a shortage of physicians willing to work in the stations. For example, in October 1988 (the last month before the implementation of the new model), the average waiting time for patients coming to the walk-in urgent care unit was 103 minutes; a year later it was 27.5 minutes. In 1988, a patient had to wait three to four weeks for an appointment. In 1990, all doctors had appointments available within one to three days. These changes are clearly reflected in the distribution of different types of visits to the doctors (Table 1.2). The excessive use of walk-in urgent care services was dramatically reduced as the accessibility and availability of regular daytime appointments and telephone consultations were improved.

Cognitively, this transformation demands that the practitioners reconceptualize the object of their work. Instead of occasional visitors, patients and their problems are to be seen as being in potential or ongoing long-term care relationships with the doctors. After the implementation of the new model, one of the physicians characterized this reconceptualization as follows:

In this new model of work, it makes sense to treat patients who have a prolonged problem actively from the beginning. You can't deal with the problem shortsightedly, like here is medicine and come back if it continues – because the patient comes back to you. It's better to spend a bit more time the first time, you'll get the benefit when

Table 1.2. *Distribution of visits to doctors before and after the implementation of the new model*

| Type of visit | Jan. 1 to June 30, 1988 | Jan. 1 to June 30, 1990 | Percent change |
| --- | --- | --- | --- |
| With appointment | 14,724 | 20,192 | +37 |
| Without appointment during daytime | 8,023 | 4,973 | −38 |
| Walk-in urgent care in the evenings | 4,946 | 3,895 | −21 |
| Telephone contacts | 3,600 | 5,277 | +47 |

it continues. I mean, do it properly right away. Previously we were tempted to do it more superficially and we hoped that the patient would go to someone else if the problem continues.

If the daily functioning of the activity system in crisis took the form of a vicious circle, the transition just described might be characterized as an expansive cycle (Engeström, 1987, 1991). An expansive cycle is a developmental process that involves both the internalization of a given culture of practice and the creation of novel artifacts and patterns of interaction. The new activity structure does not emerge out of the blue. It requires reflective analysis of the existing activity structure – participants must learn to know and understand what they want to transcend. And the creation of a new activity system requires the reflective appropriation of advanced models and tools that offer ways out of the internal contradictions. However, these forms of internalization are not enough for the emergence of a new structure. As the cycle advances, the actual design and implementation of a new model for the activity gain momentum: Externalization begins to dominate. This is schematically depicted in Figure 1.11. The expansive cycle of an activity system begins with almost exclusive emphasis on internalization, on socializing and training novices to become competent members of the activity as it is routinely carried out. Creative externalization occurs first in the form of discrete individual violations and innovations. As the disruptions and contradictions in the activity become more demanding, internalization increasingly takes

EXTERNALIZATION

INTERNALIZATION

Figure 1.11. A representation of the cyclical relationship between internalization and externalization at different points in an expansive cycle of changing activity.

the form of critical self-reflection – and externalization, the search for novel solutions, increases. Externalization reaches it peak when a new model for the activity is designed and implemented. As the new model stabilizes itself, internalization of its inherent ways and means again becomes the dominant form of learning and development.

At the level of collective activity systems, such an expansive cycle can be seen as the equivalent of traveling through the zone of proximal development discussed by Vygotsky (1978) at the level of individual and small-group learning. A key feature of expansive cycles is that they are definitely not predetermined courses of one-dimensional development. What is more advanced, "which way is up," cannot be decided using externally given, fixed yardsticks. Decisions of that kind are made locally, within the activity system itself, under conditions of uncertainty and intensive search. Yet they are not arbitrary decisions. The internal contradictions of the activity system in a given phase of its evolution can be more or less adequately identified, and any model for the future that does not address and solve those contradictions will eventually turn out to be nonexpansive.

Expertise can be understood as a system of cognition, distributed as an activity system. The type of distribution observed in the health center at the beginning of the project was one of compartmentalization. The type of distribution achieved through the expansive cycle was one of teamwork. The transition from compartmentalized expertise to team-based expertise was essentially a process of redistribution of cognition based on design from below. It can be assumed that such a design will be incorporated into the new team-based type of expert practice as a novel cognitive resource. The verification of this assumption will be a task of further analysis.

### By way of a summary

We have not been able to provide examples of all the ways in which cognition manifests itself as distributed activity. However, we hope that our brief treatment of two examples selected to represent different forms of activity and different parts of the life cycle are sufficient to make clear the affinity between cultural-historical psychology and the notion of distributed cognition. In essence, when one takes mediation through artifacts as the central distinctive characteristic of human beings, one is declaring one's adoption of the view that human cognition is distributed. Precisely how cognition is distributed must be worked out for different kinds of activity, with their different forms of mediation, division of labor, social rules, and so on. The underlying principles, however, are universal. In aggregate they constitute a cultural theory of mind.

After reading an earlier draft of this chapter, a commentator asked what seems to us to be two reasonable and interesting questions. First, why is all of this rediscovery of the idea of distributed cognition going on right now? Second, have we learned anything from this rediscovery that would allow us to say we had made scientific progress?

Why the current burst of interest in distributed cognition? In the most general terms, it is because of the widespread belief that the positivistically oriented social sciences, with their notion of cognition firmly located inside the individual, are inadequate for the task of grasping the essential nature of human experience and behavior. That psychologists are *re*discovering these ideas stems from the same source: We are replaying in new terms precisely the same debate in which Wundt, Münsterberg, Dewey, and the Russian cultural-historical psychologists formulated competing versions of a psychology that unites the natural and cultural sciences. Such attempts at unification, we believe, will come up with some way of conceptualizing cognition as a distributed phenomenon.

Have we made any progress? We are not so sure, save for the fact that we are attacking the problem having learned from the experiences of our predecessors. An additional advantage is that we have a far more sophisticated technology for representing complex, temporally extended behavior than did researchers at the end of the century. Audio and video tape recording, films, and computers have all, in their own way, enabled us to interact with the phenomena of mind in a more sophisticated way. We can now not only talk about the mutual constitution of human activities, but display it in scientifically produced artifacts. Whether these advantages will prove any greater relative to the complexities of the tasks we are asked to deal with is another matter. We believe we *can* create cognitively and socially useful forms of activity in a variety of institutional settings. But so could Dewey, Luria, and Münsterberg. Our inclination is to conclude that our progress, if any, has been slight. Goethe could be nodding his head.

We should note in closing that the joint activity of producing this chapter was distributed in a manner that is recent historically but that is increasing rapidly in frequency. During the first round of writing, one author was in northern California, the other in southern California. During the second round of writing, one author was in southern California, the other in northern Europe. One writes on an MS/DOS machine, one on a Macintosh. Three Unix systems and an electronic mail network mediated between the different text editors and linked the co-authors to each other and to support staff (including the U.S. and Finnish postal systems). It may be in no small measure owing to such new forms of joint-activity-at-a-distance that we have made the current rediscovery that thinking occurs as much among as within individuals.

# References

Anderson, R. C., Hiebert, E. H., Scott, J. A., & Wilkinson, I. A. G. (1985). *Becoming a nation of readers.* Washington, DC: National Institute of Education.

Arney, W. R., & Bergen, B. J. (1984). *Medicine and the management of living: Taming the last great beast.* Chicago: University of Chicago Press.

Bateson, G. (1972). Form, substance, and difference. In *Steps to an ecology of mind* (2d ed.). New York: Ballantine Books.

Berry, J. (1976). *Ecology and cultural style.* New York: Sage-Halstead.

Blumenthal, A. L. (1980). Wilhelm Wundt: Problems of interpretation. In W. G. Bringmann & R. D. Tweney (Eds.), *Wundt studies: A centennial collection* (pp. 435–45). Toronto: Hogrefe.

Bock, P. (1988). *Rethinking psychological anthropology.* New York: Freeman.

Boster, J. (1991). The information economy model applied to biological similarity judgement. In L. B. Resnick, J. Levine, & S. D. Behrend (Eds.), *Perspectives on socially shared cognition* (pp. 203–25). Washington, DC: APA Press.

Cahan, E. D., & White, S. (1992). Proposal for a second psychology. *American Psychologist, 47,* 224–35.

Connerton, P. (1989). *How societies remember.* Cambridge University Press.

D'Andrade, R. (1984). Cultural meaning systems. In R. A. Shweder & R. A. LeVine (Eds.), *Culture theory: Essays on mind, self, and emotion* (pp. 88–119). Cambridge University Press.

   (1986). Three scientific world views and the covering law model. In D. Fiske & R. Shweder (Eds.), *Meta-theory in the social sciences* (pp. 19–41). Chicago: University of Chicago Press.

   (1990). Culture and human cognition. In J.W. Stigler, R.A. Shweder, & G. Herdt (Ed.), *Cultural psychology: Essays on comparative human development.* Cambridge University Press.

Dewey, J. (1963). *Experience and education.* New York: McMillan. (Originally published 1938.)

Douglas, M. (1987). *How institutions think.* London: Routledge & Kegan Paul.

Edelman, G. (1987). *Neural Darwinism.* New York: Basic Books.

Engeström, Y. (1987). *Learning by expanding: An activity-theoretical approach to developmental research.* Helsinki: Orienta-Konsultit.

   (1989). *Developing thinking at the changing workplace: Toward a redefinition of expertise* (Technical Rep. 130). University of California, San Diego: Center for Human Information Processing.

   (1990). *Learning, working and imagining: Twelve studies in activity theory.* Helsinki: Orienta-Konsultit.

   (1991). Activity theory and individual and social transformation. *Multidisciplinary Newsletter for Activity Theory, 7–8,* 6–17.

   (in press). Developmental studies on work as a testbench of activity theory. In S. Chaiklin & J. Lave (Eds.), *Understanding practice: Perspectives on activity and context.* Cambridge University Press.

Engeström, Y., Engeström, R., & Saarelma, O. (1988, September). Computerized medical records, production pressure and compartmentalization in the work activity of health center physicians. In *Proceedings of the Conference on Computer-Supported Cooperative Work* (pp. 65–84). New York: Association for Computing Machinery.

Farr, R. (1987). The science of mental life: A social psychological perspective. *Bulletin of the British Psychological Society, 40*, 1–17.

Foorman, B., & Siegel, A. W. (Eds.). (1986). *The acquisition of reading skills.* Hillsdale, NJ: Erlbaum.

Fussell, S. R. & Krauss, R. M. (1989). The effects of intended audience on message production and comprehension: Reference in a common ground framework. *Journal of Experimental Social Psychology, 25*, 203–19.

Geertz, C. (1973). *The interpretation of culture.* New York: Basic Books.

Griffin, P., King, C., Diaz, E., & Cole, M. (1989). *A socio-historical approach to learning and instruction* (in Russian). Moscow: Pedagogika.

Hutchins, E. (1986). Mediation and automatization, *Quarterly Newsletter of the Laboratory of Comparative Human Cognition, 8*, 47–57.

Katz, J. (1984). *The silent world of doctor and patient.* New York: Free Press.

King, C. (1988). *The social facilitation of reading comprehension.* Unpublished doctoral dissertation, University of California, San Diego.

Laboratory of Comparative Human Cognition (1982). A model system for the remediation of learning disabilities. *Quarterly Newsletter of the Laboratory of Comparative Human Cognition, 4*(3), 39–66.

Lave, J. (1988). *Cognition in practice.* Cambridge University Press.

Leont'ev, A. N. (1932). Studies in the cultural development of the child, 3: The development of voluntary attention in the child. *Journal of Genetic Psychology, 37*, 52–81.

(1978). *Activity, consciousness, and personality.* Englewood Cliffs, NJ: Prentice-Hall.

(1981). *Problems in the development of mind.* Moscow: Progress Publishers.

Luria, A. R. (1928). The problem of the cultural development of the child. *Journal of Genetic Psychology, 35*, 506.

(1932). *The nature of human conflicts.* New York: Liveright.

(1973). *Traumatic aphasia.* New York: Basic Books.

(1978). The development of writing in the child. In M. Cole (Ed.), *The selected writings of A. R. Luria.* White Plains, NY: Sharpe. (Originally published 1929.)

(1979). *The making of mind.* Cambridge, MA: Harvard University Press.

(1981). *Language and cognition.* Washington, DC: Winston.

Macfarlane, A. (1977). *The psychology of childbirth.* Cambridge, MA: Harvard University Press.

Maniulenko, Z. V. (1975). The development of voluntary behavior in pre-school-age children. *Soviet Psychology, 13*, 65–116. (Originally published 1948.)

McClelland, J. L. & Rumelhart, D. E. (1981). An interactive activation model of context effects in letter perception, Part 1: An account of basic findings. *Psychological Review, 88*(5), 375–407.

Münsterberg, H. (1914). *Psychology: General and applied.* New York: Appleton.

Palincsar, A. S., & Brown, A. L. (1984). Reciprocal teaching of comprehension-fostering and monitoring activities. *Cognition and Instruction, 1,* 117–75.

Rubin, J. Z., Provezano, F. J., & Luria, Z. (1974). The eye of the beholder: Parents' view on sex of newborns. *American Journal of Orthopsychiatry, 44,* 512–19.

Scardamalia, M., & Bereiter, C. (1985). Fostering the development of self-regulation in children's knowledge processing. In S. F. Shipman, J. W. Segal, & R. Glaser (Eds.), *Thinking and learning skills: Research and open questions* (pp. 65–80). Hillsdale, NJ: Erlbaum.

Schwartz, T. (1978). The size and shape of culture. In F. Barth (Ed.), *Scale and social organization* (pp. 215–52). Oslo: Universitetsforlaget.

(1990). The structure of national cultures. In P. Funke (Ed.), *Understanding the USA* (pp. 110–49). Tübingen: Gunter Narr.

Shorter, E. (1985). *Bedside manners: The troubled history of doctors and patients.* New York: Simon & Schuster.

Stocking, G. (1968). *Race, culture, and evolution.* New York: Free Press.

Toulmin, S. (1981). Toward reintegration: An agenda for psychology's second century. In R. A. Kasschau & C. N. Coter (Eds.), *Psychology's second century: enduring issues* (pp. 264–86). New York: Praeger.

Valsiner, J. (1988). *Developmental psychology in the Soviet Union.* Bloomington: Indiana University Press.

Vygotsky, L. S. (1929). The problem of the cultural development of the child, II. *Journal of Genetic Psychology, 36,* 415–34.

(1960). *The development of higher psychological functions (in Russian).* Moscow: Izdael'stov Akademii Pedagogicheskikh Nauk.

(1978). *Mind in society.* Cambridge, MA: Harvard University Press.

(1987). *Thinking and speech.* New York: Plenum. (Originally published 1934.)

Wertsch, J. (1985). *The social formation of mind.* Cambridge, MA: Harvard University Press.

White, L. (1942). On the use of tools by primates. *Journal of Comparative Psychology, 34,* 369–74.

(1959). The concept of culture. *American Anthropologist, 61,* 227–51.

Wundt, W. (1921). *Elements of folk psychology.* London: Allen & Unwin.

# 2 Practices of distributed intelligence and designs for education

*Roy D. Pea*

## Introduction

Widespread conceptions of learning and reasoning invoke "intelligence" largely as a property of the minds of individuals. This belief is prevalent in educational settings, which are concerned largely with solitary intelligence. Intelligence, they say, is what testing firms test and, increasingly commonly, what schools need to be held more accountable to measuring and improving.

Problems lurk in these assumptions. Anyone who has closely observed the practices of cognition is struck by the fact that the "mind" rarely works alone. The intelligences revealed through these practices are distributed – across minds, persons, and the symbolic and physical environments, both natural and artificial. Gregory Bateson remarked that memory is half in the head and half in the world. In this chapter, I will first lay out the central ideas of the distributed-intelligence framework and then provide a background to its development, before closing with considerations of some implications for education. How we think about these relations may change what we

Portions of this chapter were originally slated to appear in a book edited by David Perkins and Becky Simmons of Harvard University's Educational Technology Center. Plans for that book subsequently foundered, and portions of my essay (Pea, 1988) appear here as a necessary pretext to subsequent work. Previous papers on this theme were first presented in April 1988 to the First Annual Cognition and Education Workshop, Bolt, Beranek and Newman, Inc., Cambridge, Massachusetts, and at the 1988 Cognitive Science Society Meetings. Related work was described at the 1989 Social Science Research Council Conference on Social Aspects of Computing (in which Gavriel Salomon and David Perkins participated) and in the 1990 American Educational Research Association Symposium on Distributed Intelligence, which led to the plan for this book. I am indebted to Christina Allen for provocative discussions of distributed intelligence, especially concerning design and the roles of human desires.

47

do with technologies in education – not only computational media, but also social technologies for supporting learning such as guided participation or peer collaboration and learning/teaching materials more broadly. While providing few answers, I hope to provoke new questions and inquiries, for distributed intelligence is not a theory of mind, or culture, or design, or symbol systems and their impact on human thought so much as it is a heuristic framework for raising and addressing theoretical and empirical questions about these and other topics.

While the relevance of these concepts is not restricted to learning in mathematics, science, and technology, I will often use examples and issues in these fields for making my points, since the roles for distributed intelligence perhaps stand out in greater relief in these domains than in other areas of learning, education, and work.

## The nature and concepts of distributed intelligence

Knowledge is commonly socially constructed, through collaborative efforts toward shared objectives or by dialogues and challenges brought about by differences in persons' perspectives. Intelligence may also be distributed for use in designed artifacts as diverse as physical tools, representations such as diagrams, and computer–user interfaces to complex tasks. In these cases, intelligence is often distributed by off-loading what could be elaborate and error-prone mental reasoning processes as action constraints of either the physical or symbolic environments.

On close inspection, the environments in which humans live are thick with invented artifacts that are in constant use for structuring activity, for saving mental work, or for avoiding error, and they are adapted creatively almost without notice. These ubiquitous mediating structures that both organize and constrain activity include not only designed objects such as tools, control instruments, and symbolic representations like graphs, diagrams, text, plans, and pictures, but people in social relations, as well as features and landmarks in the physical environment. Imagine the absence of the following resources and the detrimental effects of that absence on the activities to which they may contribute intelligence: keyboard letters, labels on instrument controls, everyday notes, well-placed questions, the use of space to organize piles of materials on a desktop, the emergent text in a written composition one is constructing. These everyday cases show the active and evolving structuring of the material and social environments to make them a repository of action mediators. Unlike other species, such as Simon's (1981) ant on the beach, whose complexity of behavior is determined more by the shape of its environment than by its mental contents, humans have desires that lead them to recraft their environments to carry out aspects of reasoning, to make reminders for action, and to get help from others. When talking about distributed intelligence, then, I mean that resources in the world are used, or come together in use, to shape and direct possible activity emerging from desire. This is not to claim, of course, that *all* intelligence is or can be so distributed, but that there is a constitutive trend in this direction to be found in cultural history, ontogenesis, and the microgenesis of activity.

The distributed-intelligence orientation that I describe, which takes these observations as central data about cognition, stands in sharp contrast to the common focus on "intelligence" as an attribute of individuals, carried primarily in internal transformations of mental representations of symbols for goals, objects, and relations. Theories of education building on these notions are concerned largely with solitary intelligence, decontextualized from its uses in activities beyond the educational. Analyses of our designs for such distributions may be more revealing for understanding cognition than are studies of the formation and transformation of mental representations that have come to define cognitive science and educational studies based on this field.

Some key interrelated concepts I will use require clarification. These include "intelligence," "activity," "distributed," "means–end adaptivity," "affordances," and "desire."

## Intelligence as distributed and manifest in activity

The primary sense of distributed intelligence arises from thinking of people in action.[1] We begin with activity, expressing

---

[1] I take the work of Leont'ev (1978a, b) on activity theory as arguing forcibly for the centrality of people-in-action, activity systems, as units of analysis for deepening our understanding of thinking. On related philosophical grounds, Wartofsky's (1979,

action rather than a state of being. In such activity, we see the *configuring* of distributed intelligence. Activity is enabled by intelligence, but not only intelligence contributed by the individual agent. When I say that intelligence is distributed, I mean that the resources that shape and enable activity are distributed in configuration across people, environments, and situations. In other words, intelligence is accomplished rather than possessed. The intentionality of activity may originate with the agent's desires or the hopes of a designer wishing to bring the affordances of a new artifact into the configuration of another agent's activity. While it is people who are in activity, artifacts commonly provide resources for its guidance and augmentation. The design of artifacts, both historically by others and opportunistically in the midst of one's activity, can advance that activity by shaping what are possible and what are necessary elements of that activity.

What is meant by *intelligence* as distributed? I use the phrase "distributed intelligence" rather than "distributed cognition," because *people,* not designed objects,[2] "do" cognition. Yet I want to capture the important fact that intelligence, which comes to life during human activities, may be crafted. There are both social and material dimensions of this distribution. The social distribution of intelligence comes from its construction in activities such as the guided participation in joint action common in parent–child interaction or apprenticeship, or through people's collaborative efforts to achieve shared aims. The material distribution of intelligence originates in the situated invention of uses for aspects of the environment or the exploitation of the affordances of designed artifacts, either of which may contribute to supporting the achievement of an activity's purpose.

Activity is achieved in means–end adaptations. These adaptations may be more or less successful. The focus in thinking about distributed intelligence is not on intelligence as an abstract property or quantity residing in minds, organizations, or objects. In its primary sense here, intelligence is manifest in activity that connects means and ends through achievements. I also do not mean "intelligent" in

1983) historical epistemology also highlights external action, or praxis, as the focus of understanding for psychological development.

[2] I leave designed objects such as "artificially intelligent" computer software aside for the moment, concentrating on noncomputational objects. Whether computer programs engage in cognition is not a topic of this chapter.

the generic folk value sense, so I reject "distributed foolishness" or "stupidity" as antonyms of "distributed intelligence." These are values at the evaluation level of the action itself (e.g., "Bank robbing is a stupid and not an intelligent act") or in terms of norms regarding, for example, the efficiency of means–end adaptivity, as in "Using a rock to hammer a nail is stupid; using a hammer is more intelligent."

### Affordances

How do tools serve as artifacts of distributed intelligence, carrying along with them new opportunities for contributing to activity, as defined by a community of users of such tools? I begin this inquiry by noting the focal relevance of works by Vygotsky, Simon, and Gibson. Each of these theorists considered questions about the distribution of intelligence between the world and the mind to be fundamental. Vygotsky (1978) placed great emphasis on the ways in which the character of social interactions and externally mediated action makes explicit certain processes that come to be internalized in the private thought of the individual. In Simon's (1981) seminal work, *The Sciences of the Artificial,* he questions whether what we often consider the complexity of some act of thought may have more to do with the complexity of the environment in which action takes place than with the intrinsic mental complexity of the activity. In pointing to the mind–environment interface, Simon suggests looking at problem solving as distributed between mind and the mediational structures that the world offers. In Gibson's (1979, 1982) work on the ecology of perception, the notion of "affordances" of objects that link perception and action is central. "Affordance" refers to the perceived and actual properties of a thing, primarily those functional properties that determine just how the thing could possibly be used. Less technically, a doorknob *is for* turning, a wagon handle *is for* pulling.

Research examining the concept of affordances is critical if we are to build a science of distributed intelligence and a more flexible design orientation to the practices of education. For many of the hoped-for goals of education, we presuppose the success of the social constructability of affordances – that one can get a learner to attend to the pertinent properties of the environment, or the designed object, or the inscriptional notations, such that the learner can join in to contribute to distributed intelligence in activity. For a given activity, and the various means for its achievement, there can be considerable variation in the ease with which one can show a learner how to exploit those means to form a system of distributed intelligence for achieving that task. This will vary with the learner's background experiences, the obviousness of the mapping between the learner's desire or goal, and the assimilation of the artifact as means toward it. Such a meeting of intentionality and artifact in activity is thus not simply the direct perceptual pickup of the affordance structure of the object or notation, as radical Gibsonians would have it. Culture and context contribute to its achievement.

Norman (1988) has done a great service both to the field of design and to psychology in developing Gibson's insights on affordances (which largely underplayed the cultural factors involved in learning to use humanly designed objects) into what he calls a "psychology of everyday things." Norman offers many examples – microwave ovens, videocassette recorders, car instrument panels, slide projectors, even water faucets – to show how affordances of objects deeply and often unnecessarily restrict their *accessibility* to the ordinary human. The point is that better design of artifacts would make it easier to accomplish certain functions. One would like to be able just to look and see what to do, and then do it, without instruction, without manuals, without complex deductions. Such "efficiency" of action is also a tacit objective of cognition in practice. Everyone can imagine a few examples of powerful representational tools that are not obvious in function (e.g., the static $x$–$y$ coordinate graph, static ray diagrams in optics) and make apparent that what Norman calls the "psychopathology of everyday things" may carry over only too well to an account of the psychopathology of instructional artifacts and representations in mathematics and science.

Lave (1988) offers many examples of "smart tools" that we may point to as illustrations of the everyday presence of such distributed intelligence. She describes how measurement activities are often achieved with special-purpose "stashes" of numerical information embodied in measuring instruments. Examples include such invisible cases as the dime-store thermometer, yardstick, auto speedometer, and home thermostat. Many of these objects have become "mythic," as Roland Barthes (1972) uses this term, in that they have become so deeply a part of our consciousness that we do not notice them. Turned from history into nature, they are invisible, un-"remarkable" aspects of our experiential world. A large number of such "smart objects," especially for measurement and for calculation, but also as reminding devices, are appearing. They are becoming especially prevalent as microprocessors enter the fabric of everyday activities by the tens of millions. Finding marketable niches for such efficiency, many of these devices reify common problem formats and automate solution-finding procedures. Examples include jogger pulse meters, automatic street locators, currency exchange calculators, world-time clocks, and weight-loss calculators.

These tools literally carry intelligence *in* them, in that they represent some individual's or some community's decision that the means thus offered should be reified, made stable, as a quasi-permanent form, for use by others. In terms of cultural history, these tools and the practices of the user community that accompany them are major carriers of patterns of previous reasoning. They may contribute to patterns of distributed intelligence configured in activity. They may now be used by a new generation with little or no awareness of the struggle that went into defining them and to adapting their characteristics to the tasks for which they were created. The inventions of Leibniz's calculus and Descartes's coordinate graphs were startling achievements; today they are routine content for high school mathematics. But as such tools become invisible, it becomes harder to see them as bearing intelligence; instead, we see the intelligence "residing" in the individual mind using the tools. This encapsulation of distributed intelligence, manifest in such human activities as measuring or computing, may arise because we are extraordinarily efficient agents, always trying to make what we have learned works usable again and again. We deploy effort-saving strategies in recognition of their cognitive economy and diminished opportunity for error (Kusterer, 1978; Scribner, 1986).

The individual still has a primacy in activity, of course. But the distributed-intelligence framework sees a much more substantial haze around the boundary of the person and shines the light of attention on the more invisible intelligence in the artifactual, physical,

symbolic, and social surrounds, as brought into relief in the config-
urations of distributed intelligence by which activity is achieved.

To sum up, knowledge is often carried in artifacts as diverse as
physical tools and notational systems such as algebraic equations.
This knowledge may come to be exploited in activity by a new learner
through a variety of genetic paths: through observations of use by
other humans and attempts to imitate it, through playful discovery of
its affordances in solitary activity, and through guided participation in
its use by more knowledgeable others. And the affordances of such
artifacts may be more or less difficult to convey to novice users of
these artifacts in the activities to which they contribute distributed
intelligence.

### Desires

Our last major concept is "desire." What initiates activities
and designs of distributed intelligence? I find it useful to begin with
Norman's (1988) approximate model of the structure of activity. His
account of seven stages of action proceeds through four stages of execution – forming a goal, forming an intention, specifying an action-
sequence plan, and executing an action, and three stages of
evaluation – perceiving the world state after the action, interpreting
the world state, and evaluating an outcome of action in relation to the
goal. Since I believe that the concept of "goal" common in cognitive
science presupposes commitment to greater articulateness and mental representation than the diffusely specified *desires* that often lead to
action,[3] it will be important to develop some basic account of desires
in order to think about the shapes of distributed intelligent activity
that emerge for people.

How do people's *desires* for a particular situation shape both their
interpretation and their use of resources for activity? Human use of
distributed intelligence in the designed environment to achieve activity goes far beyond either situational determinism or a decoding

---

[3] Agre (in press), Suchman (1987), and Winograd and Flores (1987) have provided
compelling arguments on this point, rooted in phenomenological works by
Heidegger, Husserl, and Schutz. Their arguments on the primacy of situated action
and the derivative nature of mental representation also rest on a shift of attention
toward person-acting-in-setting-with-others-and-artifacts-with-cultural-histories as
the to-be-explained rather than individual knowledge.

of the intentions behind the design of objects.While one who is using a hammer to strike a nail is, in the achievement of that activity, in an important sense collaborating with its designer, there is more to it than this. The process also involves the interpretation of resources and relationships for creative and novel activity (Schön, 1983). Resources of the world offer potential relationships, constrained by their affordances, that may not at all be mentally represented prior to a situational perception of their meaning. Their functional roles as components of a configuration of distributed intelligence may arise only in the course of desire-driven initiatives by an actor. This observation is profoundly true for designers, who are continually creating new objects and environments, interpreting their meaning, and revising their designs accordingly (Allen, 1988). Intelligence is contributed in each moment by the ways in which people interpret the things they are experiencing. We need to understand more fully the genesis of human desires, because people create, invent, and innovate as they create or act in designs for distributed intelligence. They do not simply act in habitual, static ways. The interpretation, relevance, and meaning of resources available for activity are shaped by the desires with which people come to situations.

Some basic distinctions are valuable for beginning to think through a useful taxonomy of desires. We can identify a small set of basic desires, not intended to be exhaustive, each of which constitutes a kind of experiential "moment" that a person brings to a situation for achieving activity:

1. With a *task* desire, one has a clear goal and intention, and the need is to specify an action with a particular means. If I am freezing in a cabin, my task desire for warmth may make the affordance of a chair for burning much more salient than its affordance for sitting. If my task desire were different, different properties of the chair would matter.

2. With a *mapping* desire, one falls short of mapping the achievement of projected activity back into the specific action to be taken with an available means. I know this tool may be used to achieve the activity, but I am uncertain of how the distributed-intelligence resources need to come together in design. In Norman's terms, this is a gap to be closed from intention to specification of action. I have available an outline processor instead of a typewriter for writing – my

task of writing and tool are known, but now the desire is to find the ways in which this outline processor is useful for the writing task. To close this gap between desire and action may require reflective cognition, as suggested in accounts of the breakdown of "concernfull action" (Winograd & Flores, 1987).

3. With a *circumstantial* desire, one has no specific goal or intention in approaching the situation. Instead, the desire arises opportunistically in response to one's noticing properties of the situation that emerge during action. A rubber band becomes a musical instrument; a steering wheel emerges as a percussion device for the driver listening to a song. For circumstantial desire, the role of play, of exploration of potential relations into which the object can enter, cannot be underemphasized.

4. With a *habitual* desire, one merely repeats a familiar course of action incorporating the distributed-intelligence resources of the world or other persons into one's activity. Winograd and Flores (1987, p. 32) follow Heidegger in calling such unreflective, action-embedded knowledge "ready-to-hand." The blind man tapping his cane on the pavement treats it as an extension of self; it becomes invisible in its properties as means, since it is so well integrated in activity.[4] The seven stages of action are cycled with minimal notice.

In these examples, we can see creativity emerging from situated interpretations of resources in the environment based on desires. Creativity often consists of novel interpretations in activity of desire–situation resource pairs. While more kinds of desire surely exist than the ones described,[5] we can see the importance of the concept by noting how designs for distributed intelligence are reliant upon the specific desires in an activity.

## Beginnings

How did this view of distributed intelligence arise? I can explain what it seeks to account for in terms of the paths that led to its

[4] An example often used by Wittgenstein and Merleau-Ponty, and later by Bateson (1972).
[5] For example, Ford and Nichols (1987) define a broad variety of human goals, including goals directed toward transactional accomplishments such as those of safety, sex and reproduction, self-esteem, establishing social relationships, and hunger satisfaction, and what they describe as internally oriented goals such as experiencing a sunset, having fun, feeling joy, avoiding stress, and spirituality.

development. As a developmental psychologist in the early 1980s with a long-term interest in the social foundations of cognitive growth, I became very intrigued with the increasingly prevalent use of technologies in society, including the widely hyped developments in artificial intelligence systems of the time. What consequences would this have for rethinking human development, learning, and educational goals and practice? I developed a cultural-historical perspective, influenced by the works of Vygotsky, Luria, and Cole and rooted in the theories of Vico, Hegel, Marx, and Engels, for addressing these questions. Cole and Engeström (Chapter 1, this volume) provide some historical context for this work, so I will not do so here. A fundamental aspect of this perspective is a view of human nature that, while acknowledging biological and environmental contributions, emphasizes that humankind is "reshaped through a dialectic of reciprocal influences: Our productive activities change the world, thereby changing the ways in which the world can change us. By shaping nature and how our interactions with it are mediated, we change ourselves" (Pea, 1985a, p. 169). Just as the use of physical machinery in farm labor came to mediate human interaction with nature in increasingly different ways, so too do computer technologies mediate human interactions with nature, information, and other persons in distinctly different ways. This argument is an extension of Vygotsky's (1930/ 1978) arguments in "Tool and Symbol," in which he emphasized that both physical tools and symbol systems culturally mediate human activity.

This perspective on the sociohistorical construction of human nature is also reflected in studies of the child as a "cultural invention," in which it is argued that the concept of "child" is a social and historical kind rather than a natural kind, and that children become what they are taken to be by others (e.g., Wartofsky, 1983).

I took up these issues in several different essays. In one (Pea, 1985a), I argued that computer tools serve not as they are often construed – as "amplifiers" of cognition – but as "reorganizers of mental functioning." The distinction highlighted the functional organization, or system characteristics, of human activity. Whereas amplification suggests primarily quantitative changes in accomplishments, what humans actually do in their activities changes when the functional organization of that activity is transformed by technologies.

(I explicate some of these functional shifts later in a section on Polya and distributed intelligence.)

In another essay speculating on integrating human and computer intelligence, I took a Vygotskian perspective on this question (Pea, 1985b), asking whether future computer systems could serve interactively, as adults and more able peers do now, to help guide children through zones of proximal development (ZPD), co-constructing with children their latent developmental capabilities. The central idea that emerged from these considerations was a radical one – that of considering the child–computer system as the developmental unit. I suggested an extension of the Turing test for assessing computer intelligence by means of an inability to differentiate interactive dialogues with the output of a human and that of a computer. In this extension, applied to the developmental level of the child–computer system outputs rather than the unsupported child, one would look for answers to queries concerning tasks defined to represent thinking of particular developmental levels for a child–computer system versus a child alone.

I further distinguished between "pedagogic systems," or uses of computers that focus on achieving the cognitive self-sufficiency of their users, and "pragmatic systems, which allow for precocious intellectual performances of which the child may be incapable without the system's support" (Pea, 1985b, p. 84). More recently, Salomon, Perkins, and Globerson (1991) have echoed this distinction in their characterization of effects *of* technology and effects *with* technology, a contrast to which I will return.

## Getting to distributed intelligence

Since those essays were written, there has been a substantial increase in the density and novelty of computer technologies that play important roles in augmenting human activities, in science, industry, and education. Of special relevance to distributed intelligence is the increasing use of visualization techniques in scientific inquiry.

### *Augmenting intelligence with computing*

In the case of science visualization, throughout many university and industrial research laboratories, groups and individuals are achieving their desired activities through the use of high-resolution graphics programs, often involving supercomputers, which provide manipulable "virtual realities" (Lanier, 1989; Rheingold, 1991) for modeling and reasoning about domain phenomena in science, engineering, mathematics, and design (Brooks, 1988). In this paradigm, graphic computer representations have "direct manipulation" interfaces (Hutchins, Hollan, & Norman, 1986) with action properties analogous to their real-world counterparts. Human intuitions about how to act are exploited in communication with the machine in order to narrow gaps between desires and actions.

From such labs as that of the University of North Carolina at Chapel Hill, VPL Research, National Center for Supercomputing Applications at University of Illinois, Urbana-Champaign, and NASA AMES Research Center, scientific visualization examples include topics as diverse as molecular "docking" in molecular engineering (Ouh-Young, Pique, Hughes, Srinivisan, & Brooks, 1988), travel through virtual buildings before they are constructed (Brooks, 1986), and a study of a numerically modeled severe storm (Wilhelmson et al., 1990). Furthermore, modeling and interpretation of patterns in complex empirical data in biomedical research, space exploration, geophysics, molecular modeling, and robotics have come to depend on three-dimensional (3-D) graphic rather than numerical data displays, and new 3-D designs for structuring information displays exploit human visualization skills as well (Card, Robertson, & Mackinlay, 1991). The veridicality of many of these aesthetically elegant interfaces to complex knowledge are so striking that they have come to be designated as "virtual realities" in which highly complex phenomena can be modeled, explored, and experienced in lush color and dynamics well suited to the categorizing and pattern recognition capabilities of the human visual system (Blattner & Dannenberg, 1991) and, in some cases, the proprioceptive feedback that is provided. For example, take the following description of a 1991 SIGGRAPH course by Richard Becker of AT&T Bell Laboratories:

Consider for example, measurements of temperature, humidity, barometric pressure, percentage of cloud cover, solar radiation intensity, and wind speed at a particular location at noon on 100 different days. The data on these six non-spatial variables consist of 100 points in a six-dimensional space. In this course, participants peer into such six-dimensional spaces, see the configuration of points, and visualize them to understand their complex relationships.

Note in applications of advanced computing such as these how sym-
biotic are the contributions of the scientist formulating the problems
and comparisons of interest, the designers of visualization algorithms,
and the contributions of computation and display technologies.

While such applications are beyond most K–12 settings, nonetheless dynamic 2-D and, occasionally, 3-D graphic interfaces contribute to learning and reasoning in mathematics and science education.
Perhaps most striking is the use in thousands of classrooms of
microcomputer-based laboratories with which students can investigate real-world phenomena by means of data collection using probes
that plug into the computer for such variables as temperature, pressure, light, and sound, with the generation of graphs to be interpreted
as the results of these investigations (Linn, in press; Thornton &
Sokoloff, 1990; Tinker, 1992). Again, consider the contributions
made by the teacher and curriculum materials to the framing of the
learner's investigations, the learner's perceptual and interpretive processes for looking at graphs, the technology collecting data and transforming them into data displays, and the designers behind these
innovations. Similarly striking advances have been made in developing computer tools for learning statistics in middle schools and high
schools through building and manipulating statistical models of populations (Hancock & Kaput, 1990; Rubin, Rosebery, Bruce, & Du-
Mouchel, 1988; Rubin et al., 1990; Russell & Corwin, 1990),[6] or for
learning Newtonian physics in elementary schools (White, 1988;
White & Horwitz, 1987). In each case, researchers and educators
have been surprised at the young age at which learners can participate in treatments of complex subject matter.

### *Augmenting intelligence with guided participation*

There has also been much work on designing new social arrangements and activity structures to support human learning, much
of it inspired by Vygotskian (1978) and neo-Vygotskian conceptions
of the ZPD, which argue that development occurs as the "internalization" of socially distributed cognitive processes in a "zone of

---

[6] Spatial location, shape, color, brightness, and motion are used in commercial statistics programs such as Data Desk, MacSpin, StatView, and Systat for visualizing
complex empirical phenomena and equations.

proximal development," toward autonomous performance (Brown, Chapter 7, this volume; Newman, Griffin, & Cole, 1989; Rogoff, 1990). In these conceptions of social contexts of cognitive development, adults often provide supported situations for children to perform more complex tasks than their current knowledge and skills alone would allow. Such "guided participation" (an apt phrase used by Rogoff, 1990) distributes the intelligence required to carry off the activity across child and adult. Affiliated work has elaborated a model of learning through reciprocal teaching and cognitive apprenticeships in which intelligence required to do an activity (e.g., interpret a text) is distributed across a group of peers, or a learner–mentor system (Brown, Collins, & Duguid, 1989; Collins, Brown, & Newman, 1989), as exemplified by instructional studies in reading (Palincsar & Brown, 1984), text composition (Bereiter & Scardamalia, 1986), college mathematics problem solving (Schoenfeld, 1985), and learning how to reason in geometrical optics (Pea, in press; Pea, Sipusic, & Allen, in press).

*Augmenting intelligence with inscriptional systems*

It is widely recognized that external representational systems, dependent on inscriptional technologies such as paper and pencil, computer and display, have made major contributions to the sociohistorical development of science, mathematics, and other disciplines (e.g., Cassirer, 1923; Goodman, 1978). I use the phrase "inscriptional systems" rather than "symbol systems" or "representational systems" for two reasons. First, I want to stress their external, in-the-world status, which allows for construction, review, deconstruction, and the emergence of completed structures of inscriptions that have little relation to their patterns of temporal development (Latour & Woolgar, 1986; Lynch & Woolgar, 1990). Second, both "symbol" and "representation" have taken on the cognitive sciences interpretation of *mental* representation, deemphasizing the sociohistorical fact that many of the kinds of notations that are considered to be among the languages of "thought" – such as mathematical language, written language, and scientific symbols – began their existence ontogenetically as external inscriptions whose conventions of construction, interpretation, and use in activities had to be acquired in cultural activities.

We know that inscriptional systems often pose vast problems for the learner. Mapping relations between objects in the world and the written number system are problematic for many learners, as in the well-documented difficulties of place–value subtraction or, for older learners, between algebra equations or linguistic descriptions of situations and their representation in the notation of Cartesian coordinate graphs (Confrey, 1990). Inscriptions rarely reveal their affordances for activity. It is too rarely recognized that inscriptional systems, while allowing for efficient achievement of certain goal-directed activities, also make those very activities opaque to persons not privy to the conventions for their interpretation and use, an unfortunate circumstance for learning mathematics and science. The affordances of many inscriptional systems are deeply cultural in the following sense: A person has to have been introduced to, and preferably to have participated in, the activities that give meaning to these inscriptions. After such initiations, one may have the sense of directly perceiving the patterns the inscriptional system was designed to make "obvious," but before such initiation, the conventions and uses of the inscriptions are usually obtuse. Mature users of an inscriptional system know the kinds of tasks it is good for – the questions it enables them to answer, the inferences it enables them to make – as well as its limitations. Much of this is invisible to the initiate, since such social practice does not lie "in" the representation itself, but in its roles in relation to the activities of persons in the world.

People often invent inscriptional systems for local purposes, to achieve activities that would be harder to accomplish without them. For example, in describing a microgenetic study of adolescents' invention of a notational scheme for describing velocity and acceleration, di Sessa et al. (1991) characterized the increasing sophistication of the notation as one of "transparency" or obviousness to their intended purpose. He described the talents the students revealed in describing the pros and cons of the inscriptional systems that different students invented during the several-hour session as "metarepresentational knowledge." He demonstrated how the different kinds of inscriptional systems the students invented required more or less explanation for peers to be able to interpret the mapping from inscription to the situation depicted. I argue that we see the concept of efficiency of action, and the closing of the gap from desire to achievement, as important contributors to the normative assessments of "better" inscriptional systems (Pea, 1992).

### Augmenting intelligence with situated cognition

Diverse studies, primarily on the basic mathematical reasoning that is embedded in such activities as the order loading of dairy workers (Scribner, 1985), grocery shopping (Murtaugh, 1985), and home dieting measurement activities (de la Rocha, 1986) and various street-life activities, such as street candy selling by Brazilian children (Carraher, Carraher, & Schliemann, in press; Saxe, 1988, 1990), began to reveal the powerful ways in which people use structural properties of the physical environment to carry some of the weight of what is traditionally "mental" activity in school-based mathematics tasks (Lave, 1988; Lave, Murtaugh, & de la Rocha, 1984). For example, in grocery store best-buy shopping, when mathematics is used at all, it is virtually always correct and creative in its uses of material features of unit sizes to save "mental" work in computation (Lave et al., 1984). Similar findings on exploitation of the environment to help in the doing of intelligence are provided by work on ecological memory in repetitive work tasks such as those involved in barhopping and waiting on tables (see Scribner, 1986). Such studies highlight how intelligence efficiently uses resources, drafting, or crafting the environment to achieve activity with less mental effort if necessary. These studies highlight the situated properties of everyday cognition, which is highly inventive in exploiting features of the physical and social situation as resources for performing a task, thereby avoiding the need for mental symbol manipulations unless they are required by that task. Empirical domains in which these conceptions have been further developed include reasoning about algebraic functions on a physical winch (Greeno, 1991), team navigation of a large ship (Hutchins, 1990), and carrying out photocopying tasks (Suchman, 1987).

The work on situated cognitive theory by Lave, Scribner, and others was richly descriptive and revealed aspects of human preference structures for relying on intelligence in the world in functional systems of activity. But that work did not go far enough in my opinion. It fell short in not acknowledging the fundamental roles of design in the activities of these reasoners and designers, in the achievement of action through situated cognition. These studies also did not move from "is" to "ought" – for example, by recommending that learners be prepared by education to more deeply exploit situated knowledge for action in the world; nor did they, as Norman's (1988) work came to do, exhort designers to help learners function more effectively in the world.

### Rich phenomena without a framework

I was struck by the lack of adequate conceptions of intelligence and its development to account for what was exciting and seemed to be working in new computer-enhanced work and learning environments, those studies involving new social arrangements for supporting learning, and accounts of the situated properties of everyday cognition. But what was the link?

The missing orientation came to me as I was reflecting on a story told by Seymour Papert at a meeting of National Science Foundation project officers in 1987. Papert (1980) had provided extensive neo-Piagetian arguments that when, in instruction-centered learning, one directly teaches a learner something, one robs that learner of the opportunity to discover it for him- or herself. This constructivist argument[7] has been quite influential in designs for educational technology use in schools and in other curricular approaches. A version of this argument was made at this 1987 meeting by Papert concerning Logo–LEGO research. In this research, students built LEGO machines that could be controlled by Logo programs they wrote (Resnick & Ocko, 1990). Papert described what marvelous machines the students had built, with very little "interference" from teachers. On the surface, this argument was persuasive, and the children were discovering important things on their own. But on reflection, I felt this argument missed the key point about the "invisible" human intervention in this example – what the designers of LEGO and Logo crafted in creating just the interlockable component parts of LEGO machines or just the Logo primitive commands for controlling these machines. For there are only so many ways in which these components can be combined. Considerable intelligence has been *built into*

---

[7] The MIT Epistemology and Learning Group now designates its pedagogical perspective as one of "constructionism" (e.g., Harel, 1990).

these interpart relations as a means of constraining what actions are possible with the parts in combination. What I realized was that, although Papert could "see" teachers' interventions (a kind of social distribution of intelligence contributing to the child's achievement of activity), the designers' interventions (a kind of artifact-based intelligence contributing to the child's achievement of activity) were not seen, were somehow not viewed as affecting the terms of the constructionist argument. But, of course, in either case the child was not engaged in solitary discovery, in keeping with the Piagetian metaphor of "child as scientist" – he or she could be scaffolded in the achievement of activity either explicitly by the intelligence of the teacher, or *implicitly* by that of the designers, now embedded in the constraints of the artifacts with which the child was playing.

## *Distributed intelligence mediated by design*

What was thus missing, in my view, was an explicit recognition of the intelligence represented and representable in design, specifically in designed artifacts that play important roles in human activities. This led me to work on concepts and research explicitly concerning the notion of distributed intelligence around 1987 (Pea, 1988) and described in the present chapter.

## Polya on problem solving and distributed intelligence

As an illustration of the ways in which conceiving of activity in terms of distributed intelligence reorients our perspectives on familiar phenomena, let us look at a set of familiar assumptions about the nature of problem solving from cognitive psychology. Specifically, let us briefly turn to a familiar model of problem solving from Polya's *How to Solve It* and explore how the concept of distributed intelligence relates to it. The standard problem-solving model, introduced by John Dewey (1910) early in the century and revised and popularized by the mathematician George Polya (1957), has been assimilated into the mainstream of cognitive psychology, appearing in most textbooks and accounts of problem solving. Many theorists have found its depiction in a six-stage model convenient (Figure 2.1). Research has shown the applicability of this model to writing, algebra word problem

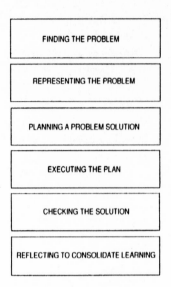

Figure 2.1. Six-stage problem-solving model.

solving, reading comprehension, electronics troubleshooting, programming, decision making, and many diverse tasks educators would like students to be able to do. It is important to note that these are not *linear* stages in a top-down process, but comprise a more *cyclic* system in which each new set of constraints created by materials the problem solver produces makes for new opportunities to be exploited in its next developments (as in writing; Pea & Kurland, 1987). This was the *first myth* to dissolve about the stages of problem solving.

The distributed-intelligence perspective provides reasons to explode a second and third myth intrinsic to the problem-solving model. Each involves dissolving the "boundaries" around the boxes.

The *second myth* is that the boxes in the model are constructions of the individual mind. Each phase may be, but is often not, the result of individual achievement. The role of others is crucial. In neo-Vygotskian research by Wertsch, McNamee, McLane, and Budwig (1980), we can see even "problem finding" as a social construction of the child with other agents, such as the mother who guides the child to "see" goals in the task of jigsaw-puzzle making. Similarly, in recent work on "anchored instruction," the Cognition and Technology

Group at Vanderbilt (1991) uses teacher guidance and carefully scripted videotapes of everyday problem solving to help students "see" the utility of concepts and strategies in mathematics and science for achieving activities in the world.

The *third myth* is that the different boxes in the model are mental constructions. They may be, but they are often not "tool-free." Crucial roles in mediating such phases of problem solving are played by external representations, features of the environment, and artifacts. "Planning a problem solution" is often mediated by external representations such as written language in lists or charts, or in diagrams serving as qualitative models of the problem situation. "Plan execution" is even automatically achieved through tools designed to save effort and to spare reliance on error-prone procedures (Engelbart, 1963; Rheingold, 1985).

So as we begin to ask, "What is distributed in distributed intelligence?" the boxes begin to crumble, and more complex formations of activity emerge:

1.  Different whole-component processes of the problem-solving model (e.g., problem finding or problem representation) may be distributed in the environment, tools, or other persons. Whole task components are typically distributed during *collaborative activities* (e.g., one person may draft a topical plan as another finds materials to allow for writing) and apprenticing (e.g., Zincanteco weaver apprentices take on part activities such a boiling thread before learning to cut fabrics for sewing; Greenfield & Lave, 1982).
2.  Parts of a whole-component process may be distributed as social constructions or as a result of processes of human-tool symbiosis (e.g., an outlining program and I work together to plan for text composition). In the social construction of plan execution during the single-word period, mother and child may build together a sentence that describes the present situation (Keenan, Schieffelin, & Platt, 1976).

Let us look more specifically at some of the ways intelligence is distributed with respect to the problem-solving model.

*Problem finding.* Goal cues are distributed in one kind of "problem finding." The need to recall what to do at an appropriate time or to cope with an overload of goals one wishes to maintain in working memory is often overcome by the use of artifacts (e.g., alarms, lists), mnemonic strategies using environmental features (such as reminder objects put in key locations), or other persons. A software program may provide timely cues to the different subtasks of writing or to planning a project development and delivery schedule. And in some structured curricula, "problem-finding" aspects of distributed intelligence are distributed in the text as adjunct questions to the reader.

*Problem representation.*    Humans often opportunistically use available objects, artifacts, or notes in representing problems – for example, milk crates are used by dairy loaders as calculating units (Scribner, 1985). A few examples will provide an illustration. In the well-known "cottage cheese" example, a weight watcher in the kitchen multiplies ⅔ by ¾ through physical objects and divisions rather than symbol multiplication (de la Rocha, 1986). Requiring specification of units, the software program Semantic Calculator helps students represent problems in appropriate terms. As a social distribution of "problem representation," a teacher suggests that a student draw a diagram model of a problem before constructing equations to solve it. And rather than requiring the *creation* of representations, computer tools often offer different representations for *selection.* Mapping between problem representations may be done automatically instead of by the student (e.g., automatic graphing of algebraic functions is now available on inexpensive calculators).

*Planning a problem solution.*    This is often made unnecessary as the gap between plan and plan execution is reduced to perceptual choice by severely reducing the number of choices. To save error and effort, algorithms for repetitive measurement or computations can be built into the artifact used to measure, so that applying the tool to the task *is* the needed action and "planning" becomes unnecessary. "Planning" a problem solution for riding a bicycle for the first time without falling over becomes unnecessary when training wheels are mounted. Research on learning to compose texts shows that it is easier to write well when one uses planning aides such as "completion" sentences: "My most important point was . . . " (Bereiter & Scardamalia, 1986).

*Executing the plan.* This is often distributed. Effortful, repetitive activities of "clerical cognition" are automated as algorithms, macros,
and templates for execution with minimal thought or off-loaded onto
tools or machines (Bush, 1945; Licklider, 1960). A typical word-
processing macro might be to "find all occurrences of 'mind'; replace
each with 'society of minds' in italics." Autochecking and autocorrec-
tion of typing mistakes are now features of many spell-checking programs. Social allocation of the part-component process of plan
execution takes place in apprenticeship learning, too, and is used by
analogy in recent work in artificial intelligence that sends computer
"agents" off to do information retrieval. Prominent examples already
in schools are strategy-supporting and outlining programs for writing
and microcomputer-based laboratories that provide hardware–
software systems for measuring and graphing changes over time in
temperature, light, or sound. For a few hundred dollars there are programs that provide equation-solving "workbenches" that automatically do complex symbol manipulations, which are prone to error
when carried out with paper and pencil.

*Error checks of solutions.* These are commonly distributed. The need
to check for errors (e.g., in calculations or programming) is often ob-
viated by blocking the very possibility of error. Error-prone activities
are made impermissible to carry out in many systems of human–computer interaction (e.g., the computer queries whether I really want to
throw away my word processor when I accidentally act to delete it).

  With this introduction in mind, let me offer an unfamiliar but typical example of intelligence "embodied" in artifacts, distributed for
use across history and minds.

### An illuminating case

  An example of distributed intelligence comes from the PBS
television show "Square One" on mathematics for children. A forest
ranger is being interviewed. Each year she measures the diameters of
trees in the forest to estimate the amount of lumber contained in a
plot of land. With a conventional measuring tape she

1.  measures the circumference of the tree (6 feet);
2.  remembers that the diameter is related to the circumference of an object according to the formula circumference/diameter equals 22/7 (or pi);
3.  sets up the formula, replacing the variable circumference with the value of 6 feet;
4.  cross-multiplies, getting 22(diameter-unknown) = 42;
5.  isolates the diameter by dividing by 22, obtaining 42/22;
6.  reduces the fraction 42/22 to 1.9 feet.

Note that to do this she has to remember the formula, set it up correctly, and then correctly do her substitutions and calculations. This procedure is error- and effort-prone. She could learn to do this automatically. She could even ask someone nearby who happens to be good at estimating. But something different happens: A new measuring tape is invented. I call it a special-purpose "direct calculation" tape for tree-diameter measures. The numbers have been scaled so that the algorithm for these calculations is *built into* the tool. She wraps it around the tree and reads off "1.9 feet" directly. The only possible errors are perceptual ones (if she does not see the number clearly) or ones caused by the use of the tape for measuring purposes to which it was not adapted.

The work done by the new measuring tape helps explain why it is wrong to say that the person using it "represents the problem," "plans a problem solution," and "checks the solution." These three phases of the intelligent activity of measuring trees are distributed in the object used for measuring, its social history of practices for engaging that embodied intelligence, and the user's memory for how to engage that tool in activity.

This example illustrates that activity is a product not of intelligence in the individual mind, but of one's memory, the structure of the resources available in the environment at hand, and one's desires, which guide the interpretation of these structuring resources. Through processes of design and invention, we load intelligence into both physical, designed artifacts and representational objects such as diagrams, models, and plans. We exploit intelligence from objects when we use them instrumentally in activities. And we often need to decouple intelligence from such objects to reuse them in novel ways. Once such intelligence is designed into the affordance properties of artifacts, it both guides and constrains the likely contributions of that artifact to distributed intelligence in activity. Obviously the measuring tape, once the formula has been compiled into its design, cannot readily be adapted to linear measurement without recrafting its scale.

### Issues in distributed intelligence

A focus on distributed intelligence is now rare in learning or educational research. The common assumption of solo intelligence as a central goal of education guides the investigation of learning, the cultivation of mental abilities, information processing, the role of misconceptions in the acquisition of new knowledge, and the design of classroom instruction, with relative disregard for the social, physical, and artifactual surroundings in which such activities take place. Many schools, technology developers, and researchers now use technologies to "enhance" education by making the achievement of traditional objectives more efficient. Many intelligent tutors and software programs in mathematics and science fit together under this strategy. Objectives for education are not reconceptualized; the computer is conceived of as a means for "delivering" key components of instructional activity – not for redistributing intelligence and new uses of students' potentials for activity and participation.

Yet the phenomena of distributed intelligence make apparent how the exploitation of external resources changes the functional systems from which activity emerges. New resources, and changing attitudes toward the integrity of their use, change the properties of what one "needs to know." Culturally valued designs for distributed intelligence in which a learner participates to achieve a specific goal will change throughout history. Stated with a different focus, and as but one example, what is considered to be the curriculum will vary when the technologies used for reasoning in a domain change (Pea, 1987).

These shifts are particularly dramatic for mathematics. As one may observe in the new curriculum and evaluation standards proposed by the National Council of Teachers in Mathematics (NCTM), the support of computer technologies has dramatically transformed the objectives and timing of the entire course of mathematics education (NCTM, 1989). For example, in K–4 mathematics, a focus on long-division operations and paper-and-pencil fraction computation has been diminished, the availability of calculators is assumed, and attention is shifted to estimation activities and a focus on the meaning of operations and the selection of appropriate calculation methods. In grade 9–12 mathematics, the presumed use of calculators, graphing utilities, statistical programs, and computer-based exploration of 2-D and 3-D figures and uses of coordinate and transformation approaches to geometry leads to recommendations for decreased attention to such activities as hand graphing of functions, paper-and-pencil solution of trigonometric equations, and axiomatic treatments of Euclidean geometry. The treatment of entirely new topics in statistics, probability, and discrete mathematics is made possible at these grade levels by visual and dynamic technological support for reasoning and learning in these areas. The NCTM standards go on to note that "calculators, computers, courseware, and manipulative materials are necessary for good mathematics instruction; the teacher can no longer rely solely on a chalkboard, chalk, paper, pencils, and a text" (1989, p. 253).

While the distributed nature of intelligence is everywhere noticeable, what consequences should these observations about distributed intelligence have for the design and practice of education? If we treat distributed intelligence in action (rather than the individual's knowledge structures alone) as the scientific unit of analysis for research and theory on learning and reasoning, new questions arise:

1. What is distributed (i.e., different components of the problem-solving process as well as the product)?
2. What constraints govern the dynamics of such distributions in different time scales (e.g., microgenesis, ontogenesis, cultural history, phylogenesis)?
3. Through what reconfigurations of distributed intelligence might the performance of an activity system improve over time?
4. What distributions and their changes over time are effective for specific goals of education?

When we think about intelligence as manifest in activity and as distributed in nature, we may wish to ask a descriptive question for learning: How *do* learners enact the cultural practices for designing, constructing, and displaying distributed intelligence in activity? We must also ask the prescriptive version of this question for education:

How *should* learners acquire such cultural practices? To answer the latter question, we will need to examine trade-offs in the design of distributed intelligence that may influence our considerations.

### *Trade-offs in the design of distributed intelligence*

It is important to observe and acknowledge distributed intelligence because successful learning (that which eventuates in the achievement of activities) often involves it and learning beset with failures often does not. Education often results in making far too many people look "dumb" because they are not allowed to use resources, whereas outside of education we all use resources. To get close to empowering more learners to do the activities that education should be enabling, intelligence should be recognized as distributed and education should elaborate the design consequences of that fact.

I have said much about design, perhaps too much for many psychologists and educators. But one central aspect of work in design is that it is very commonly posed, or at least thought about, in terms of *trade-offs*. A designed thing is, of course, but one choice among many possibilities that were considered, and even more possibilities that were never considered. Designers often are quite articulate about trade-offs (MacLean, Young, & Moran, 1989).

Why is a focus on trade-offs important? Because much of the critical discussion around distributed intelligence takes an extreme position on one or two dimensions of a design trade-off and overemphasizes it at the cost of acknowledging the more basic point that trade-offs are inevitable in design. What we quickly come to see is that we have a long way to go in working on our own design space for considering the ways in which distributed intelligence relates to learning and education. There are no easy or obvious answers. And recourse, much less reliance, on existing practice is one of the weakest arguments of all. It makes it seem as if there is little choice but to yield to existing practice, when quite different arrangements may be possible, preferable, and even practical. It does not follow that they would be easy to achieve.

Let us consider several important trade-offs in thinking about designs of distributed intelligence as examples of these issues.

*Trade-off 1: access to activity versus understanding its foundations.*     A central trade-off is that between *access* and *understanding* that may come from focusing on either tool-aided cognition or tool-unaided cognition. What opportunities are lost for learner participation in higher-level activities, and meaningful contributions rather than basic skills practice, if one does not allow for distributed-intelligence support for those activities involving artifacts and other persons? Tools may grant greater accessibility to complex mentation. More universal access among learners to participation in complex thought and activities may be gained at the expense of low-level understanding. An emphasis on learning activities requiring tool-unaided cognition may grant deeper understanding, but at the cost of blocking many individuals from engaging in meaningful whole-task problem solving because of the learning "overhead" of knowledge needed to get to the tool-unaided problem-solving process.

Whatever we find as scientists about how the dynamics of distributed intelligence work, we are still faced with the moral question of educational aims – whether they are to foster intelligence that it executed "solo," is tool-aided, or is collaborative, or in what combination for what content domains and activities. We are at a point in cultural history where these issues of tool-aided, socially shared cognition must be examined and debated on empirical grounds. What designs of distributed intelligence are effective to what ends? What are our assumptions about the patterns of distributed intelligence in society into which students must enter and productively use what they have learned?

In describing the theoretical significance of learner development being aided by both social and computational "scaffolds" to achieve more than the learner could alone, I argued some time ago:

Self-sufficiency is [not assumed to be] the telos of such learning activities. Many forms of cognitive activity may require the continuing intervention of an intelligent computer system, for effectiveness or because of their complexity. Similarly, not all cognitive tasks for which ZPDs can be arranged should be ones that the child is expected to internalize for subsequent solo performances. Solo performances are not realistic in terms of the ways in which intelligent activities are organized and accomplished in the real world. They are often collaborative, depend on resources beyond an individual's long-term memory, and require the use of information-handling tools. . . . The level of task understanding necessary for the child alone is an empirical question that remains to be answered, domain by domain. (Pea, 1985b, p. 84)

There has been a common objection to this intelligence-distribution intensive orientation that wishes to import the "efficiency drive" of everyday cognition into the classroom. For doesn't one get access to distributed intelligence at the cost of understanding and solo cognition? Doesn't such distributed intelligence make us look smarter than we are by building the clever constraints that guide the display of intelligent action as features of the social, computational, or representational environments? Along these lines, Salomon et al. (1991) distinguished two kinds of cognitive effects of technologies on intelligence: "Effects *with* technology obtained during intellectual partnership with it, and effects *of* it in terms of the transferable cognitive residue that this partnership leaves behind in the form of better mastery of skills and strategies" (p. 2). They argue for the educational utility of emphasizing effects *of* rather than *with*, so that autonomous intellectual performance can be achieved. For if not, they argue, the student is dependent on the technology, without which he or she does not understand.

The invisible nature of many tools and the support of social networks in collaboration, even those now used in the classroom, makes it apparent that this antisupport argument will not do. Pencils are allowed as memory aids, so why not have to do mathematics orally or reinvent measurement scales used in instrumentation? In the world outside school, part of knowing how to learn and solve complex problems involves knowing how to create and exploit social networks and the expertise of others, and to deftly use the features of the physical and media environments to one's advantage – like using principles of leverage and balance in judo. Socially scaffolded and externally mediated, artifact-supported cognition is so predominant that its disavowal in the classroom is detrimental to the transfer of learning beyond the classroom (also see Resnick, 1987).

Salomon et al. (1991) broach the issue of their potential conservatism in wedging the distinction between effects *with* and effects *of*, since with the widespread availability of intelligent computer tools "the question of what residues the partnership with the technology leaves might be moot" (p. 5). But they consider such tools not sufficiently prevalent yet, so "how a person functions away from intelligent technologies must be considered" (p. 5), and emergent dilemmas in the world "need an independent and capable thinking mind" (p. 5). This insistence profoundly misses several critical points concerning distributed intelligence. I have never argued that "all we should aim at are effects *with* a technology whereby intelligence is truly distributed" (p. 5). One neglected point is that distributed intelligence is largely invisible throughout life, but is broadly considered, as I have argued, to include not only computer tools, as they emphasize, but materials in the environment and the expertise available from other human beings. A second point is that this distributed intelligence is quite commonly *designed*, with consequences described in a later section. A third is that we may all want to exert a greater voice in the design of distributed intelligence, both in and out of schooling, once we recognize the designedness of intelligence. And a fourth point is that a central goal for an empowering education is to nurture the learners' attitudes and talents in designing distributed intelligence for their use and that of others, not only to participate in the designs of distributed intelligence provided by others. Finally, the general argument attributed to me that is tacit in their critique – that all thinking *should* be distributed – is wildly wrong. Of course, there will not be intelligent computer tools for every kind of task achievement conceivable, nor should there be.

*Trade-off 2: static definition of tasks versus evolving concepts of tasks.* One potential misunderstanding of the concept of distributed intelligence must be guarded against. It is the notion of distribution as *reallocation,* of dividing up cognition among mind, setting, and artifacts, or a "division of labor" among contributions to distributed intelligence. This limited notion is that there is a fixed quantity of intellectual work for the doing of some task and that this quantity can then be differentially distributed across persons and environment. The concept we are concerned with is that of *expanding* intelligence rather than reallocating it. We want to ask where the capacity for innovation exists in the concept of distributed intelligence, how we may engender ever more useful designs for distributed intelligence – whether we are considering shared activities such as cooperative learning or an individual's uses of a tool for augmenting mathematical problem-solving ability. I have argued that there is a natural tendency for humans to aspire to greater efficiency in distributing intelligence through the design and use of the physical, symbolic, and social environments in order to cope with the complexity of "mental activities." But this does not lead to a situational determinism. The flip side of this efficiency drive is the *freedom* thereby attained to explore and seek the new. Having achieved a greater efficiency by off-loading thinking into the design of the world, one then is freed up to continue to invent and innovate. Whether learning conditions foster these new opportunities is an issue of cultural choice.

Salomon et al. (1991) make an interesting contrast between two ways of evaluating intelligence for partnerships between people and technologies: *systemic* and *analytic*. The systemic attends to the aggregate performance of the person–computer system, while the analytic articulates the specific contributions made by the person and the technology to that performance. They caution against the possibilities of human deskilling and disinterest in tasks if analytic analyses reveal minimal contributions of the person to the system performance. However, this analysis appears to buy too deeply into the fixed-quantity concept.

Further, they argue mistakenly that the analytic approach is "more oriented toward the study of human potential and toward educational concerns" (p. 5) than the systemic approach, which "appraises the products of the joint abilities of person and tool." This is simplistic in at least two ways. One is in terms of the access–understanding trade-off discussed earlier – the systemic approach may be profoundly suited to education by enabling all learners to do things that would be accessible to only some learners if the analytic approach had its way. The second is that the learner may be not just the *recipient* of the intellectual tool, which contributes to high-level systemic achievement, but its *designer* – and that learner may minimize the need to contribute his or her mental activities to that performance by design. In the former case, a too conscious reliance on the analytic approach may bode ill for enabling poorly motivated and low-achieving students to engage successfully in high-level tasks to which the computer contributes. In the latter case, a too restrictive use of the analytic approach may lead to a neglect of the mindful process by which the learner designs distributed intelligence so as to make minimum use of mental process for system performance involving the computer tool.

There are various ways to overcome the deskilling problems mentioned as well, even if one were (which I am not) inclined to accept a fixed-quantity concept of intelligence contributing to task achievement by a human–computer system. First, one could treat *design* seriously and rotate the component activities (as in the six-phase problem-solving process described earlier) contributed by the human and the computer, with the objective of avoiding the possibilities of an entrapping and boring contribution of the same component activities to that task by the human. Unfortunately, some of those phases, such as problem finding and problem representation, may prove immensely difficult for the computer to contribute to the system performance. Second, I have already stressed the design aspect of distributed intelligence, one normative consequence of which involves an increasingly recognized phenomenon in the world of work – the need to "informate" (rather than automate) the workplace (Zuboff, 1988), thereby providing important opportunities for workers to contribute to the redesign of their working conditions and tools (Attewell, 1987; Barley, 1988; Bjerknes, Ehn, & Kyng, 1986; Wenger, 1991). Finally, taking a lesson from Kusterer's (1978) findings of individual differences in knowledge on the job among "unskilled workers," we would design activities that allowed participation in diverse tasks for knowledge utilization, and with as few routinized tasks as possible. Kusterer finds broader working knowledge for workers who often need to learn new things to resolve emergent dilemmas in their nonroutine work functions.

Why does the static versus dynamic definition of tasks exemplify a trade-off? Because it may be easier to develop learning materials and teacher education programs for helping students achieve static tasks, whereas if the very tasks learners undertake evolve as the tools and designs for distributed intelligence change over time, static materials and teacher preparation methods for the "delivery" of curriculum will not suffice. The trade-off becomes one of automating the delivery of standard materials and practice to the neglect of the dynamic nature of distributed intelligence versus providing continually renewable, flexibly adaptive materials and practices.

### Evolving telos: new aims of development

One of the central implications of the dialectical perspective on human nature arises when we look at the concept of development itself. Piaget sketched a view that was neo-Kantian in nature and rooted in a well-defined endpoint of formal operations (Piaget & Inhelder, 1969). By contrast, the implications of the sociohistorical view of human nature, which is manifest in a focus on the design of distributed intelligence, are more profoundly open-ended. When "development" is seen not as a descriptive concept standing in for "time" or "history," but as a *normative* concept involving the evaluation of means–end adaptations (Kaplan, 1983), and an activity–person system is defined as more or less highly developed with respect to the achievement of these ends, it becomes apparent that the system's developmental status is sociohistorically defined in terms of society's evolving metrics of evaluating means–end relations and in the ends selected themselves.

Developmental psychology thus takes on a different character when considered from this orientation. Whether under Piagetian influences or those of an information-processing approach, developmental studies have typically targeted changes in the mental structure and processes of the individual. Although social scaffolding of development is a definite emphasis in research influenced by the sociohistorical school of Vygotsky, Luria, and Leont'ev, more attention has been paid in the recent incarnations of that work to social scaffolding than to the roles of cultural artifacts and representations as carriers of intelligence (e.g., Moll, 1990; Wertsch, 1985, 1991). This is a particularly important omission in light of arguments such as those of Wartofsky (1979) that the artifact is to cultural evolution what the gene is to biological evolution – the vehicle of information across generations. Answers to the question of what develops may fundamentally change in the face of a distributed-intelligence perspective, for *systems of activity* – involving persons, environment, tools – become the locus of developmental investigation.

What I have been stressing throughout is a focus on intelligence as manifest in *activity* – dynamics, not statics. The language used by Salomon et al. (1991) to characterize the concepts involved in how they think about distributed intelligence is, by contrast, *entity*-oriented – a language of containers holding things. "Cognitive residues" are "left behind" by interactions with technologies or "carried away" from human–computer partnerships. Abilities and intelligence are "in" persons or tools. When one views intelligence as *in* activity, which I argue for in this chapter – rather than in agents or tools – the kind of clean, pure, solo intelligence of the independent and capable thinker that Salomon et al. seek to produce from education is but a theoretician's fantasy. Persons are situated in the physical, artifactual, and social worlds and continually use and redesign them to achieve the activities they desire. The distributions they so chose to design or participate in may change over time, cultural as well as ontogenetic. How social models and social pressures, and individual desires and aesthetics, come to shape these changing patterns of distribution over time is a reformulation of the basic question of developmental psychology.

### Broader consequences

There are some other noteworthy consequences of this perspective on intelligence beyond education. The scope of coverage is intentionally broad and recasts a broad variety of contemporary and historical issues (Pea, 1993). These include the impacts of text literacy on thinking; the influences of symbol systems in mathematics, logic, and science on forms of thought and activity; relations among changes in science, technology, and society (e.g., the effects of industrialization on work and the distribution of control), and new paradigms in computing, publishing, and telecommunications (Pea & Gomez, 1992). These are critical issues, since few technological inventions besides computers (and affiliated technologies involving microprocessors) have had or will continue to have as profound an impact on how people spend their time in work and on how new educational objectives are defined (Dunlop & Kling, 1991).

Seeking to understand distributed intelligence may be important because it yields sociohistorical links beyond the confines of today's cognitive science of education. For example, its results will tie into design more generally. Architects and designers are often sensitive to how human activities emerge and flow by the shapes that an environment affords (e.g., Alexander, Ishikawa, Silverstein, & Jacobson, 1977; also see Hooper, 1986). I have highlighted the sociohistorical fact that the world has been shaped by the intelligence that has been "left behind" through the activities of past persons (in artifacts, conventions, practices) and that is continually being transformed by social agents forming the current collectivity of intelligence, mediated by the individual and situated interpretation of meaning that forms the fabric of creativity and development.

Learning and design are fundamentally connected with an orientation toward distributed intelligence. Exploration and play, basic human capacities used long before the invention of today's education, are seen as important, as particular desires leading to designs of distributed intelligence. Learning can be viewed as much more than "problem solving" and more broadly in terms of each of the desires. For example, the activities of play as much create and find problems as they "solve" them. Technology design and development are also viewed differently. New technologies can support human activities by serving as experimental platforms in the evolution of intelligence – by opening up new possibilities for distributed intelligence. They are not serving, in any simple sense, as "amplifiers of intellect" or as ways to "mechanize" existing desires (e.g., off-loading particular kinds of activity in work).

## Conclusions

When we look at actual human practices, we see that human cognition aspires to efficiency in distributing intelligence – across individuals, environment, external symbolic representations, tools, and artifacts – as a means of coping with the complexity of activities we often call "mental."

Since such aspirations do not inevitably lead to the fulfillment of culturally valued goals of invention and innovation in the face of today's rapid societal and global change, a principal aim of education ought to be that of *teaching for the design of distributed intelligence.* Learning to create and willfully regulate distributed intelligence should be an aim of education for students and teachers. We should reorient the educational emphasis from individual, tool-free cognition to facilitating individuals' responsive and novel uses of resources for creative and intelligent activity alone and in collaboration. Such an education would encourage and refine the natural tendency for people to continually re-create their own world as a scaffold for their activities. For example, in mathematics and science education, one might develop a metacurriculum oriented to learning about the role of distributed intelligence in enabling complex thought. Students would come to understand and deploy heuristics for inventing cognitive technologies as participants in a knowledge-using community. They would see through their activities where the bottlenecks of complex mentation reside. They would recognize how physical, symbolic, and social technologies may provide the supports necessary for reaching conceptual heights less attainable if attempted unaided. This goal might be achieved through the examination of living, everyday examples (building from cases where they already do distributed intelligence in the world) and, perhaps, through case studies of the roles of information structures (e.g., matrices, flow charts, templates) and social structures (work teams, apprenticeships) in mediating learning and reasoning as activity systems of distributed intelligence. Students would be empowered both through the reflective use of new tools and through the invention of new tools and social distributions of activities.

In sum, we should strive toward a reflectively and intentionally distributed intelligence in education, where learners are inventors of distributed-intelligence-as-tool, rather than receivers of intelligence-as-substance. In the court of worldly experience, such learners may be far more ready not only to adapt to change but to contribute substantially to it.

## References

Agre, P. (in press). *Computation and human experience.* Cambridge University Press.

Alexander, C., Ishikawa, S., Silverstein, M., & Jacobson, M. (1977). *A pattern language: Towns, buildings, construction.* New York: Oxford University Press.

Allen, C. (1988). *Situated designing.* Unpublished master's thesis, Carnegie-Mellon University, Pittsburgh, PA.

Attewell, P. (1987). The deskilling controversy. *Work and Occupations, 14,* 327–46.

Barley, S. (1988). Technology, power, and the social organization of work: Toward a pragmatic theory of skilling and deskilling. *Research on the Sociology of Organizations, 6,* 33–80.

Barthes, Roland. (1972). *Mythologies,* trans. A. Lavers, New York: Hill & Wang.

Bateson, G. (1972). Form, substance, and difference. In *Steps to an ecology of mind* (2d ed.). New York: Ballantine Books.

Bereiter, C., & Scardamalia, M. (1986). *The psychology of written composition.* Hillsdale, NJ: Erlbaum.

Bjerknes, G., Ehn, P., & Kyng, M. (Eds.). (1986). *Computers and democracy: A Scandinavian challenge.* Brookfield, VT: Gower.

Blattner, M., & Dannenberg, R. (Eds.). (1991). *Multimedia and multimodal user interface design*. Reading, MA: Addison-Wesley.

Brooks, F. (1986). Walkthrough: A dynamic graphics system for simulating virtual buildings. *Proceedings of the ACM Workshop on Interactive Graphics*, 9–21.

(1988). Grasping reality through illusion: Interactive graphics serving science. *Proceedings of the ACM SIGCHI Human Factors in Computing Systems Conference*, 1–11.

Brown, J. S., Collins, A., & Duguid, P. (1989). Situated cognition and the culture of learning. *Educational Researcher, 18* (1), 32–42.

Bush, V. (1945, July). As we may think. *Atlantic Monthly,* 101–8.

Card, S. K., Robertson, G. G., & Mackinlay, J. D. (1991, April–May). The information visualizer, an information workspace. In S. P. Robertson, G. M. Olson, & J. S. Olson (Eds.), *Proceedings of the ACM SIGCHI Conference on Human Factors in Computing Systems*, 181–8.

Carraher, T. N., Carraher, D. W., & Schliemann, A. D. (in press). *Street mathematics and school mathematics*. Cambridge University Press.

Cassirer, E., (1923). *Substance and function & Einstein's theory of relativity*. New York: Dover.

Cognition and Technology Group at Vanderbilt (1990). Anchored instruction and its relationship to situated cognition. *Educational Researcher, 19* (6), 2–10.

Collins, A., Brown, J. S., & Newman, S. (1989). Cognitive apprenticeship: Teaching the craft of reading, writing, and mathematics. In L. B. Resnick (Ed.), *Knowing, learning, and instruction: Essays in honor of Robert Glaser.* Hillsdale, NJ: Erlbaum.

Confrey, J. (1990). A review of the research on student conceptions in mathematics, science, and programming. *Review of Research in Education, 16,* 3–56.

de la Rocha, O. (1986). *Problems of sense and problems of scale: An ethnographic study of arithmetic in everyday life.* Unpublished doctoral dissertation, University of California, Irvine.

Dewey, J. (1910). *How we think.* Boston: Heath.

di Sessa, A. A., Hammer, D., Sherin, B., & Kolpakowski, X. (1991). Inventing graphing: Meta representational expertise in children. *Journal of Mathematical Behavior, 10,* 117–60.

Dunlop, C., & Kling. R. (Eds.). (1991). *Computerization and controversy: Value conflicts and social choices.* New York: Academic Press.

Engelbart, D. (1963). A conceptual framework for the augmentation of man's intellect. In G. W. Howerton & D. C. Weeks (Eds.), *Vistas in information handling, Vol 1: The augmentation of man's intellect by machine* (pp. 1–29). Washington, DC: Spartan Books.

Ford, M. E., & Nichols, C. W. (1987). A taxonomy of human goals and some possible applications. In M. E. Ford & D. H. Ford (Eds.), *Humans as self-constructing living systems: Putting the framework to work.* Hillsdale, NJ: Erlbaum.

Gibson, J. J. (1979). *The ecological approach to visual perception.* Boston: Houghton Mifflin.

(1982). *Reasons for realism: Selected essays of James J. Gibson.* Hillsdale, NJ: Erlbaum.

Goodman, N. (1978). *Ways of worldmaking.* Indianapolis, IN: Hackett.

Greenfield, P. M., & Lave, J. (1982). Cognitive aspects of informal education. In D. Wagner & H. Stevenson (Eds.), *Cultural perspectives on child development* (pp. 181–207). San Francisco: Freeman.

Greeno, J. G. (1991). Environments for situated conceptual learning. In L. Birnbaum (Ed.), *Proceedings of the International Conference on the Learning Sciences* (pp. 211–16). Charlottesville, VA: Association for the Advancement of Computing in Education.

Hancock, C. M., & Kaput, J. J. (1990). Computerized tools and the process of data modeling. *Proceedings of the 14th International Congress on the Psychology of Mathematics Education.*

Harel, I. (Ed.). (1990). *Constructionist learning.* Cambridge, MA: MIT Media Laboratory.

Hooper, K. (1986). Architectural design: An analogy. In D. A. Norman & S. W. Draper (Eds.), *User centered system design: New perspectives on human–computer interaction* (pp. 9–23). Hillsdale, NJ: Erlbaum.

Hutchins, E. (1990). The technology of team navigation. In J. Galegher, R. E. Kraut, & C. Egido (Eds.), *Intellectual teamwork: Social and technological foundations of cooperative work* (pp. 191–220). Hillsdale, NJ: Erlbaum.

Hutchins, E. L., Hollan, J. D., & Norman, D. A. (1986). Direct manipulation interfaces. In D. A. Norman & S. W. Draper (Eds.), *User centered system design: New perspectives on human–computer interaction* (pp. 87–124). Hillsdale, NJ: Erlbaum.

Kaplan, B. (1983). Genetic-dramatism: Old wine in new bottles. In S. Wapner & B. Kaplan (Eds.), *Toward a holistic developmental psychology* (pp. 53–74). Hillsdale, NJ: Erlbaum.

Keenan, E., Schieffelin, B., & Platt, M. (1976). Propositions across speakers and utterances. *Papers and Research on Child Language Development, 12,* 127–43.

Kusterer, K. C. (1978). *Know-how on the job: The important working knowledge of "unskilled" workers.* Boulder, CO: Westview.

Lanier, J. (1989). Plenary address on virtual reality. *Proceedings of UIST: The Annual ACM SIGGRAPH Symposium on User Interface Software and Technology.*

Latour, B., & Woolgar, S. (1986). *Laboratory life: The construction of scientific facts* (2d ed.) London: Sage.

Lave, J. (1988). *Cognition in practice: Mind, mathematics and culture in everyday life.* Cambridge University Press.

Lave, J., Murtaugh, M., & de la Rocha, O. (1984). The dialectics of arithmetic in grocery shopping. In B. Rogoff & J. Lave (Eds.), *Everyday cognition: Its development in social context.* Cambridge, MA: Harvard University Press.

Leont'ev, A. N. (1978a). *Activity, consciousness, and personality.* Englewood Cliffs, NJ: Prentice-Hall.

(1978b). The problem of activity in psychology. In J. V. Wertsch (Ed.), *The concept of activity in Soviet psychology* (pp. 37–71). White Plains, NY: Sharpe.

Licklider, J. C. R. (1960). Man–computer symbiosis. *IRE Transactions on Human Factors in Electronics. HFE-1.* 4–11.

Linn, M. C. (in press). The computer as lab partner: Can computer tools teach science? In L. Roberts, K. Sheingold, & S. Malcolm (Eds.), *This year in school science 1991*. Washington, DC: American Association for the Advancement of Science.

Luria, A. R. (1979). *The making of mind: A personal account of Soviet psychology*. Cambridge, MA: Harvard University Press.

Lynch, M., & Woolgar, S. (Eds.). (1990). *Representation in scientific practice*. Cambridge, MA: MIT Press.

MacLean, A., Young, R., & Moran, T. (1989). Design rationale: The argument behind the artifact. *Proceedings of CHI'89: Human Factors in Computing Systems, April 30–May 4, Austin, Texas* (pp. 247–52). New York: Association for Computing Machinery.

Moll, L. C. (Ed.). (1990). *Vygotsky and education*. Cambridge University Press.

Murtaugh, M. (1985). The practice of arithmetic by American grocery shoppers. *Anthropology and Education Quarterly, 16*, 186–92.

National Council of Teachers in Mathematics (1989). *Curriculum and evaluation standards for school mathematics*. Reston, VA: NCTM.

Newman, D., Griffin, P., and Cole, M. (1989). *The construction zone: Working for cognitive change in school*. Cambridge University Press.

Norman, D. (1988). *The psychology of everyday things*. New York: Basic Books.

Ouh-Young, M., Pique, M., Hughes, J., Srinivisan, N., & Brooks, F. (1988). Using a manipulator for force display in molecular docking. *IEEE Robotics and Automation Conference, 3*, 1824–9.

Palincsar, A., & Brown, A. L. (1984). Reciprocal teaching of comprehension-fostering comprehension-monitoring activities. *Cognition and Instruction, 1*, 117–76.

Papert, S. (1980). *Mindstorms*. New York: Basic Books.

Pea, R. D. (1985a). Beyond amplification: Using computers to reorganize human mental functioning. *Educational Psychologist, 20*, 167–82.

(1985b). Integrating human and computer intelligence. In E. L. Klein (Ed.), *New directions for child development: No. 28, Children and computers* (pp. 75–96). San Francisco: Jossey-Bass.

(1987). Cognitive technologies for mathematics education. In A. Schoenfeld (Ed.), *Cognitive science and mathematics education* (pp. 89–122). Hillsdale, NJ: Erlbaum.

(1988). *Distributed intelligence and education* (Technical rep.). Palo Alto, CA: Institute for Research on Learning.

(1992). Augmenting the discourse of learning with computer-based learning environments. In E. de Corte, M. Linn, & L. Verschaffel (Eds.), *Computer-based learning environments and problem-solving* (NATO Series, subseries F: Computer and System Sciences). New York: Springer.

(1993). *Distributed intelligence*. Unpublished manuscript, Northwestern University, Evanston, IL.

Pea, R. D., & Gomez, L. (1992). Distributed multimedia learning environments. *Interactive Learning Environments, 2*(2), 73–109.

Pea, R. D., & Kurland, D. M. (1987). Cognitive technologies for writing development. In L. Frase (Ed.), *Review of Research in Education* (Vol. 14, pp. 71–120). Washington DC: AERA Press.

Pea, R. D., Sipusic, M., & Allen, S. (in press). Seeing the light on optics: Classroom-based research and development for conceptual change. In S. Strauss (Ed.), *Development and learning environments*. Norwood, NJ: Ablex.

Piaget, J., & Inhelder, B. (1969). *The psychology of the child.* New York: Basic Books.

Polya, G. (1957). *How to solve it: A new aspect of mathematical method* (2d ed.). Garden City, NJ: Doubleday.

Resnick, L. (1987). Learning in school and out. *Educational Researcher, 16* (9), 3–21.

Resnick, M., & Ocko S. (1990). LEGO/Logo: Learning through and about design. In I. Harel (Ed.), *Contructionist learning* (pp. 121–8). Cambridge, MA: MIT Media Laboratory.

Rheingold, H. (1985). *Tools for thought.* New York: Simon & Schuster.

(1991). *Virtual realities.* San Francisco: Whole Earth Press.

Rogoff, B. (1990). *Apprenticeship in thinking: Cognitive development in social context.* New York: Oxford University Press.

Rubin, A., Bruce, B., Conant, F., DuMouchel, W., Goodman, B., Horwitz, P., Lee, A., Mesard, W., Pringle, L., Rosebery, A., Snyder, R., Tenney, Y., & Warren, B. (1990). *ELASTIC: Environments for learning abstract statistical thinking (annual report)* (BBN Rep. No. 7282). Cambridge, MA: Bolt Beranek & Newman.

Rubin, A., Rosebery, A., Bruce, B., & DuMouchel, W. (1988). *Getting an early start: Using graphics to teach statistical concepts in high school.* Alexandria, VA: American Statistical Association.

Russell, S. J., & Corwin, R. B. (1990). *Used numbers: Real data in the classroom – The shape of the data.* Palo Alto, CA: Seymour Publications.

Salomon, G., Perkins, D. N., & Globerson, T. (1991). Partners in cognition: Extending human intelligence with intelligent technologies. *Educational Researcher, 20* (3), 2–9.

Saxe, G. B. (1988). Candy selling and math learning. *Educational Researcher, 17* (6), 14–21.

(1990). *Culture and cognitive development: Studies in mathematical understanding.* Hillsdale, NJ: Erlbaum.

Schoenfeld, A. (1985). *Mathematical problem solving.* New York: Academic Press.

Schön, D. (1983). *The reflective practitioner.* New York: Basic Books.

Scribner, S. (1985). Knowledge at work. *Anthropology and Education Quarterly, 16,* 199–205.

(1986). Thinking in action: Some characteristics of practical thought. In R. J. Sternberg & R. K. Wagner (Eds.), *Practical intelligence: Nature and origins of competence in the everyday world* (pp. 13–30). Cambridge University Press.

Simon, H. (1981). *The sciences of the artificial* (2d ed.). Cambridge, MA: MIT Press.

Suchman, L. A. (1987). *Plans and situated actions: The problem of human–machine communication.* Cambridge University Press.

Thornton, R. K., & Sokoloff, D. S. (1990). Learning motion concepts using real-time microcomputer-based laboratory tools. *American Journal of Physics, 58,* 858–67 (app. B).

Tinker, R. (1992). *Thinking about science.* Cambridge, MA: Technical Education Research Center.

Vygotsky, L. S. (1978). *Mind in society: The development of the higher psychological processes.* Cambridge, MA: Harvard University Press. (Originally published 1930.)

Wartofsky, M. (1979). *Models: Representation and the scientific understanding.* Boston: Reidel.

(1983). The child's construction of the world and the world's construction of the child: From historical epistemology to historical psychology. In F. S. Kessel & A. W. Siegel (Eds.), *The child and other cultural inventions* (pp. 188–215). New York: Praeger.

Wenger, E. (1991). *Toward a theory of cultural transparency: Elements of a social discourse of the visible and the invisible.* Unpublished doctoral dissertation, University of California, Irvine.

Wertsch, J. V. (1985). *Vygotsky and the social formation of mind.* Cambridge, MA: Harvard University Press.

(1991). *Voices of the mind.* Cambridge, MA: Harvard University Press.

Wertsch, J. V., McNamee, G. D., McLane, J. B., & Budwig, N. A. (1980). The adult–child dyad as a problem-solving system. *Child Development, 51,* 1215–21.

White, B. Y. (1988). *ThinkerTools: Causal models, conceptual change, and science education* (BBN Technical Rep. 6873). Cambridge, MA: Bolt Beranek & Newman.

White, B. Y., & Horwitz, P. (1987). *ThinkerTools: Enabling children to understand physical laws* (BBN Technical Rep. 6470). Cambridge, MA: Bolt Beranek & Newman.

Wilhelmson, R. B., Jewett, B. F., Shaw, C., Wicker, L. J., Arrott, M., Bushell, C. B., Bajuk, M., Thingvold, J., & Yost, J. B. (1990). A study of the evolution of a numerically modeled severe storm. *International Journal of Supercomputer Applications, 4* (2), 20–36.

Winograd, T., & Flores, F. (1987). *Understanding computers and cognition: A new foundation for design.* Reading, MA: Addison-Wesley.

Zuboff, S. (1988). *In the age of the smart machine: The future of work and power.* New York: Basic Books.

# 3    Person-plus: a distributed view of thinking and learning

*D. N. Perkins*

Underlying psychology's multitude of investigations are a few broad and abiding questions. One of these – or perhaps two-in-one – is, How do thinking and learning happen? Efforts to reply include those of the behaviorist tradition, with its theory of classical and conditioned reflexes; now-classic cognitive theories, with their visions of problem spaces and schemata; and the more recent perspective of parallel distributed processing, with its holographic concept of how the mind captures and deploys information.

Whatever theory you pick, there is a notable and in some ways peculiar asymmetry between the posture taken toward the person and toward the physical arena in which the thinking and learning occur. Consider, for example, a student in a course on medieval history who has developed careful, well-organized notes about 1066 and all that. Most theories of learning would say that what the student has learned lies in his or her head. Whatever is in the notebook that is not also in the student's head is not part of what the student has learned.

Not, of course, that the notebook is deemed irrelevant. The student's effort to keep the notebook in a thoughtful, organized way will have resulted in better mental encoding of a good many of the ideas also represented in the notebook, including superior understanding and retention, because of the "elaborative processing" (e.g., Baddeley, 1982; Craik & Lockhart, 1972; Pressley, Wood, & Woloshyn, 1990). Nonetheless, the notebook itself would not usually count as a container of what the student had learned, even though it

Some of the ideas expressed in this chapter were developed with grants from the MacArthur Foundation for research on thinking and its teaching, and from the Spencer Foundation for research toward a pedagogy of understanding. The author thanks the foundations for their support.

88

represents considerable cognitive investment in a well-organized memory bank, and a bank that will pay dividends when, for instance, the student writes a term paper, drawing on this well-organized resource for ideas.

Another view of the matter is certainly possible. We could take as our unit of analysis not the student without resources in his or her surround – the *person-solo* – but the person plus surround, or *person-plus* for short, in this case the student plus the notebook. We could say that this person-plus system has learned something, and part of what the system has learned resides in the notebook rather than in the mind of the student. Moreover, in learning about 1066 and all that, this system thought hard, the notebook serving as a thinking scratch pad as well as a repository of conclusions.

What should we make of so odd a way of putting the matter? A reasonable attitude might be this: Certainly one can speak of the person plus surround as a compound system that thinks and learns – but is it particularly illuminating to do so? Do insights result that might otherwise pass us by?

### Distributed cognition

The general view adopted here takes as one point of departure a conception of "distributed intelligence" articulated by Roy Pea (Chapter 2, this volume). Pea urges that we do well to reconsider human cognition as distributed beyond the compass of the organism proper in several ways: by involving other persons, relying on symbolic media, and exploiting the environment and artifacts.

The present view also reflects the distinction drawn by Salomon, Perkins, and Globerson (1991) between effects *with* and *of* information-processing technologies, effects *with* being amplifications of the user's cognitive powers during the use of a technology and effects *of* being cognitive spinoff effects that occur without the technology. The present discussion focuses on effects *with* – not only with high technologies but with what in general will be called the *physical* distribution of cognition – onto things such as computers, to be sure, but also pencil and paper or the simple tactic of leaving a folder in front of the door to remind yourself to take it to work. There will be some attention also to the *social* distribution of cognition.

The posture taken here can be summarized as follows:

1.  The surround – the immediate physical and social resources out-side the person – participates in cognition, not just as a source of input and a receiver of output, but as a vehicle of thought.
2.  The residue left by thinking – what is learned – lingers not just in the mind of the learner, but in the arrangement of the surround as well, and it is just as genuinely learning for all that.

Indeed, in the person-plus spirit we might venture a rather brash claim called the *equivalent access hypothesis*. This hypothesis asserts that thinking and learning for the person-plus depend only on what might be called the "access characteristics" of relevant knowledge – what kind of knowledge is represented, how it is represented, how readily it is retrieved, and related matters – and not whether the knowledge is located in the person or the surround. If, for example, the student can access ideas in that notebook about 1066 fairly easily, having organized it so well, what does it matter whether the ideas lie inside or outside the student's cranium?

Of course, the case cannot be pressed too far. The claim is cer-tainly not that a set of notes in the best indexed notebook or even a rapid retrieval electronic database is exactly functionally equivalent to a well-memorized battery of facts in long-term memory. Indeed, there are a number of trade-offs between the two. The real claim is more a point of principle: the litmus to be applied is function – a matter of the access characteristics of the information – not locus – a matter of which side of one's skull hosts the information.

## Cognition as information flow

Let us sharpen this notion of person-plus on the stone of a very abstract notion: a knowledge-processing system. This system might be a person filling out income tax forms, a computer in an in-surance company calculating risks, or DNA replication. In such a sys-tem, a typical information-handling episode picks up knowledge from various places in the system and operates on it, often incrementing the knowledge of the system. For example, a person-plus consisting of a person, pencil, tax forms, and instructions would, at a certain point, increment the system's knowledge with the total decrement due to the federal government.

For a broad-stroke analysis of such an episode, one might look to four categories: *Knowledge* concerns what kinds of knowledge are available, including declarative and procedural knowledge, facts, strategies, and skilled routines, in other words knowledge in the broadest sense. *Representation* concerns how the knowledge is represented – in particular, whether in ways that make it easily picked up, transported in the system, and recoded. *Retrieval* concerns whether the system can find the knowledge representations in question, and how efficiently. *Construction* concerns the system's capacity to assemble the pieces of knowledge retrieved into new knowledge structures.

The four together comprise the *access characteristics* of the system – what knowledge it includes access to, via representations that afford what access to information, by way of what retrieval paths for accessing the information, and with what access to further constructions based on that knowledge. Because of the emphasis on access, the entire perspective is called the *access framework* (Perkins & Simmons, 1988; Perkins, Crismond, Simmons, & Unger, in press).

These four categories have been chosen partly because they represent a fairly intuitive partition of the facets of an information-handling episode that can be applied to any system, involving a human or not, examining whatever kinds of knowledge, representation, retrieval mechanisms, and construction mechanisms serve the system. The access framework amounts to a general framework for what might be called an "information flow" analysis. Although all this may sound quite computeresque, no such restriction or even emphasis is intended. DNA replication or the generation of antibodies by the immune system in response to invasion are both processes that could be analyzed in such terms. Both involve certain kinds of information, encoded in certain ways and retrieved by certain paths, and the construction of new (or replicated) information structures.

However, in part the four categories were selected because they prove useful for sorting a number of findings from contemporary psychology about the conditions for good human learning. The following samples show how this sorting works.

*Knowledge.* Understanding a discipline typically involves not only "content-level" knowledge – facts and procedures – but what might be called "higher-order" knowledge about problem-solving strategies, styles of justification, explanation, and inquiry characteristic of the domain (Perkins & Simmons, 1988; Posner, Strike, Hewson, & Gertzog, 1982; Strike & Posner, 1985). In many learning situations, neither the learner nor the surround contains much of this higher-order knowledge, a situation that often obscures the meaning and motive of particular facts and procedures.

*Representation.* A considerable body of work suggests that visual mental models aid us in understanding complex and novel concepts. Able learners may construct such models or something of similar function for themselves, but less able learners benefit more when models are provided (e.g., Gentner & Stevens, 1983; Mayer, 1989; Perkins & Unger, 1989; Salomon, 1979).

*Retrieval.* Research shows that typical patterns of learning lead to "inert knowledge," that, although forthcoming on the fill-in-the-blank quiz, is not retrieved under authentic conditions of use. That is, such knowledge is represented in the system but with inappropriate retrieval characteristics. Problem-based learning, among other tactics, can help to prime such knowledge for contextually appropriate retrieval (Bransford, Franks, Vye, & Sherwood, 1986; Perfetto, Bransford, & Franks, 1983; Sherwood, Kinzer, Bransford, & Franks, 1987).

*Construction.* A number of developmental studies suggest that limitations in short-term memory create a processing bottleneck that makes certain concepts inaccessible to the learner. However, a well-designed surround can provide a surrogate short-term memory and support learners in attaining some of these concepts (Case, 1985; Fischer, 1980; Halford, 1982).

Notice that the access framework and general considerations such as those just mentioned offer an analysis of a thinking-learning system somewhat "above" the level of particular psychological theories of mechanism. The access framework does not provide a detailed theory of cognition, but rather an encompassing outline of a cognitive system at a rather high level of description. We do not have to know how the mind does what it does to profile the access characteristics of a person-plus. We only need to recognize the "black box" operating characteristics of the system and to ask whether the hoped-for pattern of information flow can occur.

For example, one does not require a detailed theory of knowledge representation to make the point that, in many learning situations, higher-order knowledge about the subject matter is *nowhere represented* in the system. One does not need a detailed theory of working memory to make the point that complex tasks and concepts are likely to overload the person-solo.

It is not the intent of the access framework to offer an account of underlying mechanism. Rather, the aim is to achieve an "information flow" analysis, and the claim is that interesting strengths and shortfalls of thinking and learning settings emerge at that level of analysis.

### The distribution of thinking and learning generally

The distributed thinking and learning of the person-plus perhaps comes most to the fore in situations of authentic and extended inquiry – a student or a professor developing an essay, an advertising executive contriving a campaign, a director mounting a play, an engineer designing a bridge. Such creative processes have been studied (e.g., Gruber, 1974; Perkins, 1981; Tweeney, 1985, 1992), but they are hardly in the mainstream of psychological inquiry. Let us use the engineer as a focus. The categories of the access framework aid in surveying the ways in which the engineer distributes the thinking and learning that must be done.

*Knowledge.* From the standpoint of knowledge, the engineer-solo, of course, brings to the task a rich technical repertoire in long-term memory. But also very important are books with tables of materials strength, formulas about stress on beams, regulations governing construction in the state where the bridge will be built, descriptions and images of the bridge site, and so on.

*Representations.* Besides mental representations, the engineer employs text, mathematical tables and formulas, and drawings to explore both structural and aesthetic alternatives. It is likely today that the engineer would utilize computer-aided design, with its powerful capacity to render and rotate three-dimensional visualizations of the project.

*Retrieval.* The engineer employs tables of contents and indexes in books, conventional table lookup processes for reading numerical tables, the retrieval resources of the computer-aided design system, and perhaps key words to probe bibliographic databases for the latest information on some point of construction.

*Construction.* The engineer works amid a surround providing massive short-term and long-term memory support through drawings and notes on paper and through the computer-aided design system. Memory aside, the setting affords computational support for a number of valuable cognitive operations. Hand calculators enable the engineer to make simple computations. The power of a computer-aided design system permits the engineer to view the evolving design from different angles with full precision, an achievement possible with pencil and paper only by tedious redrawing or building a three-dimensional model, the classic and quite serviceable approach.

Moreover, these points about the knowledge, representation, retrieval, and construction address the physical, not the social, surround. Almost certainly, the engineer is part of a team, and its collaborative processes contribute to the picture. The team, too, is part of this engineer's person-plus. Indeed, perhaps a better phrase is "people-plus" – the functioning cognitive unit is the team, plus its physical support system of scratch pads, technical tables, computer-aided design systems, and so on.

## The tacit views of psychology and education

Such stories are easy to tell whenever complex inquiry occurs. Moreover, other activities that are less thinking-intensive in the usual sense also typically involve massive environmental support. For example, the bustle of a cook in a kitchen, where not only the cookbook but the presence of implements in stored positions or out on the table ready to be used, or placed in the sink for later washing, constitutes a kind of cognitive scaffold that would make it difficult indeed for the cook to lose his or her place in the process.

In contrast, typical psychological and educational practices treat the person in a way that is much closer to person-solo. The usual laboratory subject is rarely equipped with more than pencil and paper to support cognition. This would serve nicely if studying cognition meant no more than studying the Platonic mind abstracted from the physical world. However, the claim here is that person-plus situations have emergent characteristics that substantially change the information-processing capacities of the system and that warrant investigation and understanding.

Schools mount a persistent campaign to make the person-plus a person-solo. "Person plus pencil, paper, text, almanac, encyclopedia" and so on is fine for *studying*, but the target performance is typically "person plus paper and pencil." And the pencil and paper are conceived not so much as thinking aids as a hopper into which the person-solo can pour concrete evidence of achievement.

Certainly there is justification for some concern with the person-solo. But so much seems quite misguided, for at least two reasons: (1) If part of the mission of schools is to prepare students for out-of-school performance, this perseveration on the person-nearly-solo is not "lifelike"; (2) most students have much to learn about the art of distributing cognition, and schools should help.

The cause of overemphasis on the person-solo may be this. There is a widespread belief in what I have previously called the "fingertip effect": Simply make a support system available and people will more or less automatically take advantage of the opportunities that it affords (Perkins, 1985). Were the fingertip effect a reality, there would be little need for education to worry about students learning to make the best use of support environments – ones as simple as pencil and paper or as complex as word processor, outliner, or hypertext environment.

However, considerable evidence argues that the fingertip effect is a sham. For example, investigations of the impact of word processors on students' writing have shown that the powers of structural transformation of the text afforded by word processors are hardly used at all. Instead, the students utilize this powerful mechanism primarily to make minor stylistic, grammatical, and spelling corrections and to get nice printouts (Cochran-Smith, 1991; Daiute, 1985, 1986). Experienced writers *do* use the resources for structural revision, and were doing so more painfully by hand before they began to use word processors.

But we do not have to turn to high technology to make the case that people miss some of the best uses of the physical support structures at their disposal. Research on reading strategies shows that readers can benefit enormously by taking advantage of abstracts, tables of contents, section headings, and captions in previewing an article they are going to read and by being aware of the kinds of text structures they are reading (e.g., Higbee, 1977). Yet without instruction in reading strategies, students do the straightforward thing: They read linearly from beginning to end.

Or, for example, conventional linear note taking in a class is arguably less efficacious than recourse to notational techniques that show the structure of knowledge in a better way, such as concept mapping (Novak & Gowin, 1984) or the use of a variety of graphic organizers for capturing particular patterns of ideas, such as narrative, compare–contrast relationships, or argument–counterargument (Jones, Pierce, & Hunter, 1988–9; McTighe & Lyman, 1988).

In summary, two principal points invite recognition. First, in rich contexts of inquiry and indeed in most everyday activities we find immense physical support systems for cognition; these support systems speak to all four facets of the access framework, providing (1) needed knowledge, (2) accessible representations, (3) efficient retrieval paths, and (4) constructive arenas (scratch pads, work benches, etc.) that support the making of things and the structuring of ideas. Second, the best use of these physical support systems is an art. It is not so commonly found. And conventional instruction does little to acquaint students with this art, mistakenly expecting the fingertip effect to do the job.

## The distribution of the executive function

We do not have to untangle the paradoxes of free will to recognize that cognitive organisms – even machines – have an executive function. That is, there are routines that do the often nonroutine job of making choices, operating at decision points to explore the consequences of options and select a path of action. While the preceding section examined the distribution of thinking and learning in general, it is worthwhile to focus for a while on this special case – the executive function and its distribution in various versions of the person-plus.

To relate the executive function to the access framework, making choices in complex circumstances is plainly a highly constructive act; consequently, the executive function inevitably draws on knowledge and representational, retrieval, and constructive resources. Sometimes, however, the executive function is fulfilled in a more straightforward way through memory for previous choices at similar choice points, mostly a matter of retrieval from internal or external representations of the knowledge stored about the choice point.

The executive function of a person-plus during thinking and learning can be distributed in a number of ways. We most often envision a person deciding for him- or herself. But many other scenarios occur. For example, often during instruction the teacher decides what would be best to do. The learner, to be sure, decides whether or not to go along. A text or workbook or computer-aided instruction (CAI) program has an implicit set of executive decisions built in: Read this chapter, then do this exercise. Solve this problem; depending on how well you do, the computer will provide another problem.

In cases like these, it would be easy to sloganeer about a learner's loss of autonomy, certainly an important issue. But it is definitely *not* the presumption here that this taking over of the executive function by the learning support system (teacher, book, computer, etc.) is generally a bad thing. All depends on the wisdom of the support and on whether the learner eventually has a chance to develop whatever executive functions are needed to gain from the learning experience.

Indeed, ceding the executive function to the surround is often one of the most powerful moves we can make. If the directions for assembling the components of a new stereo system are clearly written, we do best to follow them. When concerned with the capriciousness of human judgment in cases of conflicting interest, we make written contracts and laws that freeze certain patterns of decision making. Of course, all this is usually done with some latitude or power of override left to a human-solo or a social group (e.g., juries, judges), but that should not obscure the basic tactic of ceding considerable executive function to the physical surround.

There are also interesting mixed cases. The menu systems commonly used in computer interfaces leave choices to the user, but organize the options on pull-down menus that anticipate the user's likely priorities. Thus, the surround undertakes part of the normal executive function – constructing a representation of the option space. To turn for a moment to the social distribution of intelligence, clinicians commonly avoid taking over executive function for their clients, because they want to build the clients' autonomy. But they scaffold and nudge the clients in the construction of the option space. To turn to education, Mark Lepper's studies of expert tutors disclose a complex pattern of interaction in which the tutor leaves the student feeling empowered but subtly exercises enormous control on the student's path through questions and challenges of various sorts (Lepper, Aspinwall, Mumme, & Chabay, 1990).

Granted that there are many sound distributions of executive function between the person and surround, in some circumstances there is an executive function gap: Learners do not automatically know how to handle distributed executives. For example, following directions with precision (a ceding of the executive function to the source of the directions) is a very useful skill; but many learners do not seem to muster related skills of self-monitoring, checking, and attentional control and so do not track well directions that ask for high precision. For a socially oriented example, some people of all ages seem to have difficulty making decisions in group contexts; indeed, sorting out priorities in a group involves a multitude of complications and a maze of cross-talk not encountered in solo decision making.

So education might in principle give students more help in the art of distributing the executive function. In practice, however, instruction generally has its own executive shortfalls. Many instructional designs may leave students – especially weaker students – with inadequate executive function: The learner does not know and cannot readily figure out quite what to do, and the surround does not provide enough help. This is commonly the case in open-ended learning situations, such as the use of Logo when teachers are not skilled in the art of scaffolding students' activities (Papert, 1980; Pea & Kurland, 1984a, b; Salomon & Perkins, 1987). The implication is *not* that such environments should involve a strong executive function in the surround, telling learners what to do, but rather that such environments should involve enough support specifically for the executive function that students can find their way into worthwhile activities.

For example, Harel (1991) reported an experiment in which youngsters used Logo to develop simple instructional software about fractions. As is not always the case in Logo settings, care was taken to create a support structure around the students sufficient to sustain fairly systematic progress through a long-term project. While the students had considerable autonomy, notebooks, discussions, and other mechanisms scaffolded good task management. The students progressed well on the projects and gained dramatically in both programming skills and fractions understanding.

### *Transitions of the executive function during learning*

This brings us to the point that the distribution of the executive function during learning can change in various ways. In the most familiar pattern, the learner cedes executive function to the surround and gradually gets it back as he or she gains mastery over the knowledge and skills in question. The catch, in much educational practice, is that the student never gets back much autonomy at all. The educational surround typically maintains extensive executive control through the formal learning process. Then the learner leaves the educational surround to function alone, suddenly responsible for an executive function but entirely unprepared for it.

A classic example is problem selection. Conventional education does virtually all problem selecting for students, deciding which problems are worth doing and, often, in what order. Then the assignments stop. And we are puzzled when students do not see opportunities in everyday life to apply what they have learned. Such a mishap is commonly called "lack of transfer." But this is something of a misdiagnosis, because it fails to recognize that the students have never had a chance to learn the process we are hoping they will transfer – problem selection. The surprising thing is not that learners commonly miss "real-life" applications, but that from time to time students find some. This is, if anything, evidence of the remarkable reach of transfer under uncongenial conditions (Perkins & Salomon, 1988; Salomon & Perkins, 1989).

So investing the learner with needed executive function is an important, yet neglected educational agenda. At the same time, there is no intent here to beat an ideological drum to the tune of total learner autonomy. Depending on the nature of the learning objective, the learner may not ever need executive control. Consider, for example, some of the CAI environments designed to routinize skills, such as typing, word recognition, or spelling. They exercise executive function to lead the learner through the learning process, but enhanced executive functioning may not be important to the automatized skill itself.

For example, research suggests that, for some slow arithmetic learners, automatization of basic arithmetic skills is a critical bottleneck that can be eliminated by drill and practice under time pressure (Hasselbring, Goin, & Bransford, 1988). Coercive as this may seem, it is not the executive function of the student that needs developing in this case. A learning experience that pays no attention to the student's executive function but simply develops the student's automaticity and stops serves perfectly well.

Finally, it is important to recognize that in some learning situations the learner moves toward ceding more executive function rather than less. A manager learns to cede executive function to capable subordinates. A museum goer, after some experience with self-directed tours versus the use of audiopacks provided by the museum, may learn to cede executive function to the audiopack, which he or she finds can provide a better tour than a self-constructed one, at least until the person gains more experience. A married couple, thrashing out some problems, may fashion written rules for themselves, such as "We talk about finances for no more than an hour on Saturday morning." In general, in the course of learning, executive function may appropriately flow toward or away from the learner, depending on the circumstances.

To summarize, there is a complex tale to be told about the social and physical distribution of the executive function. We cede executive function to the physical, never mind social, surround much more often and for much better reasons than might at first be expected. The person-plus is often substantially empowered by ceding the executive function.

At the same time, the nuances of the game are all-important. Not infrequently a person-plus fails in an activity because neither the person nor the surround nor the two in combination provides for a good executive function for the activity. Often, instruction seizes executive control when it might be better to scaffold the executive function of the student, helping to decide but not deciding. And often, when the executive function must be transferred to the learner, the instructional surround does nothing to mediate this transition.

### The distribution of higher-order knowledge

As mentioned earlier, the "knowledge" category of the access framework distinguishes between content-level knowledge – the facts and procedures of a subject matter – and "higher-order" knowledge, including discipline-appropriate problem-solving strategies and patterns of justification, explanation, and inquiry characteristic of the discipline (cf. Perkins et al., in press; Perkins & Simmons, 1988). Higher-order knowledge in a domain includes, for example, heuristics of problem solving (e.g., Polya, 1954, 1957; Schoenfeld, 1982, 1985) and patterns of explanation, justification, and inquiry (e.g., Schwab, 1978; Toulmin, 1958). Such higher-order knowledge occurs not only in academic domains but in daily life; an example is knowledge about everyday decision making or self-management.

Elsewhere, we have argued that an appreciation of higher-order domain knowledge is very important for learning in a domain (Perkins & Simmons, 1988). Many misconceptions in mathematics and science can be traced in part to the lack of higher-order knowledge that gives the appropriate conceptions a supportive context while disclosing the weaknesses of the inappropriate conceptions.

This higher-order knowledge not only informs the construction of understandings of content-level knowledge but also provides grist for the executive function discussed in the preceding section. Problem-solving strategies and patterns of justification, explanation, and inquiry give the executive major paths of domain-relevant behavior to choose among. Lacking this higher-order structure, the executive is limited in its choices to the retrieval of content knowledge and the execution of routine procedures, such as the algorithms of arithmetic. It is the higher-order aspects of a domain that infuse domain-related activities with significance.

#### The presence of higher-order knowledge

With such points in mind, it becomes important to ask how higher-order knowledge is distributed in thinking-learning situations. Perhaps the first point to make echoes one underscored for the executive function: In many person-plus situations, there is *no* appreciable representation of higher-order knowledge either in the person or in the surround. For example, many textbooks in science simply do not touch, in any but the most superficial ways, upon the processes and commitments of science (Evans, Honda, & Carey, 1988). History books commonly say nothing at all about the epistemological basis of history: how historians generate hypotheses about the past and test them against historical evidence. Often, textbooks make little use of "mental-state terms" such as "think," "know," "infer," "assume," "conclude," and "hypothesize" (Olson, & Astington, 1990; Olson & Babu, in press). Students themselves can hardly be expected to conjure up such ideas out of nothing.

It is commonplace to note such shortfalls in conventional instructional materials. However, the point goes well beyond textbook bashing. Many innovative learning environments that dramatically improve some access characteristics of a learning situation nonetheless do not touch on the problem of higher-order knowledge.

To make this proposition concrete, consider the example of the Geometric Supposer (Schwartz & Yerushalmy, 1987), an ingenious computer program designed to restore exploration and discovery to the teaching of Euclidean geometry. The Supposer does this by way of three basic tactics. First, it makes geometric constructions extremely easy: A user can request that a triangle be drawn, an altitude be dropped, a parallel be constructed, and so on. Second, it makes measuring such constructions in order to check conjectures very easy. For example, a student can request a measurement of two sides of a triangle to see whether they are equal. Third, the Supposer makes retesting a conjecture on different versions of the same process extremely easy. For example, having begun by constructing a random triangle, dropping an altitude, and so on, the student can request that the system repeat the entire construction beginning with a new randomly chosen triangle or one the student specifies. Thus, the student can discern whether the same construction on a different triangle yields the conjectured geometric relationship again.

The Geometric Supposer is one of the best-known technological innovations in mathematics education, justifiably renowned for restoring a measure of creativity to the traditional geometry curriculum. From the standpoint of the access framework, it clearly affords improved access characteristics in a number of ways. Basically, the Supposer provides a constructive arena – in the most literal sense. The operations in this arena are executed with much more fluency and precision than a student could readily muster using a straightedge and compass. Regarding retrieval, the system affords immediate re-trieval and re-execution of the previous construction. Regarding representation, the system of course displays constructions, but also, through artful screen layout, makes plain the repertoire of constructive operations that one might apply.

Thus, the student has all the resources to proceed with higher-order inquiry in the domain of geometry. However, remember the fingertip effect, the mischievous assumption that people readily take advantage of opportunities that are there. With the Supposer, many students do not so readily see the opportunities, and many teachers do not know quite what to do to lead students to those opportunities. For the Supposer does not include any knowledge about the higher-order aspects of the domain (Chazen, 1989).

The argument here is not that the Supposer should be improved by somehow building in more higher-order knowledge to the software itself. On the contrary, the Supposer is one of my favorite examples of software design and is fine as it stands. The point, rather, is that the surrounding instruction must – and sometimes does – include artic-ulate attention to the higher-order aspects of geometry.

In general, cognitive opportunities are not in themselves cognitive scaffolds. Thoughtful, innovative technological resources that afford great opportunity for higher-order kinds of thinking and learning in a domain do not in themselves necessarily provide cognitive scaffolding.

### The locus of higher-order knowledge

Recognizing the need for higher-order knowledge in the person-plus, we can ask where its locus should be. In general, this essay has pressed the point that locus in itself is not important – whether in the surround or in the person. What counts are the access characteristics – for example, how transparently the needed knowledge is represented and how readily it can be retrieved. This was the equivalent access hypothesis advanced at the outset.

But this hypothesis does not necessarily imply that higher-order knowledge can just as well be located in the surround. All depends on whether approximate functional equivalence might be achieved – which is not so easily done with higher-order knowledge. By and large, the higher-order knowledge should be in the person (or distributed among the minds of participating persons) rather than physically downloaded.

Why is this? First of all, because higher-order knowledge is referenced more or less continuously by the executive function in complex inquiry activities. It is not like a formula that, checked once a month, might as well be buried in a book. Second, higher-order knowledge is fairly stable, not ephemeral like scratchwork, and so it might as well sit in long-term memory. Third, higher-order knowledge is relatively compact compared with the mass of facts and procedures in a domain. So there is no particular problem with the sheer bulk of it; indeed, the problem is more one of getting it to operate actively in guiding the executive function. Fourth, a person seriously involved in a discipline or caught up in the activities of everyday life functions in many surrounds – at his or her desk, the walls crowded with reference books; at meetings, with notebook in hand; washing the dishes or mowing the lawn; or hashing over a personal problem with the help of a close friend and a couple of beers. The higher-order knowledge, needed moment-to-moment in diverse settings, cannot readily be relegated to a particular physical storage system.

Accordingly, contrary to the general spirit of distributed cognition, the internalization of higher-order knowledge in a domain is particularly to be urged.

### What is a person as a cognitive agent?

We began with an asymmetry. Most views of thinking and learning lean toward the person-solo, neglecting the ways in which people employ the surround (including other people) to support, share, and undertake outright aspects of cognitive processing. In contrast, one can take a person-plus perspective on thinking and learning, treating the person plus surround as one system, counting as part of the thinking what gets done or partly done in the surround, counting as learning traces left in the surround (assuming it stays accessible) as well as the person, and in general picking the lock of a person-solo view of thinking and learning.

So when we pick the lock, do we find anything interesting in the larger space we enter? The case was made that genuine contexts of inquiry typically involve massive distribution of thinking and learning between the person and the surround. Active thinkers assemble around themselves a rich surround and interact with it in subtle ways to achieve results that would be difficult for the person-solo. Unfortunately, schools show a strong bias toward the person-solo. They rely on the "fingertip effect" assumption, presuming that people will automatically take effective advantage of the surround just because it is there. They thereby miss the opportunity to cultivate all sorts of skills concerning the artful distribution of thinking and learning.

Thinking and learning often involve ceding the executive function to the surround in worthwhile ways. No dogged vision of person-solo autonomy seems warranted. At the same time, a prevalent problem of thinking and learning occurs when neither person nor surround nor the two together supports an effective executive function. Many open-ended instructional settings suffer from this problem. Another mishap occurs when the executive function is ceded to the surround for a while during the early stages of learning, but the learner never gets it back.

Higher-order knowledge informs the executive function in important ways. Arguably, most higher-order knowledge ought to find its locus in the person; as explained earlier, it should be continuously on tap, not buried in a sourcebook or other surrogate memory. In many thinking and learning situations encountered in schools, necessary higher-order knowledge is to be found neither in the persons nor in their surrounds. Even innovations strikingly insightful in boosting other access characteristics for the person-plus commonly do not address the presence of higher-order knowledge in the system.

All of this demonstrates that a story can be told about the happenings and mishappenings of thinking and learning, employing the notions of distributed thinking and learning and the access framework to see the person-plus rather than the person-solo as the key player. This story makes salient some neglected features of cognition and throws into relief certain shortfalls of typical and even innovative education.

As Pea (Chapter 2, this volume) points out, a further potential payoff of perspectives emphasizing distributed cognition is an enlarged concept of human development. The Piagetian perspective, for example, has highlighted assimilation of and accommodation to the environment by the organism, as though the environment were given and the person there to learn to deal with it. Of course, this is true to a considerable extent. But also, people select and build their physical and social environments, and do so in part to support cognition. In this sense, there is mutual assimilation and accommodation between the person and the surround – a complex equilibration process, if you like, in the person-plus.

A Vygotskian perspective would highlight the learner's assimilation from the social surround of patterns of cognition (Vygotsky, 1962, 1978). The notion of distributed cognition would also mark the person's modifying influence on the social surround. Moreover, it would emphasize the importance of the *physical* surround alongside the social as a major factor in the cognition of the person-plus system.

Finally, many contemporary developmental perspectives make much of limitations in working memory as a developmental bottleneck, and various experimental results suggest that physical support in the surround can enable the person-plus to deal with some complex concepts that would be unmanageable for the person-solo. It would be interesting to investigate to what extent the available physical supports in person-plus settings generally absorb some of the cognitive burden of the thinking youngsters and whether they could easily absorb more of it with some adjustments.

In short, a person-plus view suggests that some basic parameters and trajectories of human development might change according to what might ordinarily be considered nuances in the surround and the person's relation to it. This is surely something we need to understand better. And it is surely possible to envision an educational process oriented more toward the person-plus, empowering learners to capitalize with greater awareness and art upon the cognitive resources afforded by the physical and human resources around them – indeed, empowering learners to construct around themselves their personal "plus," their own surround for an agenda that will evolve with that surround.

Such an educational tactic surely would be in keeping with the human trend from one-pebble-per-sheep accounting systems to hieroglyphics and on. It is notable how vigorously we human beings, given half a chance, function as agents recruiting into the cognitive enterprise not only other people but the insentient physical things around us, arranging them and refashioning them so that they become "partners in cognition" (Saiomon et al., 1991).

Reciprocally, it seems worth reflecting that at the center of every person-plus is, of course, at least one person. Indeed, any person alone is the intersect of the set of person-pluses in which that person participates. A person alone, then, becomes the queen bee in a hive of innumerable participations.

So what is the person proper – the person-solo? The tendency of our language and much of educational practice and psychological research is to say yes, the person proper is the person solo. But this paradigm needs to be rethought. Perhaps the person proper is better conceived not as the common core but the set of interactions and dependencies; not as the intersection but the union of involvements; not as the pure and enduring nucleus but the sum and the swarm of participations.

## References

Baddeley, Alan. (1982). *Your memory: A user's guide.* New York: Macmillan.

Bransford, J. D., Franks, J. J., Vye, N. J., & Sherwood, R. D. (1986, June). *New approaches to instruction: Because wisdom can't be told.* Paper presented at the Conference on Similarity and Analogy, University of Illinois, Urbana.

Case, R. (1985). *Intellectual development: Birth to adulthood.* New York: Academic Press.

Chazen, D. (1989). *Ways of knowing: High school students' conceptions of mathematical proof.* Unpublished doctoral dissertation, Harvard Graduate School of Education, Cambridge, MA.

Cochran-Smith, M. (1991). Word processing and writing in elementary classrooms: A critical review of related literature. *Review of Educational Research, 61,* 107–55.

Craik, F. I., & Lockhart, R. S. (1972). Levels of processing: A framework for memory research. *Journal of Verbal Learning and Verbal Behavior, 11,* 671–84.

Daiute, C. (1985). *Writing and computers.* Reading, MA: Addison-Wesley.

(1986, May). Physical and cognitive factors in revision: Insights from studying with computers. *Research in the Teaching of English, 20,* 141–59.

Evans, R., Honda, M., & Carey, S. (1988). *Do theories grow on trees?* Unpublished manuscript, Harvard Graduate School of Education, Educational Technology Center, Cambridge, MA.

Fischer, K. W. (1980). A theory of cognitive development: The control and construction of hierarchies of skills. *Psychological Review, 87*(6), 477–531.

Gentner, D., & Stevens, A. L. (Eds.). (1983). *Mental models.* Hillsdale, NJ: Erlbaum.

Gruber, H. (1974). *Darwin on man: A psychological study of scientific creativity.* New York: Dutton.

Halford, G. (1982). *The development of thought.* Hillsdale, NJ: Erlbaum.

Harel, I. (1991). *Children designers.* Norwood, NJ: Ablex.

Hasselbring, T., Goin, L., & Bransford, J. (1988). Developing math automaticity in learning handicapped children: The role of computerized drill and practice. *Focus on Exceptional Children, 20*(6), 1–7.

Higbee, K. L. (1977). *Your memory: How it works and how to improve it.* Englewood Cliffs, NJ: Prentice-Hall.

Jones, B. F., Pierce, J., & Hunter, B. (1988–9). Teaching students to construct graphic representations. *Educational Leadership, 46*(4), 20–5.

Lepper, M., Aspinwall, L., Mumme, D., & Chabay, R. (1990). Self-perception and social perception in tutoring: Subtle social control strategies of expert tutors. In J. M. Olson & M. P. Zanna (Eds.), *Self-inference processes: The Ontario Symposium* (Vol. 6, pp. 217–37). Hillsdale, NJ: Erlbaum.

Mayer, R. E. (1989). Models for understanding. *Review of Educational Research, 59,* 43–64.

McTighe, J., & Lyman, F. T. (1988). Cueing thinking in the classroom: The promise of theory embedded tools. *Educational Leadership, 45*(7), 18–24.

Novak, J. D., & Gowin, D. B. (1984). *Learning how to learn.* Cambridge University Press.

Olson, D. R., & Astington, J. W. (1990). Talking about text: How literacy contributes to thought. *Journal of Pragmatics, 14*(15), 557–73.

Olson, D. R., & Babu, N. (in press). Critical thinking as critical discourse. In S. P. Norris & L. M. Phillips (Eds.), *Foundations of literacy policy in Canada.* Calgary: Detselig.

Papert, S. (1980). *Mindstorms: Children, computers, and powerful ideas.* New York: Basic Books.

Pea, R. D., & Kurland, D. M. (1984a). On the cognitive effects of learning computer programming. *New Ideas in Psychology, 2*(2), 137–68.

(1984b). *Logo programming and the development of planning skills* (Rep. No. 16). New York: Bank Street College.

Perfetto, G. A., Bransford, J. D., & Franks, J. J. (1983). Constraints on access in a problem solving context. *Memory & Cognition, 11*(1), 24–31.

Perkins, D. N. (1981). *The mind's best work.* Cambridge, MA: Harvard University Press.

(1985). The fingertip effect: How information-processing technology changes thinking. *Educational Researcher, 14*(7), 11–17.

Perkins, D. N., Crismond, D., Simmons, R., & Unger, C. (in press). Inside understanding. In D. N. Perkins, J. Schwartz, M. M. West, & M. S. Wiske (Eds.), *Teaching for understanding in the age of technology.* New York: Teachers College Press.

Perkins, D. N., & Salomon, G. (1988). Teaching for transfer. *Educational Leadership, 46*(1), 22–32.

Perkins, D. N., & Simmons, R. (1988). Patterns of misunderstanding: An integrative model of misconceptions in science, mathematics, and programming. *Review of Educational Research, 58*(3), 303–26.

Perkins, D. N., & Unger, C. (1989, June). *The new look in representations for mathematics and science learning.* Paper presented at the Social Science Research Council conference "Computers and Learning," Tortola, British Virgin Islands.

Polya, G. (1954). *Mathematics and plausible reasoning* (2 vols.). Princeton, NJ: Princeton University Press.

    (1957). *How to solve it: A new aspect of mathematical method* (2d ed.). Garden City, NY: Doubleday.

Posner, G. J., Strike, K. A., Hewson, P. W., & Gertzog, W. A. (1982). Accommodation of a scientific conception: Toward a theory of conceptual change. *Science Education, 66*(2), 211–27.

Pressley, M., Wood, E., & Woloshyn, V. (1990). Elaborative interrogation and facilitation of fact learning: Why having a knowledge base is one thing and using it is quite another. In W. Schneider & F. W. Weinert (Eds.), *Interactions among aptitudes, strategy, & knowledge in cognitive performance* (pp. 200–21). New York: Springer.

Salomon, G. (1979). *Interaction of media, cognition, and learning.* San Francisco: Jossey-Bass.

Salomon, G., & Perkins, D. N. (1987). Transfer of cognitive skills from programming: When and how? *Journal of Educational Computing Research, 3,* 149–69.

    (1989). Rocky roads to transfer: Rethinking mechanisms of a neglected phenomenon. *Educational Psychologist, 24*(2), 113–42.

Salomon, G., Perkins, D. N., & Globerson, T. (1991). Partners in cognition: Extending human intelligence with intelligent technologies. *Educational Researchers, 20,* 2–9.

Schoenfeld, A. H. (1982). Measures of problem-solving performance and of problem-solving instruction. *Journal for Research in Mathematics Education, 13*(1), 31–49.

    (1985). *Mathematical problem solving.* New York: Academic Press.

Schwab, J. (1978). *Science, curriculum and liberal education: Selected essays* (I. Westbury & N. J. Wilkof, Eds.). Chicago: University of Chicago Press.

Schwartz, J. L., & Yerushalmy, M. (1987). The Geometric Supposer: Using microcomputers to restore invention to the learning of mathematics. In D. N. Perkins, J. Lochhead, & J. Bishop (Eds.), *Thinking: Proceedings of the second international conference* (pp. 525–36). Hillsdale, NJ: Erlbaum.

Sherwood, R. D., Kinzer, C. K., Bransford, J. D., & Franks, J. J. (1987). Some benefits of creating macro-contexts for science instruction: Initial findings. *Journal of Research in Science Teaching, 24,* 417–35.

Strike, K., & Posner, G. (1985). A conceptual change view of learning and understanding. In L. H. T. West & A. L. Pines (Eds.), *Cognitive structure and conceptual change* (pp. 211–32). New York: Academic Press.

Toulmin, S. E. (1958). *The uses of argument.* Cambridge University Press.

## 110   *D. N. Perkins*

Tweeney, R. D. (1985). Faraday's discovery of induction: A cognitive approach. In D. Gooding & F. James (Eds.), *Faraday rediscovered: Essays on the life and work of Michael Faraday, 1791–1867.* New York: Stockton Press.

   (1992). How Faraday invented the field. In R. Weber & D. N. Perkins (Eds.), *Inventive minds.* New York: Oxford University Press.

Vygotsky, L. S. (1962). *Thought and language.* Cambridge, MA: MIT Pres.; New York: Wiley.

   (1978). *Mind in society: The development of higher psychological processes.* Cambridge, MA: Harvard University Press.

# 4    No distribution without individuals' cognition: a dynamic interactional view

*Gavriel Salomon*

I have come neither to bury the idea of distributed cognitions, on the basis of which I am developing new computer tools, nor to praise it. For the idea is novel and provocative. However, it can be carried too far. As is the case with so many other newly coined terms, "distributed cognitions" strongly illuminates one facet of an issue, sending to dark oblivion others. For the person with the hammer, the whole world looks like a nail; glass, toes, and skulls become endangered species. The same applies, I think, to distributed cognitions. The individual has been dismissed from theoretical considerations, possibly as an antithesis to the excessive emphasis on the individual by traditional psychological and educational approaches. But as a result the theory is truncated and conceptually unsatisfactory.

The issue of where cognitions reside, particularly when discussed in an educational context, cannot be dealt with in an either (in one's head)/or (distributed) fashion. We have to consider the possibility that, while cognitions can be distributed, they need a few "sources" for this distribution such that they can operate conjointly. We also have to consider the possibility that each of these so-called sources, or intellectual partners, can also grow such that each subsequent joining of partners will become more intelligent.

Before we proceed, however, I would like to make a few comments about the word "distribution." To be sure, the term means the absence of a clear, single locus, as when family responsibilities or financial investments become distributed over different individuals or portfolios. But this, of course, is not the whole story. Distribution also means sharing – sharing authority, language, experiences, tasks, and a cultural heritage. Unlike cognition and ability, which are traditionally seen to reside solely inside the individual (leading to the

111

inevitable disregard for social, situational, and cultural contexts), distributed cognitions do not have a single locus "inside" the individual. Rather, they are "stretched over" (Cole, 1991; Lave, 1988); they are "in between" and are jointly composed in a system that comprises an individual and peers, teachers, or culturally provided tools.

We can elaborate on the notion of cognitions as "stretched over" by borrowing a useful metaphor from recent formulations of connectionism (without necessarily subscribing to connectionists' tenets). Bereiter (1991), in an attempt to relate connectionism to educational matters, offers a model of Frisbees, four of which are clamped to a room's four walls and connected to others by rubber bands, with the whole network suspended in midair. The network, so suspended, first vacillates and then comes to rest, creating a particular pattern. To achieve a desired pattern, many subtle adjustments must be made, since any modification of one rubber band connecting two Frisbees will affect the whole network. Assume that a large number of adjustments have been made such that whenever the same four Frisbees are clamped to their designated walls, the network produces the same desired pattern. It can be said to have "learned" the pattern. But where does this learning reside and where is its knowledge? As Bereiter points out, it resides neither in the Frisbees nor in the rubber bands. Rather, it is *distributed* across the whole network.

Although I will try to show that not all cases of distributed cognitions are of the same nature, still, all of them share one important quality: The product of the intellectual partnership that results from the distribution of cognitions across individuals or between individuals and cultural artifacts is a joint one; it cannot be attributed solely to one or another partner. As Pea (1985) has put it, "Intelligence is not a quality of the mind alone, but a product of the relation between mental structures and the tools of the intellect provided by culture" (p. 168). The diagnoses rendered by a physician working with colleagues or with an intelligent expert system are the products of the distributed cognitions, "stretched over" the whole system.

In this chapter I wish to inquire into the nature of distributed cognitions and the role that conceptions of individuals' cognitions ought to play in constructing a conceptually satisfying theory of it. I will address this issue by raising three central questions and a number of accompanying ones: First, do we need to include the individual's cognitions, representations, and mental operations in the theoretical formulations of distributed cognitions? Differently put, can we afford *not* to include the individual in such theorizing? Second, since my answer is that we cannot afford the construction of a theory of distributed cognitions without *explicit* reference to the individual, are distributed and individuals' solo cognitions interrelated? If so, how? Third, based on the answers to the preceding questions, what educational implications can be derived in terms of goals and practices?

### Do we need to consider the individual?

I shall deal with the first question by raising four others: (a) How distributed are people's cognitions in daily life? (b) Are there cognitions that cannot be distributed and thus, by their very nature, are in the individual's territory? (c) Can we make do in our theoretical formulations without reference to individuals' mental representations? (d) Can the development of joint, distributed systems be accounted for satisfactorily without consideration of how the individual partners develop? As will become apparent, these questions cannot be answered solely by reference to empirical findings and observations. Empirical findings, by necessity, are based on *a priori* assumptions that already entail answers to the questions we want to answer. A researcher's choice to examine how social contexts affect individuals' minds (e.g., Hatch & Gardner, Chapter 6, this volume) or a researcher's choice to observe only behaviors and cognitions in a social or technological context (e.g., Lave, 1988; Saxe, 1988) are already based on the assumption that individuals' cognitions are or are not of theoretical interest.

### *How distributed are people's cognitions in daily life?*

Although it is undeniable that many human actions are socially and technologically distributed and that many of these distributions entail what Pea (Chapter 2, this volume) calls "off-loading" cognitions onto others or onto technical implements, it is also undeniable that not *all* cognitions, regardless of their inherent nature, are distributed *all the time*, by *all individuals* regardless of situation, purpose, proclivity, or affordance.

This not only is a rather obvious observation, but also follows from the very nature of the distributed-cognitions argument. This argument is based on a number of assumptions. One is that, if cognitions are *distributed*, then by necessity they are also *situated* (Brown, Collins, & Duguid, 1989) since the distribution of cognitions greatly depends on situational affordances (Lave, 1988; Pea, Chapter 2, this volume). In this light, it can be argued that, if cognitions are so situation-bound, then their *distribution* would surely also depend on situational and other local conditions and affordances. In some situations, particularly the ones that afford it, cognitions are distributed, while in others, notably when distribution is impossible, impractical, or the affordances are not recognized, they are not. Sitting at my desk thinking about the arguments I want to present in this chapter, I cannot but rely on my own cognitive repertoire; there is little in this austere surrounding that affords much cognitive distribution of any notable quality. Thus, if cognitions sometimes are and sometimes are not distributed, then no theory about distributed cognitions can afford to ignore the (probably many) cases and opportunities when cognitions are not distributed.

### *Are there cognitions that cannot be distributed?*

The idea of distributed cognitions is based on a second implicit assumption, namely that all cognitions *can* be distributed. This assumption can be questioned, however, for there is the possibility that some cognitions – due to their inherent nature – cannot be. Perkins (Chapter 3, this volume) attempted such an approach, claiming that, while most kinds of cognitions can be distributed, the only ones that cannot be pertain to higher-order knowledge of a field. Such knowledge, he claims, lacks many of the attributes that enable distribution onto one's physical or social surround, and thus must be seen as residing (and must be cultivated) in the individual. However, higher-order knowledge is not the only kind of cognition that is perhaps not distributable in the sense presented here.

Consider an argument advanced by the philosopher John Searle (1984). While criticizing the "strong" version of artificial intelligence, the one that equates mind with a thinking machine, he argues that, although the machine might behave *as if* it were thinking, all it does is simulate the *syntax* (set of operating rules) of thinking; it does not have the *semantics* (actual meanings) of the symbols it manipulates. Similarly with computers. They are indifferent to whether the zeros and ones stand for numbers, letters, or whatever. To illustrate his point, Searle uses the by-now-famous Chinese room metaphor, in which a non-Chinese-speaking person is seated in a sealed room with two baskets of Chinese symbols (meaningless to him or her) and with a book of rules in *English* prescribing in great detail and accuracy which symbols should go with which. A string of symbols is slipped under the door (the people outside the room call it a "question") and the person inside it responds to it according to the book of rules. He or she hasn't got a clue to what the whole thing is about or that the outsiders treat the response as an "answer."

Now, some people might say that the activity of receiving and "answering" questions in Chinese is distributed and that the whole system – room, baskets, rules in English, the non-Chinese-speaking individual – *jointly understand's* Chinese. ("Understanding," here, is taken to mean more than just having a representation of some declarative knowledge; see Perkins & Simmons, 1988.) However, as Searle points out, this joint system, while adhering to syntactical rules, does not comprehend the semantic content of the strings of symbols it produces; it even may not know that the strings consist of symbols that stand for something beyond themselves. As he writes (1984, p. 31): "If my thoughts are to be *about* anything, then the strings must have a *meaning* which makes the thoughts about those things." It thus becomes clear that the system, lacking semantic understanding, understands nothing. Even if the individual in the room had been supplied with yet another ledger containing the semantic meanings of the symbols, it would have been he or she who could have shown some understanding, *not* the "system." Joint systems can share semantic understanding in the sense of arriving at common meanings, but these will not be distributed in the sense of being "stretched over," "off-loaded," or "in between," as presented earlier; they will always be part of the individual's mind.

*Can we make do without reference to individuals' mental
representations?*

Admitting individuals' cognitions into theoretical formulations of distributed cognitions is based on a distinction between "in-
the-head" cognitions in the form of representations and processes
applied to them, and "distributed" cognitions in the sense of jointly
emerging cognitions. This distinction, although traditionally hon-
ored, can be challenged. The argument in favor of including the individual might be seen as implying that the individual is equipped
with a certain toolbox of knowledge and skills (represented in some
form) that he or she applies according to the cues, perceived demands, and social givens and affordances of the situation and the activity to be carried out. However, this assumption is challenged by
Lave (1988) and by others (e.g., Laboratory of Comparative Human
Cognition, 1983) who have developed the idea of distributed cognitions on the grounds that activities are so highly context-bound and
the processes involved in an activity so varied from one social and distributed setting to another that the distinction between the cognitive
"toolbox," the context, and the activity becomes untenable (compare
school math with "street math"). Thus, Lave (1988) points out that
"the same people differ in their arithmetic activities in different settings in ways that challenge theoretical boundaries between activity
and settings, between cognitive, bodily, and social forms of activity,
between information and value, between problem and solution" (p. 3).
    This raises difficulties for the argument I am developing here.
Once the possibility is acknowledged that an activity, with both its
knowledge and process components, changes situationally, one may
question the idea that some cognitions are distributed some of the
time. Rather, Lave argues that in typical, real-life situations, one engages in the *process of knowing* as part of one's actual activity in the
world, not (just) in the application of preexisting knowledge and
skills. According to Lave, it is impossible to separate the processes
(of, say, problem solving) from their products, the cognitions brought
forth to a situation from those that develop in action, and the static
from the dynamic elements of thinking. Instead of discussing "the
person" (and thus what in "the person" can or cannot be distributed)
one ought to discuss the person-acting-in-settings whereby cogni-

tions are "distributed – stretched over, not divided among – mind, body, activity, and culturally organized settings (which include other actors)" (1988, p. 1). The idea of distributed cognitions constitutes a shift of attention *away* from such questions as how distributed and not-distributed cognitions interrelate and places a greater emphasis on the whole person's activities in specific situations. As Pea (Chapter 2, this volume) argues, intelligence is accomplished rather than possessed. In this sense, *representations* – the traditional domain of the individual's cognitive repertoire and the "material" mentally operated upon – also become downplayed as less relevant than the situated actions and cognitions one constructs in situ.

Indeed, this is a rather basic assumption underlying the radical distributed-cognitions perspective. If what counts is the situated action within which cognitions are "stretched over," not just divided up, among partners, then what need do we have for the concept of psychological representation? And if there is no need for mental representations, then the division between cognitions that can and cannot be distributed becomes irrelevant.

A similar claim is made by Winograd and Flores (1987) on the basis of the philosophies of the biologist Humberto Maturana and the existential philosophers Hans Georg Gadamer and Martin Heidegger. Not surprisingly, these views resemble the assumption implicitly underlying the idea of distributed cognitions. Winograd and Flores's (1987) argument is based on a phenomenological view that denies the distinction between a person who is (subjectively) perceiving something and the so perceived (objective) world. This commonly held view is replaced by the idea of *being-in-the-world* (the German *Dasein)*, or what Winograd and Flores, following Heidegger, call *thrownness* – being actively embedded in an ongoing activity where behavior is very much governed by the context and the activity itself. They write: "We have primary access to the world through practical involvement with the *ready-to-hand* – the world in which we are always acting unreflectively. Detached contemplation can be illuminating, but it also obscures the phenomena themselves by isolating and categorizing them" (p. 32). If we focus on "concernfull" activity instead of on detached contemplation, the status of mental representations is, by necessity, called into question: "In driving a nail with a hammer (as opposed to thinking about a hammer), I need not make use of any explicit representation of the hammer. My ability to act comes from my familiarity with *hammering*, not my knowledge of *a hammer*" (p. 33).

Where, then, do reflection and representation belong? According to Winograd and Flores, situated action is primary, and representation secondary, at best: "Representation [is] a derivate phenomenon, which occurs only when there is a breaking down of concernful action. Knowledge lies in the being that situates us in the world, not in reflective representations" (p. 74). Indeed, while you are chairing a meeting you are "thrown into the world" and act without much on-the-spot reflection; reflection may emerge later on when you are (re)considering the meeting: "In a sense you have a representation of the situation, with objects [two disagreeing factions] and properties [their goals and personalities], but this was not the understanding you had to work with as it was developing" (p. 35). What, then, is knowledge? According to this view it is *not* "the storehouse of representations, which can be called upon for use in reasoning and which can be translated into language" (p. 73). Rather, "Knowledge lies in the being that situates us in the world, not in reflective representation" (p. 74).

Herein lies the affinity between the view developed by Winograd and Flores (see also Thompson, 1989) and the distributed-cognitions perspective as presented by Pea (1987; see also Chapter 2, this volume) and others. For both views move away from seeing the individual as the major unit of analysis, replacing it with a much larger unit – the system of individuals in a social, cultural, technological activity setting. As Winograd and Flores (1987) write:

The key of much of what we have been saying . . . lies in recognizing the fundamental importance of the shift from an individual-centered conception of understanding to one that is socially based. Knowledge and understanding . . . do not result from formal operations on mental representations of an objectively existing world. Rather, they arise from the individual's committed participation in mutually oriented patterns of behavior that are embedded in a socially shared background of concerns, actions, and beliefs. (p. 78)

But not all is lost for representations even in Winograd and Flores's formulation. Although they demote representations to a secondary role in one's daily actions, they nevertheless allow for such things as the understanding of a (social or technological) system: "In interacting with [a technical] system we tend to treat it in the same way we treat organisms – we operate by perturbing it and observing the results, *gradually building up an understanding of its behavior"* (p. 95, emphasis added). Yet this understanding can be stored only as a representation that will be brought to the fore when a *subsequent* "concernfull action" of ours with the system breaks down, requiring us to reflect again. One would expect such reflection, based as it is on representations, to have at least some (or a great deal of) influence on subsequent events into which we are "thrown." Seeing actions as a sequence rather than a string of unrelated events, one cannot but consider the role that individuals' representations play.

### *Can the development of distributed systems be accounted for without consideration of individuals' development?*

The fourth leg of the inquiry into the potential role played by individuals' cognitions is based on the assumption that systems of distributed cognitions grow and develop. The emphasis on only the socially (or culturally) distributed nature of cognitions with no regard for the individual's inputs, the exclusive attention to the here-and-now of one's situated actions, and the disregard for the potentially important role played by one's knowledge and skills yield a rather lopsided picture; it is a *snapshot frozen in time* that captures but half of the process. For how does the joint, distributed system change over time? How can we account for the observation that the quality of the products of a joint social or technological system often changes from one occasion to another? Indeed, "our experience of the world does not appear as a mosaic of unconnected fragments" (Laboratory of Comparative Human Cognition, 1983, p. 340). In the Frisbee analogy presented earlier, knowledge is distributed throughout the whole network; but affecting a change in the network requires changes in its components – the length or strength of one or another rubber band or the position of one or another Frisbee clamped to a wall. Similar arguments follow from the fields of family therapy (Watzlawick, Weakland, & Fisch, 1974) and organizational change (Weick, 1979), fields that also face the problem of dealing with joint, distributed systems. There, as here, change is brought about by affecting the cognitions or behaviors of one or another member (the choice very often is pragmatic) whereby a quasi-stationary equilibrium is upset, thus requiring all other components to adjust.

The underlying assumption here is that changes do occur and that a description of how a person plus others or plus technological tools jointly operates at one point in time does not account for such changes. In this light, it can be argued that, although cognitions can be and often are distributed, that human action is indeed contextual and that the Heideggarian argument of thrownness-in-the world may have conceptual appeal, nevertheless these are but "stations" in an ongoing developmental process: Distributed cognitions, thrownness, and contextual actions interact with those elements one traditionally attributes to the mind of the individual: mentally represented knowledge and skill.

### How do individuals' and distributed cognitions interact?

Four arguments lead me to conclude that distributed and individuals' cognitions must be examined in interaction: There are numerous actions and instances that do not entail any distribution of cognitions; there is the possibility that some cognitions may not be distributable; representations, even if we acknowledge (and I do not) that they play only a secondary function, exert some influence on daily actions; and it is impossible to account for developments in a system of distributed cognitions without reference to individuals' changed cognitions. This, however, leaves us with the questions of how these elements interact and – perhaps more elementary than that – what we mean by "interaction."

Interaction usually means that independent entities affect one another reciprocally, the model case being billiard balls hitting one another (Altman, 1988). However, this is not what the idea of distributed cognitions is based on (e.g., Lave, 1988; Pea, 1987; see also Pea, Chapter 2, this volume). Rather, it is based on the notion that the distributed system of cognitions is more than the sum of its components; thus, its operations cannot be understood by examination of its isolated parts, and the system should be examined as a whole. The components of the system, to the extent that they are of any interest, do not interact, for they, unlike billiard balls, do not exist as isolated entities. These assumptions resemble to an impressive extent Dewey's formulation of transactional relations:

> If inter-action is procedure such that its inter-acting constituents are set up in inquiry as separate "facts," each in independence of the presence of others, then *Transaction* is Fact such that no one of its constituents can be adequately specified as "a fact" apart from the specification of the other constituents of the full subject matter. (Dewey & Bentley, 1946, p. 536)

Does this mean that the individual and the distributed system cannot be separated and thus their mutual influences cannot be studied? William James (1884) rejected such a radical approach, which he termed "absolutism," mockingly stating that it would follow from the approach that "if any member, then the whole system; if not the whole system then nothing" (pp. 282–3). The philosopher Denis Phillips (1976), while criticizing such "holistic" approaches as entailing paradoxical contradictions, offers helpful clarifications. To study a system assumed to entail more than the sum of its components, one needs to assume neither (a) that its components are *fully* determined by the whole system, not having any existence of their own, nor (b) that they are totally independent of the system affecting one another without being changed themselves in *some* but not all of their characteristics through the interaction. In more concrete terms, interaction would mean that while, indeed, the joint products of a cognitively distributed system (e.g., a jointly designed plan of action) cannot be accounted for by the operations of its isolated components (the inputs from the members of a planning team), each partner can still be seen as having qualities of his or her own, some of which (e.g., unique expertise) enter the distributed partnership and are affected by it reciprocally, while other qualities may not be so influenced.

This is very much in line with what Bandura (1978) has termed "reciprocal determinism":

> By their actions, people play a role in creating the social milieu and other circumstances that arise in their daily transactions. Thus, . . . psychological functioning involves a continuous reciprocal interaction between behavioral, cognitive and environmental influences. (p. 345)

Altman, describing his transactional approach to the study of human behavior in social context (1988), identifies the various components in a distributed system and the way each of them affects, even defines, the others and is affected and partly defined by them:

> There are no separate actors in an event; instead, there are "acting relationships," such that the actions of one person can only be described and understood in relation to the actions of other persons, and in relation to the situational and temporal circumstances in which the actors are involved. (Altman & Rogoff, 1987, p. 24)

Yet in describing his research with groups isolated for 4 to 10 days in terms of territoriality, performance, self-disclosure, and other behaviors, Altman (1988), observes that these studies "reflected equivalent emphases on both social units and psychological processes, making it possible to shift a social unit emphasis to a psychological process emphasis, depending on how one wanted to view the findings" (p. 270). In other words, while one can choose to study a conglomerate by treating its elements as supposedly indistinguishable, one can also separate the whole into its interacting units and study them for their own qualities.

I wish to adopt the idea of reciprocal influences à la Phillips, Bandura, and Altman as the model for the interaction (or transaction) between individuals' cognitions and distributed ones. This reciprocal interaction takes place within *activities* in which cognitions are shared. These activities provide the opportunity for individuals' skills to enter into distributed, intellectual partner-like situations (see Moll et al., Chapter 5, and Brown et al., Chapter 7, this volume), while also affording the opportunity for the practice of skills (e.g., Scribner & Cole, 1981). Specifically, the general hypothesis would be that the "components" interact with one another in a spiral-like fashion whereby individuals' inputs, through their collaborative activities, affect the nature of the joint, distributed system, which in turn affects their cognitions such that their subsequent participation is altered, resulting in subsequent altered joint performances and products (Figure 4.1).

Consider, by way of an example, how junior high school students employ their initial essay-writing skills with a computerized guidance-providing tool – the Writing Partner. This is a prototypical case of distributed cognitions between young writers and a semi-intelligent tool. Clearly, writing quality improves *while* the students are employing the tool. But this activity also leaves certain cognitive residues in the form of an improved ability (or, at least, tendency) to

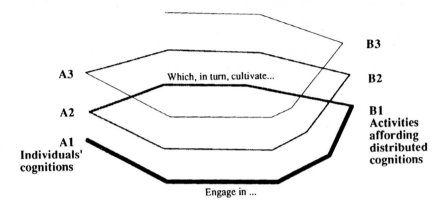

Figure 4.1. The reciprocal relations between individuals' cognitions and distributed cognitions.

self-regulate in a way that is similar to the guidance provided by the tool. This leads to improved essay writing even when the tool is not being used (Zellermayer, Salomon, Globerson, & Givon, 1991). We could easily imagine how these students, employing a somewhat more advanced tool that provided even higher-level guidance, would write higher-quality essays, which might further develop their writing-related skills.

The idea of a spiral-like development whereby distributed (or at least culturally shared) cognitions and one's own "solo" competencies are reciprocally developed by each other has parallels in adjacent fields of study. Consider, for example, Goody's (1977) idea that the development of means of communication affects modes of thought. The process, according to Goody, is spiral-like. New powers afforded by writing systems transform cognitive processes, which, in turn, affect the kinds of literate activities one engages in, and these, in turn, lead to the development of yet more powerful means of communication. Bolter (1984), similarly, postulates reciprocal influences between technologies that a culture comes to regard as "defining technologies" (e.g., the clock, the computer), the shared metaphors that these lead to (man as God's clockwork, the mind as a computational machine), and the kinds of technology usage that these metaphors lead to (the use of the computer to simulate the behavior of a paranoid patient; Colby, 1981).

Gigerenzer (1991) makes a similar case with respect to the way scientific discoveries are made, following what he coined the "tool-to-theory" heuristic:

Inferential statistics . . . provided a large part of the new concepts for mental processes that have fueled the so-called cognitive revolution since the 1960's. Theories of cognition were cleansed of terms such as restructuring and insight, and the new mind has come to be portrayed as drawing random samples from nervous fibers, computing probabilities, calculating analysis of variance, setting decision criteria, and performing utility analyses. (p. 255)

But the process is not only from tool to theory; it also works in the opposite direction: The new conception of mind as that of an intuitive statistician has affected the kinds of experiments designed, the kinds of data collected, and the kinds of new statistical procedures developed. A reciprocal process indeed.

The reciprocal, spiral-like processes just described can serve as close approximations to what might well be the interrelations between distributed and not-distributed cognitions. In fact, this follows directly from Vygotsky's writings. While Vygotsky (1978) heavily emphasized the socially distributed nature of cognitions, he also saw in this a means to cultivate the *individual's* competencies:

. . . learning awakens a variety of internal developmental processes that are able to operate only when the child is interacting with people in his environment and in cooperation with his peers. Once these processes are internalized, they become part of the child's independent developmental achievement. (p. 90)

Underlying this conception of reciprocal relations is the expectation that the partnership with others or with cultural artifacts will change over time. This change has the *appearance* of being distributed, but in fact it occurs first in the minds of the participants, which leads to changes in the quality of subsequent joint performances and the products that these yield. The participants learn how to use the technology more effectively, how to interrogate and guide each other more skillfully during reciprocal teaching, how to get more out of a computerized model builder, and the like. The partnership whereby cognitions are distributed can be said to leave *cognitive residues* in the form of improved competencies, which affect subsequent distributed activities.

Findings tend to support this contention. For example, Campione, Brown, Reeve, Ferrara, and Palincsar (1991) found that reciprocal teaching in one subject area led to cognitive residues that were manifested in improved performance in other areas later. Similarly, research by Salomon, Globerson, and Guterman (1990) and by Zellermayer et al. (1991) has shown how partnerships with specially designed computer tools that provide ongoing expert-like guidance affect readers' and writers' ability to practice self-guidance, thus gradually affecting the way their cognitions become distributed during subsequent partnerships.

This contention does not resolve the debate between the traditional emphasis on individuals' solo development, operations, and competencies and the more radical conception of distributed cognitions. Rather, it dissolves it by arguing that if development and growth are to be considered as not only static snapshots of an isolated point in time, then one should neither consider solo competencies without considering activities entailing distributed cognitions, nor consider distributed cognitions without considering their possible cognitive residues.

In sum, the claim that individuals' representations totally account for their intellectual activity is an overstatement as much as is the claim that partnerships with tools or peers totally account for the quality of the process or that the activity itself fully accounts for it. Different factors participate in the process interactively, although their specific influence may vary under different circumstances. In the absence of an opportunity for much intellectual partnership, solo representation, abilities, and the demands of the activity will dominate; in the presence of a well-rehearsed activity, the social or technological partnership and competencies may dominate, and in the presence of a very powerful tool that does much of the thinking for or with the individual, the tool will dominate.

### A challenge to the interactive view

The conception presented here is still based, however, on a distinction between the individual and his or her surroundings, focusing, among other things, on the cognitive residue that the distributed activity leaves in the individual. But this focus can be challenged on the grounds that what really counts is not what individuals have learned to do on their own, but rather how the partnership through distributed cognitions changes what they do and how they do it during that partnership. As Olson, Torrance, and Hildyard (1985) have pointed out with respect to literacy: "It is misleading to think of literacy in terms of consequences. What matters is what people do with literacy, not what literacy does to people" (p. 15).

Cole and Griffin (1980), addressing this issue, developed the argument that while cultural artifacts, particularly those related to literacy, may have some cognitive residues, these residues are in fact quite modest in comparison with the changes brought about in the way people function when literate. To use a distinction offered by Salomon, Perkins, and Globerson (1991), the emphasis shifts from a search for the effects *of* distributed activities to a search for the effects *with* them. While the former pertain to cognitive residues in the mind of the individual, the latter pertain to the structure of the activity when the tools and social surrounds for distributed cognitions are available. Thus, considering writing systems, Cole and Griffin (1980) argued, "The notion that writing systems and their sequelia in the modern world represent cultural tools that amplify mind has been found inadequate to represent the transformations in activity that literacy engenders" (p. 362).

The validity of this argument cannot be denied, but it can be argued, as before, that it does not describe the whole picture of partnership through cognitive distribution. In order to enter into an intellectually useful partnership with peers or with computer tools, in order for one's activity to undergo transformations, transformations that come about through the distribution of cognitions, one must have certain competencies and proclivities that themselves are developed through the practice provided by the partnership. Competency, as Olson (1986) points out, is "a product of the relationship between the structures of the mind and the properties of 'technologies of the intellect' " (p. 351).

Such competencies, called into play during operation with culturally provided tools or during partnerships with peers, might be quite specific – they are brought about by the requirements of the distributed activity and they may upgrade its quality subsequently. In the absence of changes in such competencies, the transformation of activities is thwarted. Such transformations – the ability to think rationally while relying less on memory (a transformation afforded by print) or the ability to construct increasingly more complex multi-variate models (afforded by semi-intelligent computer tools) – could not take place without the individual's growing mastery of the specific skills and knowledge that the distributed activity requires. In the absence of such changes in the individual's competencies, the quality of the distributed activity cannot change. What would we say of individuals who off-load some of their cognitive processing onto a computerized expert system without having learned to provide it with appropriate inputs or to read its outputs properly, without having learned to doubt the system's accuracy or without mastering the skill needed to weight the alternatives it provides?

Still, there is an important element highlighted by Cole and Griffin (1980): the role of the cultural and social contexts in which activities, particularly distributed ones, take place. It is interesting to note the important role attributed to cultural sharing of cognitions (not necessarily *distribution* of such, in the sense described earlier) by Goody (1977), Bolter (1984), Gigerenzer (1991), and Weick (1979). The technologies that affect minds and whose use is affected as a consequence have the status of *"defining* technologies" (Bolter, 1984). And scientific tools, to affect theory development, have to become *institutionalized* (Gigerenzer, 1991). Technologies that have not attained a "defining" status or that have not been "institutionalized" do not have such impacts. Heider's theory, based as it was on a factor-analytical statistical metaphor, was not accepted, because it was not institutionalized among experimental psychologists. The same theory, however, became widely disseminated a bit later through Harold Kelly's statistical ANOVA model, which was regarded with great respect (Gigerenzer, 1991).

Scribner and Cole (1981), having found only highly specific cognitive effects of the Vai literacy (a literacy not accompanied by schooling), argued: "As the technology of a society becomes more complex and it becomes more closely integrated into world affairs, we can expect the number and variety of literacy practices to increase, bringing with them new skills or more complicated versions of old skills" (p. 258).

Extrapolations from these considerations and conjectures may suggest a modification of the interactive model I presented earlier. To the extent that an activity, carried out in a distributed manner, becomes *socially accepted, widespread,* and *varied* (e.g., reciprocal teaching spreading to a variety of frequently employed team activities in classrooms), one could expect the skills it calls upon and practices to become more generalized and serve *other* activities as well. Thus, the distributed activity of building hypothetical models with a powerful computerized tool may cultivate skills that are highly tool- and situation-specific (Mandinach, 1989). However, when the activities of model building and tool use become integrated into daily school activities, are perceived as socially important and consequential, then the skills developed through these distributed activities may become far more general and thus enter into a wider range of shared activities.

## Educational implications

The conception of distributed cognitions presented here is based on the idea of reciprocal and spirally developing interactions between individuals' cognitions and socially and technologically distributed ones. Two implications for education follow: First, there is an implication concerning the cognitive goals of education, once the phenomenon and importance of distributed cognitions have been acknowledged; second, there is an implication concerning the desired design of distributed learning activities, particularly those that entail computerized tools.

### Educational goals

My point of departure is based on an article of belief: In a rapidly changing world, one of the most crucial outcomes one expects of education is students' ability to handle *new* situations and meet *new* intellectual challenges. This would include the ability to off-load intellectual tasks onto the technological and social environment, as well as other, less distributed competencies whose development *results* from the intellectual partnership afforded by situations of distributed cognitions.

The idea of distributed intelligence, as presented by its more radical proponents, emphasizes mainly the performance of a joint system of individuals and peers or cultural artifacts. It puts a premium on *performance* and tries to account for it by reference to situational determinism. In this sense it pertains to what Salomon et al. (1991) have called the effects *with* a technology or social system. The argument is that since so much of our cognitive activity is carried out by off-loading onto the cultural, technological, and social world around us anyway, the question of the effects *of* (i.e., the cognitive competencies produced by the partnership available for employment in its absence) is a moot one. The question of how to use opportunities of distributed cognitions to cultivate individuals' solo competencies is, so it is argued, a bit old-fashioned, for it treats situations of distributed cognitions as no more than means to old "cognitive cultivation" ends. As Olson (1986) points out, "Almost any form of human cognition requires one to deal productively and imaginatively with some technology. To attempt to characterize intelligence independently of those technologies seems to be a fundamental error" (p. 356). For example, we would not think of testing, let alone cultivating, people's artistic ability without the use of a medium such as brush and paint. The same could be argued with respect to intelligent computer tools. Once they have been developed and are available, the question of how to cultivate in students abilities that do not require such tools is unnecessary (Pea, Chapter 2, this volume). I would like to argue against this position from two educationally based perspectives: a pragmatic perspective and a normative one.

As the old saying goes, you can never cross the same river twice. And since each time you cross a river it is a different one, presenting new demands and choice points, you had better have available a few river-crossing skills that you can adjust and apply to the current challenges; merely using the same procedure that worked the last time you crossed the river won't do. That procedure, though of course it brought you safely to the other side, has merit now only to the extent that it taught you something useful for making a second and somewhat different crossing. This would be true even if you had crossed by means of a "superintelligent" boat, with self-guiding navigational devices and strong-current-avoiding sensors. You could off-load all of your navigational skills onto the boat's navigational mechanism. But given the quick pace of change in landscape and topography, what would you do if you faced an entirely new and unexpected stretch of marshland? Would you wait for version 7.1 of the boat to arrive, the one designed specifically to handle marshlands?

I am presently engaged in studying a computerized Writing Partner that provides continuous on-line metacognitive-like guidance during writing, designed on the basis of Bereiter and Scardamalia's (1987) research on the psychology of composition writing. The idea is to help young writers move from "knowledge telling" to "knowledge transforming." Obviously, I expect that, after a while, writing performance *with* the tool, in which the writer's intelligence is coupled with that of the tool, will yield qualitatively better writing. But I would also expect the guidance provided by the tool to become "internalized" such that writers would gradually become more independent of the tool, guiding themselves just as they were guided by the tool. The pragmatics here are based on two assumptions. First, writing also takes place in the absence of superintelligent tools, and second, metacognitive cultivation spills over to other domains, facilitating performance where no intelligence-sharing capabilities are likely to emerge (e.g., reading, informed decision making about real-life issues). Findings from our past research (Salomon et al., 1989; Zellermayer et al., 1991) strongly support these assumptions. Pragmatically speaking, limiting ourselves to the effects *with* a technology, not trying also to attain effects *of* it would mean totally forgoing the possibility that our students could learn to solve different kinds of problems under a variety of conditions, even when no opportunity for distributed cognitions exists.

This brings me to a brief discussion of the normative issue. Given the potentials of intellectual partnership through distributed cognitions, many skills could disappear in the same way that the skill of deriving a square root has disappeared. There is nothing wrong with deskilling. But what should or should not be deskilled? Here the availability of powerful intellectual partnerships with the distributed intelligence they afford is no normative guide. As argued by Sarason (1984), "Because something can be studied or developed is in itself an insufficient base for doing it however wondrous it appears to be in regard to understanding and controlling our world" (p. 480).

Moreover, we should beware of the translation of a *description* of how people operate in daily life, off-loading their intelligence as they sometimes do onto that of the environment, into an educational *pre-*

*scription.* The way the weight watcher, observed by Lave (1988), solved the cottage cheese problem is *not* necessarily the way an educated person *should* have solved it. Efficiency of performance, so strongly emphasized when distributed intelligence is advocated, is not all there is in education. Pea (Chapter 2, this volume) argues that human cognition aspires for efficiency; unfortunately, for the sake of the same cognitive economy it also aspires for clear-cut categorization, automaticity, simplicity, and, hence, inadvertently, *mindlessness* (Langer, 1989). While this is perhaps the natural way of human tendencies, we need not accept it. We need to respect the way just plain folk go through life, as we should respect the natural course of cognitive development; but – being in education – we do not have to accept these as absolute limitations that cannot be overcome by proper educational intervention (Resnick, 1981).

Most important, however, through the activity of writing with the expert-like Writing Partner, onto which one can off-load much of one's cognitive burden of writing and composing, one also learns something about writing. Over time and with much practice, writing skills are fine-tuned ("cognitive residue") and become part of one's representational system – making the user better able to self-regulate his or her own cognitions. This, in turn, may be manifested in both the user's improved ability to get more out of an even more sophisticated writing tool and the user's improved ability to communicate through writing when no such tool is available. One may prefer to cultivate more of the former than of the latter, but this is a matter of normative preferences, constraints, and pragmatic possibilities.

In sum, given the conception of distributed cognitions I have tried to develop, the challenge of employing intellectual partnerships based on the distribution of cognitions cannot be shunned. For both pragmatic and normative reasons, one ought to see in situations entailing distributed cognitions not only ends in themselves but opportunities for the development of cognitive residues that might serve students when on their own.

## The design of tools for intellectual partnership

Situations and tools for distributed cognitions should be designed in such a way as to provide opportunities to cultivate desired cognitive residues rather than limit them. As argued by Scardamalia, Bereiter, McLean, Swallow, and Woodruff (1989):

> It is not the computer that should be doing the diagnosing, the goal-setting, and the planning. It is the student. The computer environment should not be providing the knowledge and intelligence to guide learning, it should be providing the facilitating structure and tools that enable students to make maximum use of their own intelligence and knowledge. (p. 54)

The problem is that not all situations in which cognitions are distributed, particularly when intelligent computer tools and tutorial programs are used, satisfy this design condition. Indeed, not all situations of distributed cognitions are the same, and the differences between them are important from a design point of view.

The examples of situations involving the distribution of cognitions presented in this volume span a rather wide range that illustrates the near ubiquity and variability of distributed cognitions as well as the kinds of intellectual partnerships that the distribution of cognitions entails. This range, however, has an interesting attribute. When examined more closely, it appears to consist of at least two classes of distributed cognitions. The first consists of cases in which, as Pea (Chapter 2, this volume) describes it, one *off-loads* one's cognitive burden onto a tool or onto human partners. Here elements of one's social or artifactual surroundings typically carry a crucial part of one's cognitive burden: the shopping list that "remembers" for us, the computer program that graphs or computes for us, or the teacher who guides the student in lieu of the student's self-guidance. The totality of the cognitive activity, to an extent, is a matter of *division of labor:* The computer does the computation while the user provides the inputs; the list does the remembering while the person does the shopping; and so on.

The second class consists of cases in which cognitions are distributed not so much as a division of labor (although some of it still exists), but as a shared activity, as when two individuals plan together or solve a problem jointly. Consider a couple of these: cooperative learning, teamwork, teacher–student interaction during the process of learning to read (Cole & Engeström, Chapter 1, this volume), writing with a computer program that entails expert-like, and metacognitive-like guidance (Zellermayer et al., 1991). One might say that in such cases one partner in the system of distributed cognitions (human or not) stimulates, prods, guides, or otherwise redirects thinking, or activates specific retrieval paths, in the other partner. Although there might be a modicum of cognitive off-loading, the main characteristic of such cases is in fact quite different. There is much *guided stimulation* – or better, *qualitative scaffolding*, whereby one partner activates, provides meaning to, and possibly directs the cognitive activity of the other and thereby qualitatively changes the activity. The children who jointly solve science problems do not so much off-load their cognitive activity on one another as reciprocally scaffold it. The experience may have a lighter cognitive burden (social psychologists would identify it as the notorious "distribution of responsibility"), but this is not its hallmark.

The tools, teamwork, or teacher behaviors that are more akin to the off-loading type are less likely to cultivate desired cognitions than those tools and other partnerships that are of the qualitative scaffolding kind. The former, it might be pointed out, are more likely to lead to *de*skilling than to the cultivation of skill mastery (thus taking us back to the normative issue). They circumvent, even do away with, cognitive demands, making even complex intellectual activities accessible to less than skilled individuals who could not have carried them out otherwise (March, 1987). Their strength is also their weakness: By affording off-loading of (sometimes) crucial skills and knowledge, such tools or social arrangements afford higher-level accomplishments but few opportunities for the cultivation of the crucial cognitions so off-loaded.

### Summary

I began this chapter with a feeling of uneasiness. While the idea of distributed cognitions is novel and important, the way it is presented and defended is unnecessarily one-sided, excluding from theoretical considerations the cognitions of the individual and thus leaning toward situational determinism. I find such determinism conceptually limiting; any theory of distributed cognitions that leaves the individual out of consideration is unsatisfactory. I addressed three questions. The first was, Do we need to consider the individual or can we construct a conceptually satisfying theory of distributed cognitions that does not include individuals' cognitions? The answer was that we cannot afford to ignore the individual, for at least four reasons. One is that daily observations and experiences provide us with ample cases in which cognitions are *not* distributed. The second is that there might be a number of classes of cognitions – higher-order knowledge (Perkins, Chapter 3, this volume) and even processes, skills, and operations (as distinguished from declarative knowledge) – that might not be distributable. The third reason is that even in the most radical formulations of activity-in-setting (e.g., Lave, 1988; Winograd & Flores, 1987), there is no way to get around the role played by individuals' representations. Even when demoted to a secondary role, representations cannot be dismissed, because they are called upon when the smooth execution of an action is blocked, requiring reflection. Finally, I argued that the total dismissal of individuals' cognitions in favor of situated and distributed cognitions provides only frozen pictures of states that neither develop nor grow. To account for changes and developments in the performance of joint, distributed systems, one has to consider the role played by the individual partners. The conclusion I reached was that distributed cognitions and individuals' cognitions need to be seen as affecting and developing each other.

This led to the second question, How do distributed and individuals' cognitions "interact"? In exploring this issue, it became apparent that we can neither see this interaction as taking place among totally different and independent entities (such as the interaction among billiard balls), nor totally ignore the roles played by the different interactants by subscribing to a totally "holistic" view. The resolution, following Altman (1988), Bandura (1978), and Phillips (1976), is to postulate a reciprocal relationship between individuals' and distributed cognitions whereby (a) each of the interactants retains its identity while (b) *reciprocally* affecting, even defining (giving meaning to) the other. This yields a conception of spiral development according to which "any change made anywhere will eventually itself be changed by the consequences it triggers" (Weick, 1979, p. 77). Such a conception follows quite well Vygotsky's (1978) account of socially based development. The conclusion I reached was that one ought to include in a theory of distributed cognitions the possibility that joint systems require and cultivate specific individual competencies ("cognitive residues"), which affect performance in subsequent distributed activities.

Last, I addressed two educational implications that follow from the proposed conception of spiral interactions between individuals' and distributed cognitions. The first implication pertained to educational goals in the cognitive domain. Here, I argued, one should regard situations of distributed cognitions not only as ends in themselves but, more important, as means for improving mastery of solo competencies. I based this on two considerations. Pragmatic considerations suggest that in a rapidly changing world we ought to equip students with competencies that will allow them to operate intelligently outside of situations of distributed cognitions and activities. Normative considerations suggest that descriptions of performance in situations of distributed cognitions are no educational guide; they do not always provide desirable educational prescriptions. And the fact that powerful partnerships can now be created between students and intelligent computer tools does not in and of itself mean that they are always desirable.

The second educational implication concerned the design of situations of distributed cognitions, particularly the ones that entail reliance on intelligent technologies. In light of the conception I have tried to advance, I argued that such situations should be designed to promote or scaffold, rather than limit, the cultivation of individuals' competencies. Partnerships with powerful tools that are characterized mainly by cognitive off-loading may improve (joint) performance, even redefine intellectual tasks, but they may block (even deskill) the development of useful skills.

In sum, the two extremes – the psychology of individual competencies and that of distributed cognitions – ought to be accommodated within the same theoretical framework. No theory of distributed cognitions can do justice to the understanding of human activity and the informed design of education without taking into consideration individuals' cognitions. The same applies to the flip side of this argument: No theory of individuals' cognitions would be satisfactory without taking into consideration their reciprocal interplay with situations of distributed cognitions.

## References

Altman, I. (1988). Process, transaction/contextual, and outcome research: An alternative to the traditional distinction between basic and applied research. *Social Behaviour, 3,* 259–80.

Altman, I., & Rogoff, B. (1987). World views in psychology: Trait, interactional, organismic and transactional perspectives. In D. Stokolis & I. Altman (Eds.), *Handbook of environmental psychology* (pp. 1–40). New York: Wiley.

Bandura, A. (1978). The self system in reciprocal determinism. *American Psychologist, 33,* 344–58.

Bereiter, C. (1991). Implications of connectionism to thinking about rules. *Educational Researcher, 20,* 10–16.

Bereiter, C., & Scardamalia, M. (1987). *The psychology of written composition.* Hillsdale, NJ: Erlbaum.

Bolter, D. J. (1984). *Turing's man: Western culture in the computer age.* Chapel Hill: University of North Carolina Press.

Brown, J. S., Collins, A., & Duguid, P. (1989). Situated cognitions and the culture of learning. *Educational Researcher, 18,* 32–42.

Campione, J. C., Brown, A. L., Reeve, R. A., Ferrara, R. A., & Palincsar, A. S. (1991). Interactive learning and individual understanding: The case of reading and mathematics. In L. Tolchinsky-Landsmann (Ed.), *Culture, schooling, and psychological development* (pp. 136–70). Norwood, NJ: Ablex.

Colby, K. M. (1981). Modelling a paranoid mind. *Behavior and Brain Sciences, 4,* 515–34.

Cole, M. (1991). On socially shared cognitions. In L. Resnick, J. Levine, & S. Behrend (Eds.), *Socially shared cognitions* (pp. 398–417). Hillsdale, NJ: Erlbaum.

Cole, M., & Griffin, P. (1980). Cultural amplifiers reconsidered. In D. R. Olson (Ed.), *The social foundations of language and thought: Essays in honor of J. S. Bruner* (pp. 343–63). New York: Norton.

Dewey, J., & Bentley, A. F. (1946). Interaction and transaction. *Journal of Philosophy, 43,* 505–17.

Gigerenzer, G. (1991). From tools to theories: A heuristic of discovery in cognitive psychology. *Psychological Review, 98,* 254–67.

Goody, J. (1977). *The domestication of the savage mind.* Cambridge University Press.

James, W. (1884). Absolutism and empiricism. *Mind, 9.*

Laboratory of Comparative Human Cognition. (1983). Culture and cognitive development. In W. Kessen (Ed.), *Handbook of child psychology* (Vol. 1, pp. 295–356). New York: Wiley.

Langer, E. J. (1989). *Mindfulness.* Reading, MA: Addison-Wesley.

Lave, J. (1988). *Cognition in practice.* Cambridge University Press.

Mandinach, E. B. (1989). Model-building and the use of computer simulation of dynamic systems. *Journal of Educational Computing Research, 5,* 221–43.

March, J. G. (1987). Old colleges, new technology. In S. B. Kiesler & L. S. Sproul (Eds.), *Computing and change on campus* (pp. 16–27). Cambridge University Press.

Olson, D. R. (1986). Intelligence and literacy: The relationships between intelligence and the technologies of representation and communication. In R. J. Sternberg & R. K. Wagner (Eds.), *Practical intelligence: Nature and origins of competence in the everyday world* (pp. 338–60). Cambridge University Press.

Olson, D. R., Torrance, N., & Hildyard, A. (Eds.). (1985). *Literacy, language and learning.* Cambridge University Press.

Pea, R. D. (1985). Beyond amplification: Using the computer to reorganize mental functioning. *Educational Psychologist, 20,* 167–82.

(1987). Integrating human and computer intelligence. In R. D. Pea & K. Sheingold (Eds.), *Mirrors of mind: Patterns of experience in educational computing* (pp. 128–46). Norwood, NJ: Ablex.

Perkins, D. N., & Simmons, R. (1988). Patterns of misunderstanding: An integrated model for science, math, and programming. *Review of Educational Research, 58,* 303–26.

Phillips, D. C. (1976). *Holistic thought in social science.* Stanford, CA: Stanford University Press.

Resnick, L. B. (1981). Social assumptions as a context for science: Some reflections on psychology and education. *Educational Psychologist, 16,* 1–10.

Salomon, G., Globerson, T., & Guterman, E. (1990). The computer as a zone of proximal development: Internalizing reading-related metacognitions from a reading partner. *Journal of Educational Psychology, 81,* 620–7.

Salomon, G., & Perkins, D. N. (1989). Rocky roads to transfer: Rethinking mechanisms of a neglected phenomenon. *Educational Psychologist, 24,* 113–42.

Salomon, G., Perkins, D. N., & Globerson, T. (1991). Partners in cognition: Extending human intelligence with intelligent technologies. *Educational Researcher, 20,* 10–16.

Sarason, S. B. (1984). If it can be studied or developed, should it be? *American Psychologist, 39,* 477–85.

Saxe, G. B. (1988). Candy selling and math learning. *Educational Researcher, 17,* 14–21.

Scardamalia, M., Bereiter, C., McLean, R. S., Swallow, J., & Woodruff, E. (1989). Computer-supported intentional learning environments. *Journal of Educational Computing Research, 5,* 51–68.

Scribner, S., & Cole, M. (1981). *The psychology of literacy.* Cambridge, MA: Harvard University Press.

Searle, J. (1984). *Minds, brains and science.* Cambridge, MA: Harvard University Press.

Thompson, W. I. (1989). *Imaginary landscape: Making words of myth and science.* New York: St. Martin's Press.

Vygotsky, L. S. (1978). *Mind in society: The development of higher psychological processes.* Cambridge, MA: Harvard University Press.

Watzlawick, P., Weakland, J., & Fisch, R. (1974). *Change: Principles of problem formulation and problem resolution.* New York: Lawton.

Weick, K. E. (1979). *The social psychology of organizing.* Reading, MA: Addison-Wesley.

Winograd, T., & Flores, F. (1987). *Understanding computers and cognition.* Reading, MA: Addison-Wesley.

Zellermayer, M., Salomon, G., Globerson, T., & Givon, H. (1991). Enhancing writing-related metacognitions from a computerized Writing Partner. *American Educational Research Journal, 28,* 373–91.

# 5 Living knowledge: the social distribution of cultural resources for thinking

*Luis C. Moll, Javier Tapia, and Kathryn F. Whitmore*

> Human "mindedness" is not an essentially "interior" feature of mental life: rather it shows itself outwardly, in the way human beings distribute their total activity and attention among the available objects or targets of activity.
>
> Toulmin (1985, p. 12)

In this chapter we report on a study that, along with several colleagues, we are conducting in households and classrooms within predominantly Mexican, working-class communities in Tucson, Arizona. The primary purpose of this work is to change or improve classroom teaching by drawing on the knowledge and skills found in local households (see, e.g., Moll & Greenberg, 1990). As in previous work (e.g., Moll & Díaz, 1987), we have relied on a combination of ideas borrowed from sociohistorical psychology (e.g., Cole & Engeström, Chapter 1, this volume; Vygotsky, 1978, 1987) and from anthropology (e.g., Erickson, 1982; Lave, 1988; Vélez-Ibáñez, 1988). In both approaches there is a strong emphasis on analyzing the powerful, mediating role of culture in human intellectual performance; combined, these two approaches also facilitate an understanding of the cultural resources that mediate thinking as distributed dynamically in interpersonal relationships among people, their artifacts, and their environments (see also Pea, Chapter 2, this volume).

From our perspective, then, the distributed character of thinking is a given, an essential characteristic of human beings. However, as Cole and Engeström (Chapter 1, this volume) point out, "Precisely *how* cognition is distributed must be worked out for different kinds of activity, with their different forms of mediation, division of labor, social rules, and so on." This is the goal of this chapter: to present an "ethnographic" view of the social and cultural dynamics of two key

139

activity settings, households and classrooms. In both settings we are interested not only in what Erickson (1982) called the "immediate environments of learning," how specific learning contexts are socially constituted by adults and children, but in the broader social system that helps define the nature of these environments and determine what tools and resources are available for the participants' actions (see, e.g., Greenberg, 1989; Moll & Greenberg, 1990; Vélez-Ibáñez, 1988).

It is precisely this last idea, which we call the "social distribution of cultural resources," that we want to elaborate here. We do so by presenting two examples from our data. The first one borrows from our case studies of households that show how these settings, and the actions of the persons that constitute them, must be understood in relation to broader historical and economic factors. These factors, as we shall explain, constrain and shape, but do not totally determine, life within households. Household members are *active* in coping with, in changing, indeed, in mediating the very conditions under which they live. In particular, we will highlight in our example how household members develop strategies to obtain and distribute (material and intellectual) resources through social relationships. We use the term "funds of knowledge" to refer to the diverse social networks that interconnect households with their social environments and facilitate the sharing or exchange of resources, including knowledge, skills, and labor essential for the households' functioning, if not their well-being (for details, see Greenberg, 1989; Vélez-Ibáñez, 1988, in press; Vélez-Ibáñez & Greenberg, 1989).

We then turn to a classroom example, selected not from a "traditional" classroom but from a "whole-language" classroom, which takes the social distribution of learning and thinking as a central organizing principle (see Goodman & Goodman, 1990; Moll & Whitmore, in press). We selected this example not only because it provides a revealing contrast to "traditional" classrooms, but because classrooms such as this one represent good analogs to the households we study: where the participants use social processes and cultural resources of all kinds to mediate their activities, including their acquisition of knowledge. This classroom also illustrates, as does the household analysis, the great power of social arrangements in determining how and why people acquire knowledge. As Goodnow (1990) has emphasized, "The social environment does not take a neutral view towards the acquisition of knowledge and skill, but is instead highly interested, and often directive, controlling or even denying access to information" (p. 260).

It is by studying individuals, as we do, within the social networks that make up these settings that it becomes clear how, as Cole and Engerström (Chapter 1, this volume) put it, "cognition is complexly distributed in all forms of human activity." From this perspective, mental activity is not as much an in-the-head phenomenon as it is, to use Lave's (1988, p. 1) term, "stretched over" persons, activities, and settings. That is how it shows itself "outwardly," to borrow again from Toulmin (1985, p. 12), "in the way human beings distribute their total activity" – through human beings' constant, mediated exchanges with their environments. We will conclude by discussing some of the implications of this perspective for the education of the children with which we work.

### Living knowledge in the households

In no other setting do these mediated exchanges become more fully visible than in household life. A specific household's social structure is determined by a variety of factors, including the personal and labor history of the family, socioeconomic conditions, political, legal, and cultural considerations, as well as the social networks to which it belongs. In the example presented here we highlight many of the factors typical of Mexican households within close proximity to the U.S.–Mexican border, such as the rural history of the family, the transnational experiences of family members, the instability of employment within a segmented labor market, and the special, multiple roles of social relationships in the functioning of the households (Tapia, 1991; Vélez-Ibáñez & Greenberg, 1989). The example also illustrates what La Fontaine (1986) has called the "fluid reality" of the households, the changes in household composition, residence, jobs, and social relations; it is within this fluidity that the experiences of families must be understood. In all cases, children are participants in the household activities, not merely bystanders. Sometimes their participation is central to the household's survival, as when the children contribute to the economic production of the households or mediate the households' relationships with outside institutions – for example, using their knowledge of English to correspond with the school or government offices. This totality of household experiences, part of every child's learning environment, helps constitute children's funds of knowledge (Moll & Greenberg, 1990).

### The Sánchez household

This household[1] consists of seven persons, including three adolescent sons born in Nogales, Sonora (Mexico), a 12-year-old boy (Santiago) born in Tucson, Arizona, and a girl of 4, also born in Tucson. Their parents, Berta and José Sánchez, were born, respectively, in Cananea and Nogales, Sonora. The family has been living continuously, since 1984, in Tucson and, since 1986, in their present residence, a public housing, two-story apartment unit. The apartment has three bedrooms, two bathrooms, a modest living room, and a small kitchen–dining room. The apartment is located in one of the Mexican *barrios* (neighborhoods) in the south of Tucson. A Mexican bakery, a small market, and a videotape rental store are located nearby. Newspapers and magazines in Spanish (and English) are sold at the market, and the videotape store has a large collection of Mexican movies. There are several Mexican restaurants in the neighborhood, as well as a soup kitchen for the homeless and poor. There is also a large park about three blocks south of the apartment, where Roberto and Ricardo, two of the adolescent sons, like to play baseball.

The history of this family is complex, with much cross-border movement, usually in search of jobs, as is common with working-class Mexican families in this region of the country. Both Mr. and Mrs. Sánchez have relatives in Nogales, Sonora, with which they stay in close contact, in addition to Mrs. Sánchez's relatives in Tucson and in other towns in Arizona. Her mother was born in Phoenix, Arizona, but her family eventually settled in Nogales, Sonora. Her father was born in Arizona and his family lived in Nogales, Arizona (across the

---

[1] This example borrows from the dissertation of Javier Tapia (1991) and from the case study summaries of James Greenberg (see Moll, Vélez-Ibáñez, & Greenberg, 1989; Vélez-Ibáñez & Greenberg, 1989). Also see Heyman (1990) and Vélez-Ibáñez (in press). The household study, as well as the classroom analysis, was partially funded by OBEMLA Contract No. 300-87-0131; we appreciate their support.

border from Nogales, Sonora). He was a migrant farm worker following the harvests in Arizona and California. Like many Mexicans during the Depression, Mrs. Sánchez's father was forcibly "repatriated" to Mexico (even though he was a U.S. citizen) and settled in Nogales, Sonora. There he met and married Mrs. Sánchez's mother, and they had seven children. Mrs. Sánchez was born in Nogales in 1954 and went through the eighth grade there. When she was 17, she married José Sánchez, and a year later they had the first of their five children. About 10 years ago Mrs. Sánchez's family moved to Tucson to be near her mother's sisters. However, because Mrs. Sánchez was already married, she remained in Nogales with her husband and children until deteriorating economic conditions in Mexico led them to move to Tucson in 1984.

José Sánchez is also from a border family. He was born in 1949 in Cananea, Sonora, a mining town near the border. His father had been raised in Cananea and had various jobs, including repairing ships, fixing cars, and working in the post office. As part of his work for the postal service, he was transferred to Nogales, Sonora, when José was young. Although the postal service was a secure government job, the elder Sánchez needed more money than his salary could provide to support his wife and five children. As a sideline, he opened a car repair shop next to his house. When José was a youngster he, along with his brothers, helped their father repair cars after school and during vacations. José went through the 11th grade, before dropping out. He learned to play the guitar in school, and made some money playing in band, musical skills that, as we shall see, would later serve him well. Around the time José got married, his father procured him a job as a mailman. Nevertheless, he continued to work in his father's repair shop part time and to play occasionally with the band.

Mr. Sánchez recalls that the family was happy in Nogales, Sonora. He had a "good" job with the postal service and part-time work in his father's shop. He held the post office job from 1967 to 1984, with a six-month hiatus in 1978, when the family tried to immigrate to Arizona. At the time, poor economic conditions in Mexico led to a dramatic decrease in the family's purchasing power. The government also began several austerity programs leading to the cancellation of many benefits for postal workers. As things got worse, Mrs. Sánchez suggested that they might fare better in Arizona.

In 1978 the family first attempted to immigrate to Arizona. Since Mrs. Sánchez's parents are U.S. citizens, they applied for permanent residency in the United States. They moved to Phoenix with some of her relatives to await their documents. However, Mr. Sánchez was unable to secure employment and returned to Mexico, and in the interim Mrs. Sánchez, along with the three older children, moved to Tucson with some cousins. After the birth of Santiago (who is now 12), the entire family returned to Nogales, Sonora, to join Mr. Sánchez.

In 1980, Mrs. Sánchez initiated the procedures to obtain citizenship and reinitiated the process of residency for the entire family. The family arrived in Tucson once again in 1984. The move to Tucson was facilitated by a number of relatives and friends who helped them obtain jobs. They moved into an apartment in a public housing complex where Mrs. Sánchez's mother lives. Mr. Sánchez soon found a job working in a pecan factory in Sahuarita (a small town near Tucson), but worked there only a few months before a *compadre* (a close friend or godfather to an offspring) found him a better job as a carpenter in a furniture factory. His wife, after working for three years in a restaurant making *tortillas*, found a better job (with the help of a sister) in a potato chip factory, where she is still employed today. In May 1989, Mr. Sánchez was laid off his job at the furniture factory, and unable to find employment in Tucson, he took a job playing with a band in Nogales, Sonora. Unfortunately, because of documentation problems, the band cannot play in the United States, and playing only in Mexico limits Mr. Sánchez's potential earnings. Nevertheless, with the money his wife earns, and with the discount on rent and food stamps they receive because Mr. Sánchez is "unemployed," they are able to get by financially. However, because Mr. Sánchez must commute often to Nogales, Sonora, he is looking for a regular job in Nogales, Arizona, that would also allow him to keep playing in the band. If successful, the entire family would move to Nogales, Arizona.

This unstable employment situation and the constant search for better jobs is typical of many working-class families. Because of low wages, the members of the Sánchez family have had not only to move from one country to another, but to jump from one sector of the labor market to another, holding several jobs and pooling their wages. In the process they have acquired broad "funds of knowledge" that help them survive and develop. Some of these funds of knowledge, given the appropriate context or circumstances, are transferred intergenerationally. For example, all of the Sánchez children play musical instruments. Roberto, the oldest son, has become a proficient musician and, although still in high school, has begun to play professionally with a young band in Nogales, Sonora. Mr. Sánchez encouraged him to play with the band as long as the boy maintained good grades in school, and with the idea that he would later join the father's band. Roberto often accompanies his father to Nogales, Sonora, where he now has a girlfriend, establishing a new generation of cross-border relationships.

While very important, this historically accumulated knowledge alone is insufficient to help families cope with difficult economic conditions and the unpredictability of employment. Families must also depend on their social relationships, especially with kin, to gain access to or exchange resources on either side of the border. Although friends and relatives may provide significant assistance in times of crisis, most exchanges occur in such a routine and constant fashion that people are hardly aware of them. These mundane exchanges take a variety of forms, such as labor services, access to information, including help in finding jobs or housing and knowledge about dealing with government agencies, and various forms of material assistance besides money such as sheltering visitors. Again, the Sánchez family illustrates how each of these forms of exchange help the household to cope with its economic situation and how family members mobilize the funds of knowledge distributed in their social networks.

One of the most basic forms of assistance in the Sánchez family social network revolves around child care. There are five children in the family, aged 4 to 18. The older children could take care of the younger ones after school, but the 4-year-old cannot be left alone during the day while the parents work. Mr. and Mrs. Sánchez, however, are surrounded by relatives. Not only do Mrs. Sánchez's mother and sister live in the same apartment complex, but if she cannot look after the children, she has three brothers and two sisters living nearby that she can turn to, not to mention some six cousins who live in Tucson. She also has a sister in Amado, Arizona (a nearby town), and her husband, in fact, takes the boys to school each morning on his way to the clothing factory where he works in Tucson. Such assistance is by no means limited to Mrs. Sánchez's side of the family. Because his wife works, Mr. Sánchez does much of the housework and often takes his daughter with him to Nogales, leaving her with his parents or sisters while he is at work. And just as Mrs. Sánchez's mother's home is the central node for exchange among her siblings in Tucson, Mr. Sánchez's parents' house is the nexus for exchange among his kin in Nogales, Sonora. For example, one of his sisters, who works as a secretary/bookkeeper in one of the *maquiladoras* (assembly line workers) in Nogales, is divorced and has moved back in with her parents. She pays her parents to take care of her son (although not the going rate) while she is at work.

Another important set of services that the Sánchez's relatives and friends provide for one another is their labor. For example, because of the nature of men's jobs in the labor market, knowledge about car repairs is ample in this population. Mr. Sánchez, usually assisted by one of his sons, often helps friends and relatives repair their cars. Similarly, his relatives were helping him build a house in Nogales, but when the family moved to Arizona, work on the house was abandoned. Labor services are also essential to family enterprises. When Mr. Sánchez's father retired from the postal service about three years ago, to compensate for the loss of income the elder Sánchez opened a *tanichi* – a tiny grocery store. However, his son-in-law Ramón, who is a teacher and administrator at a technical school in Nogales, soon got the elder Sánchez a job teaching car mechanics at the school. His new duties left him little time for the two businesses, so he handed over the garage to his brother to run and asked his daughter Silvia to take care of the grocery store (he gives her some money for this work).

All in all, however, labor and material services are of less importance to the households than is the exchange of funds of knowledge. Indeed, help in finding jobs, housing, better deals on goods and services, and assistance in dealings with government agencies and other institutions is of far greater significance to survival than are the material types of aid these households provide one another. For example, Mrs. Sánchez has helped two of her sisters get jobs at the potato chip factory where she works and is trying to help another sister get work there as well. She has also used the funds of knowledge developed through their immigration experiences to help Mr. Sánchez's sister and husband qualify for the "amnesty" program. She has also assisted them in applying to the state's medical care program, which paid the costs of their baby's delivery. She also helped them get an apartment in the public housing complex where they live and helped them get food stamps. In each case, because they speak little English, Mrs. Sánchez or one of her sons has gone with them to these public agencies and has filled out all the appropriate forms.

Because families must deal with several government agencies and institutions, they constantly mobilize funds of knowledge about these institutions distributed in their social network. For instance, when we contacted the Sánchez family about this study, Mrs. Sánchez invited her brother (an elementary schoolteacher in the Tucson public schools) to be present when we came to explain the project; only when he was satisfied with our explanation did the family agree to participate. Similarly, when they receive mail from agencies or notices from school, they often turn to their sons, who are more fluent in English, for help in interpreting them. Sharing funds of knowledge also occurs systematically in other realms. For instance, Mrs. Sánchez and her sister-in-law regularly go through the newspaper together looking for food specials and comparing prices.

Households depend on their social networks in order to cope with complex and changing circumstances. Consequently, they are willing to invest considerable energy and resources in maintaining good social relations with its members by participating in family rituals – birthdays, baptisms, *quinceañeras* (adolescent girls' "debutante" parties), showers, weddings, Christmas dinners, outings, and so on (for details, see Tapia, 1991). Such formal rituals, however, are but one mechanism through which social networks are maintained. As important, or more so, are visits – informal rituals themselves. Not only do the Sánchez family often have guests, but they visit their friends and relatives almost daily. This frequent contact helps them both to maintain important social ties and to renew and update funds of knowledge in this social world on which they depend constantly.

In the quest for survival, especially within unstable labor markets, Mexican families have followed a dual strategy: Individuals acquire a broad spectrum of skills that allows them to jump, if need be, from one sector of the labor market to another; and because information is the key to survival in this environment, they maintain good relations with a social network of friends and relatives who have access to a variety of funds of knowledge. These funds of knowledge are socially inherited and culturally reproduced and developed (or discarded), and their distribution is a constant and dynamic characteristic of household life.

### Living knowledge in the classrooms

Our second example comes from classrooms that, in contrast to typical classrooms characterized by regimentation and control (Goodlad, 1974), are organized flexibly to facilitate the creation of diverse and changing relationships among the participants. The role of the teacher in these classrooms is that of a mediator, in the Vygotskian sense: to provide guidance, strategic support, and assistance to help the children assume control of their own learning (see Moll & Whitmore, in press).

The curriculum, rather than following a prescribed series of activities, is mutually constituted by the children and the teacher. As we will show, instruction builds on the children's interests. The content is learned through the different social relations and activities that the teacher facilitates in consultation with the children. This process is mediated in the sense that the teacher controls it strategically, indirectly, with tact. The classroom functions through multiple, mediated exchanges of knowledge, where the children, as well as the teacher, are active teachers and learners. It is this interdependence of adults and children, and how they use social and cultural resources for developing thinking, that make such classrooms informative case studies of distributed cognition.

#### *A holistic classroom*

This third-grade classroom[2] consists of 27 children, 12 boys and 15 girls, who either come from the neighborhood, or *barrio*, surrounding the school (16 children; the school is located about four

[2] The data reported here were collected by Kathryn Whitmore as part of her dissertation research. The example also borrows from a report by Moll et al. (1990), from Moll and Whitmore (in press), and from Crowell (in press).

blocks from the Sánchez household) or travel from other neighborhoods in the city (11 children) as part of a magnet desegregation program.[3] As is common in these classrooms, there is considerable diversity in the children's language and literate abilities. Fifteen of the children are monolingual English speakers and readers; the rest are bilinguals, several completely fluent in Spanish and English.

The classroom is physically organized to facilitate the distribution of activities and the use of multiple resources, especially books, as part of the activities. There are several large tables in the room that, along with the ample carpeted floor area, provide work space for the children and adults. Cubicles and cupboards are used by the children for storing their personal belongings, but the school supplies (pencils, paper, crayons, etc.) are for the classroom community. They are all within easy access of the children and are clearly labeled in both languages. A piano, loft, and the teacher's desk, partially concealed by a large cabinet, allow children places to hide away and work, read, or simply visit.

As one walks through the room at any given time, one notices that books are everywhere: They are shelved near the group meeting area marked with a sign that reminds the children to return the books they have borrowed. There is a box stuffed to overflowing with books published by individual children and collaborative small groups, and other books are stacked on the windowsill across the room. Books about the general topic of study are categorized in bins, for easy access. These books range in type from popular picture books, to cartooned information books, to adult nonfiction and "coffee table" books. The books not only provide information in English and Spanish for the students' thematic research, but are frequently chosen by the children for "free" reading.

---

[3] Readers not familiar with the politics of race in North America may not know this term. It is usually meant to depict a school located in a working-class African-American or Latino neighborhood that has been made attractive to middle-class Anglo-Saxon families because of a special characteristic, for example, an emphasis on teaching with computers. The hope is that these families will voluntarily send their children there to integrate what would otherwise be an ethnically or racially segregated school. Alternatively, desegregation schools may be located in predominantly Anglo neighborhoods and minority children are bussed to them. All desegregation programs receive additional funding, programs, and personnel, including, for example, fine arts teachers, counselors, computer equipment, and the like.

Still more books can be found elsewhere in the room. When the teacher was preparing a new literature set for author studies, a shelf of these books was marked "Favor de NO llevar libros de aquí. Estoy preparando los próximos estudios literarios. Please do NOT take books from here. I'm preparing for our next literature study groups. Ms. C [signature]." The children's selections from the library are in yet another box, waiting to be exchanged at their next visit. A peek into the children's cupboard areas reveals books they are taking home to continue reading and books they are bringing from home to read and share with others.

In addition to the books and reading materials, other functional print adorns the classroom. Two alphabets hang in the room, one in English and one in Spanish. Classroom rules, agreed upon and signed dramatically by the children and teachers, are posted near the door. Schedules that remind participants of activities such as guitar lessons and time in the loft are nearby their associated work areas. The products of the children's thinking are displayed on the walls in the form of charts and other public documents, such as webs representing brainstorming sessions, data collected during math and science experimentation, ongoing records of thematically organized activities, and lists of questions children are actively engaged in answering.

A revealing example of distributed thinking in this classroom comes from the literature study groups. The teacher uses these groups to enable the children to share their reactions, analyses, and questions about children's trade books with their peers and teachers. The children read silently, individually or with a friend, before the group meets for discussion. In addition to reading a variety of literature, the children learn biographical information about authors and illustrators, compare varied pieces of writing, extend their reading into writing and illustrations through literature logs and other writing projects, analyze plots, characters, settings, and other literary elements, and create story maps, among other activities. These literature study groups are organized according to the interests of the children; they allow the children opportunities to study literature with readers of all abilities, as well as readers of two languages, and provide the children with frequent opportunities to mediate one another's learning through shared literacy experiences.

The materials for literature study groups vary. They may be, for example, text sets related to a common concept (such as native Americans), genre-based sets (such as fairy tales), or author-based sets. In preparation for a group of literature studies centered around authors, the teacher brings to the classroom a large number of books (often from 20 to 50, but sometimes more than 100) in text sets according to author. The children choose which author they wish to study and in which language they wish to read, possibly in both. Each group meets daily, about two times per week with the teacher or an assistant and at other times independent of adult assistance.

The following example describes three typical third-graders and their interactions in one of these literature study groups. In particular, it illustrates how children form a social network wherein they exchange funds of knowledge within a classroom context in a manner similar to, although much more concentrated than, that in the households in our study.

### Reading about war

Aaron is an active, blond-haired, brown-eyed boy who is popular with his friends and successful in school. His parents are professionals and have volunteered Aaron and his sister for attendance at this bilingual school. Aaron has several areas of expertise to share with his classmates and teachers on a regular basis: He is a talented artist, he knows a great deal about his favorite animal and pet, the gecko, and he is aware and articulate about his Jewish cultural background. Aaron's skills in art and drawing surface almost daily as his peers ask him for advice and assistance with illustrations and artwork. He shares his knowledge about reptiles through presentations of research on the topic and during casual discussions with friends. Aaron's sociocultural history as a Jew provides him with a strong expert role in the class several times during the year, such as when he and his family members share Jewish holidays and traditions with the class, and especially during a literature study group related to the Holocaust, as we will elaborate later in this section.

Susan, like Aaron, is a volunteer from outside the community of the school. Her father is an investigator and her mother a teacher in a nearby border town. Susan is an exuberant, freckle-faced girl who prompts interesting discussions and open sharing of ideas and opinions, and encourages all children, particularly her closest friends, to take risks. Susan's most prominent interests relate to language: oral and written language in English and her rapidly developing bilingualism in Spanish. These interests led Susan to develop and produce a bilingual play that was performed at another school and to provide the class with a constant source of authentic questions that sparked and maintained lively conversations throughout the year. Susan's questions will be highlighted in the transcripts reproduced later.

Lolita, who is a quiet girl and very successful academically, lives in the *barrio* surrounding the school. He first language is Spanish and her working-class family speaks only Spanish at home. She has attended a bilingual school since kindergarten and is now fully bilingual and biliterate, comfortably speaking, reading, and writing in either Spanish or English. Lolita's knowledge about language and her skills in each give her a special area of expertise in the classroom. She is one of the few children who can truly communicate with any other member of the class, regardless of choice of language. Therefore, Lolita is called upon by monolingual and monoliterate classmates and adults to translate, to peer-teach, and to collaborate on bilingual projects in school. Lolita's bilingual knowledge and willingness to help out enabled a monolingual Spanish speaker, Marisela, to participate in the English gifted class this year. Lolita was also Susan's main informant about Spanish during the school year.

These three children, among others, decided to participate in the same literature study group during the spring semester. The group came together through their mutual interest in and questions about a major event in their lives at the time – the Persian Gulf War. The war had dominated talk in the classroom all winter as children raised questions, discussed options, and sought answers in the newspapers and on television. The teacher, however, was disturbed by what she felt was the glorification of war by the media (see Crowell, in press) and was compelled to offer a different, more human, compassionate, and realistic image of war to her students. She developed a literature set that consisted of a wide variety of children's books, both fiction and nonfiction, all centered around the themes of war and peace. She offered this text set to the entire class as one choice for their next study group.

Aaron, Susan, and Lolita selected this literature study group, along with five other children. They met as a group several times a week, sometimes with an adult and sometimes on their own, to read, discuss, and interpret the books. All of the books dealt with wars that occurred before the children were born: the U.S. Civil War, World War II, and the Vietnam War. Through their studies, the children used their developing knowledge about wars of the past to understand a war of the present. The following segments capture the children's discussions as well as the transformations that occurred as they explored such a meaningful, yet difficult topic.

The children spent the first several days reading the books. They often read in pairs, Susan and Lolita read with each other, and Aaron read with his friend Travis. As the children read, they kept notes in their literature logs and used "Post-it" notes to mark questions and comments on the books. During the first group discussion a fair amount of time was required to decide what to talk about and how to proceed. The children decided that they wanted to talk about a different book during each session and immediately focused on the book *Rose Blanche*, by Roberto Innocenti (1985), as a starting point.

The book is about Nazi Germany. It tells a captivating story about a small girl who discovers children in a concentration camp and secretly takes them food daily. She continues her visits as the war ends and finds one day that the barbed-wire fences have been torn down and that the children are gone. As she stands in confusion, a shot is fired by advancing soldiers; she never returns home, but spring returns to Germany and wild flowers grow around the broken fences.

One of the students raised a question that became a point of discussion for the entire group: Travis wondered why Rose Blanche, in an early illustration in the book, carried a Nazi flag. The illustration was puzzling to the group because Rose Blanche worked so diligently and bravely to help the children in the concentration camp. This contradiction is symbolic of the innocence of children in war, and these third-graders struggled to understand this abstract point. Their discussion revealed a great deal of information about what we could call this group's funds of historical knowledge:

SUSAN: Why *does* she have a Nazi flag?
AARON: She was German or something.

TEACHER: Did you talk about that together, the two of you? [referring to Aaron and Travis's earlier discussion while reading the book together]
AARON: Yeah.
TEACHER: What did you say to him?
AARON: Well, I kind of just started to answer a few of his questions but I don't remember.
TEACHER: What do you think she is? Do you think she's a Nazi?
SUSAN: No.
AARON: I don't know. I think she is really German, but she . . .
TREVOR: Maybe she was forced to do that.
AARON: I doubt it.
TREVOR: She might be part German.
SUSAN: What is a Nazi? Is it a German-Jewish?
AARON: Nazi is a . . . is a German, who uh . . .
COLIN: Kind of like the Ku Klux Klan.
TREVOR: Yeah.
SUSAN: How can they tell if they are Jewish or someone different?
AARON: Well, if they have raggedy clothes they usually say these words.
SUSAN: What if they are really rich and dressed up fancy and they're Jewish?
AARON: If they're not rich they might take you. If they're Jewish, they'll definitely take you.
TREVOR: I don't like the looks of the concentration camp.
AARON: Anyone who is different is in that concentration camp. Than them. Maybe Hitler might have been in the Klu Klux Klan. He might have [inaudible]. And then . . . he might have taken them to their place.
TEACHER: It's kind of interesting to think about if Nazi Germany was here right now, who are the people that they would round up?
SUSAN: Would they round us up, maybe?
AARON: They might round up me.
TEACHER: Why, because you're Jewish?
AARON: Yeah.
SUSAN: They're here right now!?
[The discussion continues]

In this early discussion the children demonstrate their different levels of knowledge about the historical period of World War II, and they begin to develop roles in the group that will pervade the rest of the literature study, a sort of division of labor in the exchange of knowledge. For example, Susan, who has less information, never hesitates to ask poignant questions that cause the children to think, to interpret, and to talk meaningfully. Aaron, however, is at ease answering questions about this important time in his own cultural history. He has a fair amount of accurate knowledge about the period and contributes a perspective that links the children to the story of Rose Blanche and to the present. The teacher, who is also Jewish and has considerable knowledge about the Holocaust, refrains from entering the conversation too frequently. She intentionally allows Aaron to answer the other children's questions, builds on their knowledge with more information, and asks open-ended questions to bring focus to the group and encourage individuals to participate.

The conversation continues as the children try to understand the horrendous reality that a few people can so powerfully control the lives and deaths of others. Colin and Aaron share a recent experience of observing White supremacists at the local university:

SUSAN: Aaron, would they maybe have took you?

AARON: I don't think so 'cause I'm white?

TEACHER: I don't know if the skinheads have that kind of power in the United States as the Nazis had in Germany. Here we accept anybody who is different? Right?

TREVOR: Yeah. I'm glad we do.

TEACHER: Are you?

TREVOR: Or else we wouldn't have Jewish friends?

SUSAN: No, what if we accepted Saddam Hussein?

TREVOR: Ooh, I mean . . .

TEACHER: What do you think about that?

LOLITA: Well, if he got nice with all of them.

AARON: But I don't think that would ever happen.

The conversation continues as the children compare facts about Hitler and Saddam Hussein, with Aaron providing a great deal of information about Hitler, such as his abusive childhood and his suicidal death, and even speculating whether Saddam Hussein had a similar childhood.

Two days later, the group meets again. They return immediately to their first question: Why was Rose Blanche holding a Nazi flag? Travis is particularly uncomfortable with his lack of understanding, and he pushes the group toward a higher level of analysis of the text and the illustrations. On this day the children discuss the non-Jews who were captured and imprisoned in concentration camps. Just as on the first day, the children use the present to understand the past, and the past to clarify the present:

AARON: But Mrs. C. [the teacher], did the Germans . . . a few of the Germans that weren't Nazis, 'cause they were different, and they weren't Nazis?
TEACHER: I remember reading that some of the people who were sent to concentration camps or were killed weren't just Jews, but like Gypsies . . .
AARON: Yeah.
TEACHER: And the people who were mentally ill.
SUSAN: What's Gypsies?

Susan's question initiates a lengthy discussion about Gypsies, stereotypes, and how the Gypsies were controlled by the Nazis. Aaron provides a link to the present by discussing the homeless people who sleep in a park near the school. The conversation then shifts to the ending of the book, the death of Rose Blanche, and the questions about her death. The children hypothesize how it happened, presenting different scenarios, since it is not clear in the book who killed her. As the session draws to a close, Elizabeth, a member of the group, asks her first question. Notice how confidently the group responds to her; also note Susan's new insight.

ELIZABETH: Why did they take that little boy?
AARON: They are taking him to a concentration camp.
SUSAN: Because he is Jewish.
AARON: He is either different or he is Jewish.
SUSAN: They [the Nazis] don't like anybody but themselves, the Nazis, and they think everybody else is different.

In the days ahead, the children discussed other books, including *Faithful Elephants*, a book by Y. Tsuchiya (1988) about the fate of zoo elephants during World War II. The children's discussion (this time without the teacher present), which became quite emotional, focused on the inhumane treatment of animals in the story, the incredible sadness of it, and similar stories about incidents that had occurred in the zoo in Kuwait during the recent war. The children also read and discussed *My Hiroshima*, a book by Y. Morimoto (1987) about the bombing of that city by the United States and the suffering of its residents. This discussion, which also took place without an adult present, began as follows:

TRAVIS: I think it's a sad book. It has really good illustrations.
COLIN: But it's sad how all their friends were killed.
AARON: And they get buried.
TRAVIS: This is sad.
SUSAN: It's real.
TRAVIS: Yeah. It's real. And it tells you all the skin's burning and everything. It shows it.
COLIN: It's gross.
TRAVIS: There's a bad smell. And there's glass in that kid's feet.
[A bit later in the discussion]
SUSAN: I think it's really sad that the child was trying to wake up his dead mother.
TREVOR: There's a pool of blood right . . .
TRAVIS: I know. That's what I hate in these books. There's a whole bunch of . . .
AARON: I didn't get in the story what war this was.
SUSAN: It was the Vietnam War. [A misconception later clarified by the teacher]
TREVOR: And we dropped bombs on them.

The students are dumbfounded by the reality of the United States having dropped an atomic bomb on innocent people. They then make a strong connection between the story about the bombing of Hiroshima and the fighting in Iraq and Kuwait:

TRAVIS: They could've bombed on like an air force base, not where people were innocent. That would be just like Iraq coming over here and bombing us, and we're innocent. Or like we going over there and bombing innocent people, which did happen . . . And Iraq bombing Israel.
TREVOR: They were bombing innocent people that weren't even in the war.
AARON: I know, they were bombing Israel.

The theme of innocence, which began with their reading of *Rose Blanche*, continued with the zoo animals in *Faithful Elephants*, and was graphically depicted in *My Hiroshima*, becomes the key concept that connects the different books for the children. They begin to compare the books and evaluate their worthiness:

SUSAN: It's [*My Hiroshima*] better than any book we've read, except for *Rose Blanche*. I think they are both good.

TRAVIS: But we have not talked much about other books. I like *The Wall* [a book about a father and son visiting the Vietnam War Memorial in Washington, D.C.]. That was pretty good.

AARON: But these two books are the best.

TREVOR: Yeah, the sadder they are, the gooder they get.

The children determine that "good" books are the ones that make you ask hard questions, that make you think, that cause you to feel emotions as you read. The discussion of each new book contributed to a new understanding of the topic, of the other books, and, as we shall see, of themselves.

Six weeks after the beginning of the study group, the children and the teacher met for a final discussion. It was time to draw some general themes from the group, to share final thoughts, and to bring closure to an emotional and intellectual experience. The teacher asked the children to discuss how the books they read had influenced their thinking about war, if they helped them understand what was happening in the Persian Gulf, or to make any other comment. Their responses were dramatic and revealing:

TREVOR: I've changed my thoughts about war. I used to like to play war, but now it makes me sick.

TRAVIS: I felt the same way as Trevor did . . . Now I just don't play that way any more because I think it's so gross, after I read those books.

AARON: I did both [play with toy soldiers and act out war games] but when I was reading the books, I didn't play with them that much.

Susan and Colin also shared a new understanding of war:

SUSAN: I thought in wars everybody got killed. But then in the Iraqi war, when they were like fighting the air war, I didn't believe there was such a thing as an air war. I thought there was only a ground war, and then how only twenty people got killed in the air war. I learned a lot. I thought that everybody . . .

TEACHER: There weren't many Americans [killed], right?

COLIN: There were only about twenty-five.

TEACHER: I just wonder about the Iraqis.

SUSAN: That's what I mean, the Americans.

TEACHER: So when you say only twenty people got killed, you mean twenty Americans.

SUSAN: Uh, huh.
COLIN: Only twenty-five got killed, but we killed *hundreds*.

We take these discussions as examples of distributed thinking in this particular classroom. But it is not just individual children sharing their thoughts that is important; also significant is the inseparability of their thinking from the multiple, converging factors that constitute the lessons – the children's histories, the relevance of their readings, the teacher's strategic mediations, the time allotted for reflection, the urgency of the topic, and the transformative power of the children's dialogues. This lesson, and this classroom, represent a complex, and collective, zone of proximal development, to use Vygotsky's (1978) metaphor.

## Conclusions

Toulmin (1985) observed that it is only when we consider mental activity in the context of everyday life "that its *outer directedness* becomes finally clear" (p. 17, emphasis in original). Our examples were meant to capture not only this "outer directedness," the mediated character of life, but how individuals always form part of connecting relationships that bind them, and their mental activities, together.

From our perspective, both households and classrooms are conceptualized as culturally mediated systems of knowledge – systems of living knowledge (see also Cole & Engeström Chapter 1, this volume). Our analysis reveals both the collective nature of their activities and the diversity of these human knowledge systems, including its various constraints (Glick, 1985). The households we have studied are similar in that they exist within specific sociohistorical conditions, most prominently within a border-region, working-class labor market, and they have developed similarly organized and structured networks of relationships for the exchange of funds of knowledge; they are all different in that each has developed unique strategies and arrangements to subsist and progress based on their personal and labor history, current conditions, and options for the future.

Our classroom analysis, at a different level, reveals a similar, if not analogous, sociocultural system at work. This classroom faces more or less the same external constraints as any classroom in a school system. However, it has managed to mediate these constraints by developing a socially distributed system that makes strategic use of the funds of knowledge of the children and adults. It is not only that this classroom is highly literate, requiring multiple uses of literacy to "live" within this community, but that children become important, indispensable, thinking resources for one another, as exemplified in the lessons we described.

What are the educational implications of our work? What does our perspective buy us in terms of the education of Latino or other language-minority working-class children? First of all, it facilitates a critical redefinition of these children's households as settings that contain ample cultural and intellectual resources. These households are not intellectually barren, socially disorganized, or part of some sort of apathetic and passive, if not pathological, "underclass"; nor are they lacking in cognitive resources or in the family's capacities to develop, acquire, or use knowledge. As our case study suggests, household members are not simply passive respondents to often difficult external constraints, but active, intelligent agents using multiple, socially distributed funds of knowledge in mediating these constraints and in "getting ahead." Each household, along with its interconnections to other households, contains accumulated funds of knowledge that are essential for material survival and that are constituted by the present and previous generation's repertoire of information, abilities, skills, and experiences (see, e.g., Vélez-Ibáñez, in press). The concept of funds of knowledge is also important because of its special relevance to teaching. It is specific funds of knowledge pertaining to the social, economic, and productive activities of people in a local region or community, not "culture" in its broader, anthropological sense, that represent a strategic resource for classrooms. We are currently experimenting, in close collaboration with teachers as co-researchers, with ways to document and make accessible for teaching the funds of knowledge available within their students' households (see, e.g., Moll et al., 1990; Moll, Amanti, Neff, & Gonzalez, 1992; Moll & Greenberg, 1990).

Our classroom case study also represents a critical redefinition, in this instance, of how classrooms could be organized to create a system for teaching and learning in which the teacher takes maximum advantage of the students' interests and knowledge to address academic goals. Our example highlights how, within such a distributed system, children can draw on the resources of teachers, materials, and, most important, one another to shape and direct their academic activities. Indeed, a goal of the teacher is to teach the children how to exploit the resources in their environment, how to become conscious users of the cultural resources available for thinking, be it a book, their bilingualism, the library, or other children. In this light, the typical classroom, with its control and management, its drills and worksheets, looks very strange – isolated children and teachers not making use of their powerful resources for thinking: one another, their books, their ideas, interests and experiences, in short, their funds of knowledge.

Our analysis has also led us to appreciate the critical mediational role of social relations in individual lives, whether in households or in classrooms, and the paramount importance of these relations in understanding human activity, especially mental activity. It is the thorough "socialness" of human-"mindedness" that impresses us. Our case studies show persons operating in relation to and with what we have called funds of knowledge. These funds of knowledge may certainly be thought of as individual possessions, the cognitive residues of actions (Salomon, Chapter 4, this volume), but they may be more appropriately, and productively, conceptualized as characteristics of persons-in-activity: where the individual is understood as an active, living being, transacting with many, changing environments, most prominently other human beings. As Minick, Stone, and Forman (in press) have put it, and our case studies illustrate, "Educationally significant interactions do not involve abstract bearers of cognitive structures, but real people who develop a variety of interpersonal relationships with one another in the course of their shared activity in a given institutional context." It is also not a matter of selecting between person-solo versus person-plus (Perkins, Chapter 3, this volume); that, we think, misses the point. It is a matter of how persons and their social and cultural worlds are inseparable, thoroughly embedded in each other, and, as such, how their thinking is irreducible to individual properties, intelligences, or traits.

## References

Crowell, C. G. (in press). *Living through war vicariously with literature.* In K. G. Short, Smith, K., & Patterson, L. (Eds.), *Teachers are researchers: Reflection and action.* Newark, DE: International Reading Association.

Erickson, F. (1982). Taught cognitive learning in its immediate environments: A neglected topic in the anthropology of education. *Anthropology and Education Quarterly, 13*(2), 149–80.

Glick, J. (1985). Culture and cognition revisited. In E. Neimark, R. De Lisi, & J. Newman (Eds.), *Moderators of competence* (pp. 99–116). Hillsdale, NJ: Erlbaum.

Goodlad, J. (1984). *A place called school.* New York: McGraw-Hill

Goodman, Y., & Goodman, K. (1990). Vygotsky in a whole language perspective. In L. C. Moll (Ed.), *Vygotsky and education* (pp. 206–22). Cambridge University Press.

Goodnow, J. (1990). The socialization of cognition: What's involved? In J. Stigler, R. Shweder, & G. Herdt (Eds.), *Cultural psychology: Essays on comparative human development* (pp. 259–86). Cambridge University Press.

Greenberg, J. B. (1989, April). *Funds of knowledge: Historical constitution, social distribution, and transmission.* Paper presented at the Annual Meetings of the Society for Applied Anthropology, Santa Fe, NM.

Heyman, J. (1990). The emergence of the waged life course on the United States–Mexico border. *American Ethologist, 17*(2), 348–59.

Innocenti, R. (1985). *Rose Blanche.* Mankato, MN: Creative Education.

La Fontaine, J. (1986). An anthropological perspective on children in social worlds. In M. Richards & P. Light (Eds.), *Children of social worlds: Development in a social context* (pp. 10–30). Oxford: Polity Press.

Lave, J. (1988). *Cognition in practice.* Cambridge University Press.

Minick, N., Stone, C. A., Forman, E. A. (in press). Introduction: The integration of individual, social, and institutional processes in accounts of children's learning and development. In E. A. Forman, N. Minick, & C. A. Stone (Eds.), *Contexts for learning: Sociocultural dynamics in children's development.* New York: Oxford University Press.

Moll, L. C., Amanti, C., Neff, D., & Gonzalez, N. (1992). Funds of knowledge for teaching: A qualitative approach for connecting households and classrooms. *Theory into Practice, 31*(2), 132–41.

Moll, L. C., & Díaz, S. (1987). Change as the goal of educational research. *Anthropology and Education Quarterly, 18*(4), 300–11.

Moll, L. C., & Greenberg, J. (1990). Creating zones of possibilities: Combining social contexts for instruction. In L. C. Moll (Ed.), *Vygotsky and education* (pp. 319–48). Cambridge University Press.

Moll, L. C., Vélez-Ibáñez, C., & Greenberg. J. (1989). *Fieldwork summary – community knowledge and classroom practice; Combining resources for literacy instruction* (OBEMLA Contract No. 300-87-0131). Tucson: University of Arizona, College of Education and Bureau of Applied Research in Anthropology.

Moll, L. C., Vélez-Ibáñez, C., Greenberg. J., Whitmore, K., Saavedra, E., Dworin, J., & Andrade, R. (1990). *Community knowledge and classroom practice: Combining resources for literacy instruction* (OBEMLA Contract No. 300-87-0131). Tucson: University of Arizona, College of Education and Bureau of Applied Research in Anthropology.

Moll, L. C., & Whitmore, K. (in press). Vygotsky in classroom practice: Moving from individual transmission to social transaction. In E. Forman, N. Minick, & C. A. Stone (Eds.), *Contexts for learning: Sociocultural dynamics in children's development.* New York: Oxford University Press.

Morimoto, Y. (1987). *My Hiroshima.* New York: Viking.

Tapia, J. (1991). *Cultural reproduction and funds of knowledge in U.S. Mexican households.* Unpublished doctoral dissertation, University of Arizona, Tucson.

Toulmin, S. (1985). *The inner life: The outer mind,* Vol. 15 (1984 Heinz Werner Lecture Series). Worcester, MA: Clark University Press.

Tsuchiya, Y. (1988). *Faithful elephants.* Boston: Houghton Mifflin.

Vélez-Ibáñez, C. G. (1988). Networks of exchange among Mexicans in the U.S. and Mexico: Local level mediating responses to national and international transformations. *Urban Anthropology, 17*(1), 27–51.

(in press). U.S. Mexicans in the borderlands: Being poor without the underclass. In J. Moore & R. Rivera (Eds.), *Issues of Hispanic poverty and underclass.* Beverly Hills, CA: Sage.

Vélez-Ibáñez, C. G. & Greenberg, J. (1989). *Formation and transformation of funds of knowledge among U.S. Mexican households in the context of the borderlands.* Paper presented at the Annual Meeting of the American Anthropological Association, Washington, DC.

Vygotsky, L. S. (1978). *Mind in society.* Cambridge, MA: Harvard Universty Press.

(1987). *Historia del desarollo de las funciones psíquicas superiores.* La Habana, Cuba: Editorial Cientifico-Técnica.

# 6 Finding cognition in the classroom: an expanded view of human intelligence

*Thomas Hatch and Howard Gardner*

Ned and Gerald are in their kindergarten classroom, playing at the sand table. Ned suggests that they make a tunnel. Gerald quickly replies that they cannot make a tunnel because they need wire to hold the sand in place. The idea is quickly forgotten, and the boys go on to make a castle. In another part of the room, at the art table, Kenny and Mark are hard at work:

Mark says he's going to make "Bebop." (Bebop is a character from the "Teenage Mutant Ninja Turtles" television shows and movies.) He turns to Kenny, who is sitting next to him. "Kenny, how do you make Bebop?"
  "You can copy mine," Kenny says.
  "Okay. Oh, I need black, right?"
  "You have to use black," Kenny echoes.
  Kenny tells Mark how to make something.
  "That big?" Mark wonders.
  "Yep. That big."
  Mark asks what Kenny has drawn on top of Bebop's head. Kenny responds by pointing at his picture. "What is that? That? That's his mohawk . . . "

These are simple scenarios not unlike others that occur everyday in many homes and classrooms. Nonetheless, they raise significant questions about the nature of human cognition.

According to a traditional view, the intelligence found in this classroom has three basic characteristics: it is a single, general problem-

The work reported here was supported by a Spencer Dissertation Fellowship to the first author and by grants to the second author from the W. T. Grant Foundation, the Spencer Foundation, and the Rockefeller Brothers Fund. We thank the community and school that supported our research. Our special thanks go to the teacher and all the parents and students with whom we worked. The writing of this chapter benefited from the comments of Gavriel Salomon and Ray Nickerson.

164

solving ability; it is located inside the head of each individual; and the intelligence of each individual is relatively stable from one situation and one setting to another. From this perspective, Gerald appears to have the intelligence to make a tunnel in the sand. He may be able to describe precisely what materials he would need and what he would have to do. He can, in the abstract, figure out how to make such a construction. Whether or not he actually has the needed materials or goes on to build a tunnel is irrelevant.

In contrast, Mark seems to lack the skills and knowledge he needs to make a satisfactory representation of the Ninja Turtle character. The fact that Mark is capable of solving this problem with assistance is considered to have no bearing on his general problem-solving capacity.

In both cases, the traditional view holds that if one observed the children in different settings – Gerald in a sandbox with wire or other tunnel-making materials, Mark at an individual desk without the assistance of his peers – their capacities to make a tunnel or to draw "Bebop" would remain unchanged. Similarly, if Kenny were asked to draw another subject, one would expect him to show about the same level of skill in both drawings; in fact, an entire intelligence test – the Goodenough Draw-a-Man test (1926) – is predicated on this very assumption.

In this chapter, we challenge these traditional claims. We do so by suggesting that factors or "forces" at three different levels – which we term "personal," "local," and "cultural" – contribute to the cognition in this classroom. We argue that we need to expand the scope of such terms as "cognition" and "intelligence" to include the conditions under which problems are discovered and solved and within which skills are developed.

In the first part of the chapter, we introduce this perspective by drawing on a number of the alternative views of cognition presented in this volume, as well as from an ecological perspective on behavior (Barker & Wright, 1954; Bronfenbrenner, 1979; Lewin, 1951). In the second part of the chapter, we employ this expanded view in a study of the activities and skills that several children engage in during "free play" in kindergarten. In conclusion, we consider how such a view may provide a better understanding of the variability in people's skills and intelligence from one situation to another.

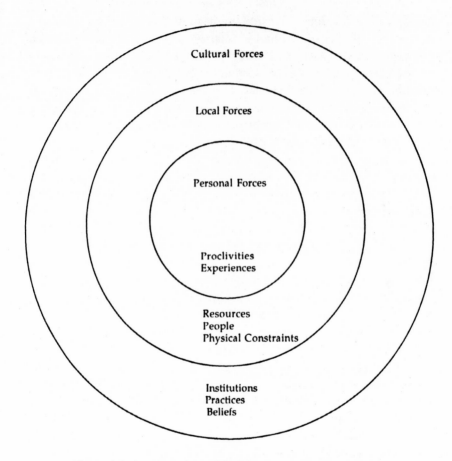

Figure 6.1. A concentric model of the forces affecting cognition.

## A concentric model of cognition

From our perspective, it is useful to think of the cultural, local, and personal forces at work in any situation in terms of a series of
concentric circles (Figure 6.1). In this "concentric" model, the forces
that operate at each level help to shape the activity and skills of all
people, including children like Gerald, Mark, and Kenny. Changes in
the forces at any one of these levels can contribute to changes both in
what people do and in what they are capable of doing (Bronfenbrenner, 1979). As a consequence, it makes no sense to consider Gerald's

tunnel-making skills or the drawing skills of Mark and Kenny without also taking into account the conditions that allow those skills to be expressed.

### Cultural forces

In the concentric model, the outermost circle represents the institutions, practices, and beliefs that transcend particular settings and affect a large number of individuals. Several widely cited studies from what Gardner (1990) has termed a "contextual" perspective have demonstrated the impact of such cultural forces as schooling (Scribner & Cole, 1981), child-rearing practices (LeVine, 1979), and language practices (Heath, 1983) on the abilities that people display and develop. When these cultural forces are taken into account, intelligence can no longer be conceptualized as an isolated property located solely inside a person's head.

While cultural forces influence many aspects of people's lives, they have three principal effects on behavior. Cultural forces influence the kinds of skills people can exhibit, the way those skills are developed, and the purposes to which they are directed. Thus, the fact that Gerald can use his spatial and fine motor skills to dig a tunnel rests on the fact that he lives in a culture where tunnels are familiar objects and where playing freely in the sand is an accepted classroom practice for young children. Similarly, if Mark and Kenny were transported to another culture where drawing is not a common pursuit for children or adults, they might find themselves using their spatial skills for navigation, tracking, or some other culturally valued activity. Even in another culture where drawing is prized, there is no guarantee that Mark or Kenny's spatial skills would be developed in the same way. In a classroom in China, for example, instead of drawing whenever and whatever they liked, Mark and Kenny might find themselves seated at desks meticulously copying a picture according to a teacher's instructions (Tobin, Wu, & Davidson, 1989). Further, it is doubtful that the children would be using their drawing skills to depict Ninja Turtles. Such differences in classroom activities can contribute to differences in the artistic development of children from different cultures (Gardner, 1989) as well as to differences in their academic achievements (Stevenson, Lee, & Stigler, 1986).

*Local forces*

The middle circle has been a particular concern of those who take a "distributed" perspective on intelligence (Cole & Engeström, Chapter 1, this volume; Pea, Chapter 2, this volume). The focus here falls on those resources and people who directly affect the behavior of an individual within a specific "local" setting. Local settings include typical habitats like the home, the classroom, and the workplace (Barker & Wright, 1954; Bronfenbrenner, 1979). From this perspective, little is accomplished by individuals working in isolation with only their minds to guide them; instead, individuals depend on a wide variety of tools, people, and other resources to help them carry out their activities. Thus, while Gerald has a notion about how to create a tunnel in the sand, as he points out he is not capable of creating that tunnel without wire.

At this level, it is proper to think of intelligence as shared by individuals and all the human and nonhuman resources they use. When mark chooses to depict the same subject as Kenny, refers to Kenny's picture, and solicits Kenny's assistance, the two boys share the capacity to produce the cartoon figure. Removing Kenny from the situation would affect Mark's capacity to draw the figure and his level of skill in the drawing process.

Those who take a "situated" perspective also emphasize the importance of local contributions to intelligence. According to this view, intelligence cannot be separated from the particular conditions in which it is deployed (Collins, Brown, & Newman, 1989). Problem-solving behaviors that are effective in one "local" setting may not apply or may not be produced in others: a strategy used to solve a math problem in the classroom may not be generated or may not be effective for calculating best buys in the grocery store (Lave, 1988) or for figuring out how to fill an order in a milk packing plant (Scribner, 1984). From this perspective, Mark would not necessarily display the same level of drawing skill in a setting where he was expected to work on his own, nor would Kenny be expected to perform at the same level if he were required to draw subjects that were unfamiliar to him.

Although some resources, people, or practices might exert the same influence throughout a particular setting, many settings can also be divided into distinct areas such as rooms, workstations, and play areas. If the materials, participants, and activities differ from one room or area to another, the affordances of each location and the "local effects" may be different as well. According to Gibson (1977), "affordances" are "facts of the environment" – functions that can be carried out given the properties of both the setting and the people (or animals) who occupy that setting. Put simply, art areas usually afford drawing, painting, and other art activities, while sand tables afford the building of sand castles and other constructions. In terms of materials, affordances describe the uses to which those materials can be put. Thus, a pencil affords drawing, a paintbrush affords painting, and shovels afford digging. As a consequence, Gerald might not show the same level of skill at the art table as he does at the sand table; if asked how to make a tunnel with the crayons and paper available at the art table – materials that would require Gerald to express his knowledge in a different form – Gerald might not have the answer.

## Personal forces

The innermost circle of the concentric model represents the attributes and experiences that individual children bring with them to many of the "local settings" where they spend their time. While traditional theories have focused on intelligence as a general problem-solving ability, they have failed to take into account both the wide variation in people's abilities and the vast array of individual differences that influence the development of those abilities. In contrast, from a "pluralistic" perspective, both endogenous factors such as genetic proclivities and exogenous factors such as personal experiences within a given culture influence the activities in which children choose to become involved and the abilities they subsequently develop. Given the tight interweaving of genetic proclivities and experience in the development of intelligences, these endogenous and exogenous factors often prove difficult to separate. Nonetheless, it is still possible to identify them as personal forces – influences children carry with them from one local setting to another.

In one "pluralistic" approach, Gardner (1983, 1990) argues that people exhibit a profile of intellectual strengths and weaknesses that includes at least seven different sets of abilities or "intelligences." Gardner deliberately spans both endogenous and exogenous forces by suggesting that there is no pure "aptitude" that can be assessed apart from a person's experience in particular domains such as language, music, and mathematics. For example, not only is the spatial intelligence that Mark displays in his drawings influenced by the culture and by Kenny's assistance; it is also a manifestation of the facts that Mark draws infrequently at home and that his parents show more interest in and provide more support for activities like writing, reading, and math. Correspondingly, Gerald's knowledge of tunnel making is related to his previous experiences with tunnels and in working with sand in other settings.

It is at the personal level that this concentric view differs both from alternative conceptions of intelligence and from the ecological perspective on development.[1] We disagree with the traditional view, which places abilities in the head and stipulates that certain skills and performances necessarily follow from these abilities; yet we recognize that individuals have the potential to use certain skills or intelligences or to achieve certain levels of performance (see Salomon, Chapter 4, this volume, for a related argument).

From our point of view, the setting or culture can certainly prevent Gerald from implementing his tunnel-making knowledge. At the same time, we argue that even in a culture with tunnels and in a setting with wire and sand, a lack of experience in playing with sand or deficits in the fine motor skills required for delicate digging could render Gerald incapable of constructing a tunnel. Nonetheless, experience in sand play and fine motor skills are not themselves sufficient to guarantee that Gerald could make tunnels in any culture, under any conditions. Similarly, the setting may include the resources and people that allow Mark to show a higher level of spatial skill in his drawings than we would normally expect; but even in a supportive setting, his lack of experience in drawing and the limits of his spatial intelligence will affect his performance.

[1] For example, Bronfenbrenner (1979) describes the ecological environment as a set of nested structures, but his innermost level corresponds to the local setting.

## *The interdependence of forces*

In this concentric model, intelligence is enmeshed in all of a person's activities, past and present, and embedded in the local settings and cultures in which those activities are carried out. From this perspective, cultural, local, and personal forces are interdependent. An individual's intelligences, interests, and concerns are formed in interactions with peers, family members, and teachers, constrained by available materials, and influenced by cultural values and expectations. The skills and interests a particular child brings into a setting may lead teachers or parents to rearrange the local setting and to provide different materials. Cultural values and expectations change over time with shifts in the interests and skills of individuals and alterations in the constitution of local settings.

As a consequence of this interdependence, no single formula determines which skills a person will use and develop. The effects of this triad of forces depend on their composition and alignment at a given site and a given point in time. For example, the influence of the personal and local forces may differ in different societies. In one society (e.g., China), a person's skills and interests may be overwhelmed by cultural and social pressures and may not play as large a role in a person's activity or development as they do in another society (e.g., the United States).

Even within the same culture, the influence of these forces may differ from one individual to another. For one individual, personal interests and abilities might have a much greater influence on behavior than they do for another individual who is more socially inclined. Over time, individuals develop, new groups are formed, innovative materials are introduced, and the culture evolves. These shifts create different pressures and contribute to changes in the activities of individuals and the skills they develop. Change the culture, switch settings, or focus on a different area of the classroom, and there is likely to be a change in the skills an individual can display as well. But that change will not be a random one. It will be in accord with the forces at work in the "new" situation. With a knowledge of how these forces operate, we can gain a better understanding of how a person is likely to perform in a variety of situations; and we may be able to expand the focus of education from the skills inside our heads to the situations in which we use them.

### An examination of the concentric circles in a kindergarten

In the remainder of this chapter, we examine the influence of cultural, local, and personal forces on the activities of two kindergartners during free play. The results are drawn from a larger study of four kindergartners during six months of observations. The study took place in a "child-centered" kindergarten at a public school located in a low- to middle-income district. The observations were conducted four mornings a week, and each of the four children was observed for two 45-minute periods every week. At the end of each morning, the notes and transcriptions of portions of audiotapes were used to construct narratives describing the activities of the children who were observed. In order to code the children's activities, the observer reviewed the narratives and divided the children's behavior into episodes (Barker & Wright, 1954; Bronfenbrenner, 1979; Stodolsky, 1988). If these episodes lasted less than five minutes, the children's activity was marked as "shifting." When episodes lasted for more than five minutes, they were defined as the children might have done so if it had been possible to ask them (for a related procedure see Reed & Csikszentmihalyi, 1983). Whenever possible, the children's spontaneous statements were used to define their activities.

This kindergarten classroom during free play serves as an especially informative setting for such a study because it contains distinct play areas within which the cultural and local forces are different, and it allows individual children to take advantage of their proclivities and experience in making decisions about which skills to use. In this chapter, we focus on activities at the art and sand tables because they represent some of the most significant local differences among the areas of the classroom: the art table supports independent product-making activities, while the sand table encourages group pretend play. For present purposes, we focus on the activities of the two boys in the study – Kenny and Mark.

If a traditional view of intelligence is correct, the skills and performances that Kenny and Mark display in the classroom should be

largely immune to the differences in the cultural and local forces at
work at the art and sand tables. Instead, the children's activities
should reflect differences in their personal forces and proclivities.
The classroom observations, however, show that both cultural and local forces have a significant effect on the activities the children pursue, the skills they use, and the levels of performance they achieve.
The children's personal forces – particularly the interests and proclivities they show at home – play an important role in their development, but that role changes from child to child and from one area of
the classroom to another.

### Activities at the sand table

Kenny and Mark each bring to the sand table distinct personal forces. Kenny has no sandbox at home, but his parents report
that he has always had considerable interest in construction activities.
His creative use of building materials also suggests that spatial intelligence is one of his strengths. Correspondingly, his parents provide
him with a wide range of building materials, including several varieties of Legos and blocks, which he can use to exercise his interests
and develop his spatial skills. In contrast, Mark's parents explain that
he spends relatively little time in construction activities and does not
show any proclivities in the spatial area. Instead, their statements
about Mark's keen interest in other people and his unusual sensitivity
to the needs and desires of others suggest that interpersonal intelligence is one of his strengths.

Despite these distinct intelligences and interests and despite the
fact that the boys have the freedom to engage in a wide range of activities, in many areas of the classroom they share a limited repertoire
of activities. This phenomenon is already evident at the sand table
during October (the first month in which activity records are kept).
During this month, most of the boys who play at the sand table work
in groups; together they make cakes and waterfalls. Of the 13 observation periods during which either Kenny or Mark spends time at the
sand table, the boys are always at work with other children (on nine of
those occasions both boys are present). During those observation periods, Kenny or Mark (or both) are engaged in an activity at the sand
table for five minutes or more 12 times. Of those 12 times, they make

either cakes or waterfalls seven times (58%). On three occasions they fill up buckets with sand and treat them and refer to them as "cakes." On four occasions they pour sand through a series of sifters or funnels and call this a "waterfall" or a "waterfall cake." Even the three instances when a single subject for the children's activity is not clear ("shifting"), these same activities are often conducted, although only for brief periods of time. Only after November 2, when the teacher adds water to the sand, do their activities change; but once again the children limit themselves to a handful of activities. Five of the eight constructions they make between November 7 and December 1 are either tunnels or pyramids (62%). After that time, the boys play at the sand table on only two more occasions during the observations.

*Cultural and local support for group activities.*    Under some conditions the boys' interests and intelligences might push them in different directions; but at the sand table the cultural and local forces encourage them to work together, share in the same activities, and exercise the same skills. Throughout this country, sand tables and sandboxes are social settings. At the cultural level, they are places in which children are expected to engage in pretend play with their peers.

For the most part, the local forces at work at the sand table in this classroom reinforce these expectations. The sand table itself is quite small, and as a consequence the teacher limits participation to four or sometimes five children. Usually, the table is filled to capacity, and it is virtually impossible to work independently. In addition, the sand, unlike blocks, Legos, and many other materials in the kindergarten, cannot be divided easily. With a table of such small size, what the children do in one part of the sand affects what happens to the sand in the rest of the table. As one child states in an interview, the size and sturdiness of his castles are affected by what his neighbors do; even if someone simply moves sand that is near his castle and not technically a part of it, the castle could collapse.

In the context of these cultural and local forces, the children share in the construction process. For example, when making cakes and waterfalls, the boys all help to fill up a single bucket or all pour sand through a series of sifters or funnels. One or two children often attempt to control the activity and occasionally they take turns as the "baker," who coordinates the "cake making":

Mark, Bobby, Charlie, and Kenny are playing at the sand table. They are making a cake, and Mark has been the baker.

"I'm the baker after Mark," Kenny declares.

"Done," Mark proclaims.

"Okay, it's my turn to be the baker." Kenny puts an empty bucket in front of himself. Someone starts to put some sand in, but he stops him. "No, I didn't ask for anything yet." Then he points to each of the others in turn. "You're the butter man, you're the egg man, and you're the flour man . . . " Now Kenny calls out each of the ingredients individually, usually indicating that a particular person should dump another handful of sand into the bucket.

When digging tunnels, the boys often coordinate their efforts by selecting (or proclaiming) one or two children as the "digging judges." Their jobs are to tell all the children where, and often what, they can dig. Kenny (K) explains this to an interviewer (I):

I: What were the digging judges?

K: Umm they got to dig, and choose who got to dig and stuff.

I: How come you needed to have digging judges?

K: Because we dig holes and tunnels so they can get all the way around and stuff.

I: Uh huh, but why did you need digging judges for that?

K: Because I mean then everybody would just be digging and then the roof would fall down.

Through these uses of their interpersonal skills, the children are able to partition the tasks. As a consequence, like the team of engineers that Perkins (Chapter 3, this volume) alludes to, the "functioning cognitive unit" at the sand table is often a group of children. Correspondingly, the use of their skills and their performance cannot be separated from the work of the group, and few differences are evident in either their interests or their skills.

*Local limitations at the sand table.* Given these cultural and local forces, it is not particularly surprising that Kenny and Mark often work together. What is surprising is that they engage in the same activities over and over again. If their skills are simply contained in their heads, Kenny and Mark should be able to carry out a much wider range of activities. Instead, it is as if the sand table is stocked with a limited number of things the children can do. The local forces contribute to these limitations both by encouraging the repetition of activities and by placing constraints on the specific activities in which the children can engage.

As Pea (Chapter 2, this volume) and Perkins (Chapter 3) point out, the arrangement and rearrangement of the environment can function as a memory aid. Thus, people are not required to remember on their own what they were doing or what was successful and adaptive. For Kenny and Mark, the sand itself serves as a record of their activities of the recent past and a prompt for future pursuits. Because cleanup at the sand table involves placing a large board over the top, the cakes and tunnels the children make are often preserved from one period and one day to the next. These arrangements can remind them of their previous activities. Further, the "remains" can give children who were not originally involved ideas they may not have thought of "on their own," thereby contributing to the spread of skills from one child to another. As a result, the children have numerous opportunities to observe and build upon their peers' creations and the ideas represented in them. Salomon (Chapter 4, this volume) speaks of the "cognitive residue" that remains with people after they have carried out an activity. In this case, the sand provides a "contextual residue" – physical traces of activities – that the children can interpret and upon which they can build.

In addition to supporting the repetition of activities, two pieces of evidence suggest that the local forces play a central role in constraining children's activities and the skills they can display: (1) These activities are unique to the sand table; and (2) the change in the children's activities and the skills they display are associated with a change in the affordances of the sand. In the classroom, pouring and working with sand are obviously restricted to the sand table. There is no restriction, however, on representing cakes or waterfalls with other materials. The children could pretend to bake cakes in the dramatic play area, build waterfalls with blocks, or draw cakes and waterfalls at the art table. Nonetheless, these concentrations on cake and waterfall making are unique to the sand table. In the dramatic play area in October, Kenny and Mark engage in a different (but still limited) set of activities: six of the seven times that they engage in an activity for more than five minutes, they take on pretend roles of media-related characters and popular toys: Ninja Turtles, Karate

Kid, or Foodfighters (action figures based on different kinds of food). While this evidence is not conclusive, it suggests that there is something unique to the sand table – and not to the children who play there – that contributes to their activities.

The impact of the local forces is further demonstrated by the fact that the most striking shift in the boys' activities at the sand table is tied to a change in the affordances of the sand. As Gerald's comment about the need for wire indicates, during October the children are unable to make many typical sand constructions like tunnels. Correspondingly, when the boys are making cakes and waterfalls, the sand is dry. The dry sand, along with the shovels, buckets, and sifters that are provided, affords activities like digging, sifting, and pouring. As a consequence, in October the sand table is better suited for mixing sand in a bucket and calling it a cake, or pouring sand through a sifter and calling it a waterfall, than it is for making tunnels and pyramids. On November 2, however, when the teacher adds water to the sand, she dramatically changes the affordances of the area. As the girls pointed out one day, wet sand can function "like cement." It cannot be sifted or poured, but it can be packed and shaped into tunnels, pyramids, and other constructions. Thus, the addition of water to the sand changes what the children are capable of doing. Before that time, it is of little use to say that either Kenny or Mark has the skills needed to make tunnels. Their skills are, literally, embedded in the sand.

*Summary.* Although Kenny could be displaying and developing his skills in the construction of tunnels and pyramids while Mark uses his skills to make cakes and waterfalls, they both choose to make the same things at the same time. Kenny and Mark appear to have the freedom to do whatever they like, but the observations suggest that the possibilities are significantly limited by the cultural and local forces. In October it is as if, instead of simply choosing between using a sifter and using a bucket, the boys perceive opportunities to make specific objects – cakes and waterfalls. Over time, through changes in the local setting, new possibilities are discovered. As a consequence, the children perceive the materials and the area in a different way – as a place where tunnels and pyramids can be made. Their activity is not only recorded in the sand; it endows the sand table with meanings that serve as the basis for the use, exercise, and distribution of particular skills.

### Activities at the art table

Just as they bring distinct personal forces to the sand table, Kenny and Mark bring different backgrounds, interests, and intelligences to the art table. According to his mother, Kenny has always done a lot of coloring, and during the period of the observations he has been doing "pages and pages and pages" of drawing. In contrast, Mark's parents report that he does not color or draw much and that he does not show particular skill in this area. These comments are confirmed by a review of the drawings that the boys make at home and that both parents are asked to collect during the six months of the observations. Throughout that time, Mark makes only 3 drawings while Kenny makes 44. Although it is possible that Mark's parents do not keep all of the drawings he makes at home, there is no reason to doubt the reliability of their collection; they are also asked to save the pictures that Mark brings home from school, and that collection includes 10 of the 11 pictures that Mark makes while he is being observed.

In addition to these differences in the boys' interests, the drawings that are collected reflect the differences in the boys' spatial intelligences that also are apparent in their construction activities. The pictures that Mark makes at home consist largely of stick figures with few colors or details, but Kenny is able to create a wide range of figures. By Christmas, Mark's figures still bear little relationship to one another, yet Kenny is able to depict his figures in profile and in relation to one another in representational scenes.

Some of these differences in the boys' personal forces are reflected at the art table. They usually arrive at the art table together, but then go on to make different works. On only five occasions do they work on pictures of the same subjects at the same time. A closer look reveals that Mark's drawings are heavily affected by the local influences of other peers. In fact, Mark almost always makes his choice of subject matter after others have stated their preferences. He usually selects a subject – like Ninja Turtles – that is either similar or identical to the drawings on which Ned or another one of his friends has already embarked. Of the 11 drawings that Mark makes while he is being observed, 7 are based on the works of friends around him (64%).

In contrast, for Kenny, neither the local setting nor the people who share it with him have much impact on the drawing skills he displays. Of the 13 drawings that Kenny produces during periods when he is observed, only 4 are based on the works of another child at the table (30%). Instead, his drawing activity and the development of his skills are tied to interests he pursues both at home and at school. Even though the setting is entirely different, the pictures Kenny's parents collect at home parallel his works at school both in content and in skill: Seven of the 13 drawings (53%) that he makes in the classroom while he is being observed contain some of the same subjects that he depicts in pictures he makes at home.

It is almost as if Kenny and Mark are at work in two different places. For Mark, the art table is much like the sand table: a place where he can engage in activities with his friends. For Kenny, however, the art table is a place where he can pursue interests that are independent of his peers. Ironically, the cultural and local forces play a central role in enabling Kenny and Mark to conduct their activities at the art table in such different ways. In contrast to the sand table, where both cultural and local forces encourage the boys to work together on a limited set of activities, not all of the cultural and local forces at the art table push in the same direction.

*The culture of art.* On a cultural level, art is often viewed as an activity in which permanent products are made by individual authors. In many cultures including this one, the artist is depicted as someone who works alone; finished products are placed in frames, homes, and museums, where they can be seen and admired. In schools, for the most part, these cultural differences are reinforced. Students work on their own to create, and usually to take home, permanent products (Gearhart & Newman, 1980). For example, in many classrooms throughout the country, separate pieces of paper and easels are set out for each child, and children are usually asked to sign their products; such individual demarcations are rarely made with either sand constructions or block buildings (Kuschner, 1989). Thus, many aspects of the culture of art inhibit the sharing and distribution of skills that are encouraged at the sand table. This dichotomy does not have to exist, however. In another culture where there are no museums, frames, or signatures, teachers might encourage children to work together and distribute their skills. They might expect all the children to work on the same piece of paper or to leave their pictures out so that their peers can add embellishments and new ideas.[2]

*The local setting of art.*     Through activities in other schools, playgrounds, and at home (and perhaps some exposure to museums and other "cultural institutions"), it is likely that many of the children in this classroom are already familiar with the cultural forces that support this dichotomy between artwork and sand play. At the art table, local forces like a "finishing routine" reinforce the cultural bias toward individual authorship and reduce the chances that the children will be able to build on the skills their peers display. When the children decide that they are finished with their work, the teacher asks them to write their names on their pictures and to put the pictures away in their cubbies to be taken home at a later time. Only on a few occasions does the teacher put the children's artworks up on the walls, and, as a result there are few reminders of their previous art activities. At the sand table, no such "finishing routine" exists. When the children tire of playing in the sand, they simply abandon their work and move on, leaving behind the traces of their activities.

At the same time, some of the local forces afford the children a chance to share their ideas and skills and to engage in collaborative activities. The art table is a long table where as many as 10 children can work side by side. No individual places or easels are set up; the children can observe each other's work, and they are able to converse freely about the things they make. As a result, there are numerous opportunities for children to learn from one another, to draw the same pictures, and to develop the same skills as their peers.

*Social interactions in the arts.*     Because of the conflicting nature of these cultural and local forces at the art table, it is largely up to individuals to take advantage of, or ignore, the work that goes on around them. On the one hand, for Kenny – a child with spatial pro-

---

[2] It is worth noting that, although the teacher in this classroom occasionally urges the children to work on the same piece of paper, more often than not the children themselves divide the paper in half and make their own drawings.

clivities and a distinct interest in drawing – it does not matter whether he is surrounded by his peers in the classroom or sitting at home; in both settings, the drawing skills that he displays are the same. On the other hand, for Mark – a child for whom social interactions and personal relationships are very important – the art table, like the sand table, is a place where his activities and skills are heavily dependent on the peers who share the setting with him.

When Mark draws on his own in the classroom, he shows the limited spatial and artistic skills that are revealed in the drawings he makes at home; but when Mark works on the same subjects as his peers in the classroom, he uses his interpersonal skills in order to get advice and assistance. By using his friends as resources and getting them to distribute their skills, Mark is able to demonstrate a much higher level of performance. Illustrating Vygotsky's "zone of proximal development" (1978), Mark produces works with the help of his peers that are clearly more advanced than the drawings he completes on his own. Instead of drawing stick figures, Mark depicts the Turtles much more realistically, with full bodies and appropriately shaped arms and legs. In addition, the figures include characteristic details and colors.

Mark's reliance on the local support of his peers to complete these "advanced" pictures is most clearly illustrated when the observer returns to the classroom for a visit in May. He asks Mark to come to the art table and draw a picture of a Ninja Turtle at a time when none of Mark's friends are there to assist him. The resulting drawing shows some development since September – colors and a few details make the drawings more mimetic – but the Turtles he draws more closely resemble the stick figures he makes at the beginning of the year than those he creates with the support of his friends.

*Personal interests in the arts.* Given the fact that, in contrast to Mark, Kenny shows roughly the same drawing skills both at home and at school, Kenny's art activities appear to support a traditional view of abilities or intelligence. It seems reasonable to suggest that if Kenny can create a picture at one time or under one set of conditions, he should be able to draw it again at another time or under another set of conditions. Nonetheless, a closer examination of Kenny's drawings suggests that the skills he displays cannot be separated from the subjects he chooses to draw. While Mark's interpersonal proclivities help to determine how his skills will be used and developed, Kenny's drawing skills are defined by his changing interests in particular fantasy characters.

In the first few months of the year, when he often draws "Halloween" monsters, Kenny usually depicts figures singly or side by side. Characteristic colors and details – Dracula's black cape and fangs and Frankenstein's green skin – are included; but the figures do not comprise specific scenes. They bear little relation to one another and simply "float" on the page. In December, he is more likely to draw scenes that represent Nintendo video games or media characters like Batman. In these pictures, actions are represented and some attempts are made to draw figures in profile. Details like Batman's mask and Freddie Krueger's hat still make the figures identifiable, but the drawings are done in pencil and only one is colored in. In January, when Kenny describes his subjects in vague terms like "monster" and "bad guy," the figures are still placed in scenes and are even more likely to be depicted in profile. At the same time, many of his characters – even those he refers to specifically as being from "Duck Tales" and "Simon's Quest" (Nintendo games) – are hard to identify. They are "generic" figures that lack characteristic details and resemble what can only be referred to as "blobs."

Further evidence that Kenny's drawing skills are tied to his interests in specific subjects is supplied when the observer asks Kenny to make a drawing in May. The observer makes the request while Kenny is at the art table with his friends – under typical local conditions. But instead of allowing Kenny to draw one of the characters that populate his pictures at the time, the observer asks Kenny to draw Dracula – one of his favorite subjects from earlier in the year. In contrast to his earlier pictures of Dracula, the figure that he draws is not a very realistic representation. Halfway through the process, Kenny even stops and declares, "I decided I didn't want to draw Dracula. I decided I just wanted to draw made-up monsters." Kenny goes on to produce one of the "generic" figures that have been his preferred subjects since January. Under these conditions – when he is assigned a subject that is not included in his current repertoire – he is unable to complete the task satisfactorily.

*Summary.*    At the art table, the cultural and local forces neither necessitate that Mark and Kenny share ideas and distribute their skills nor prevent them from doing so. As a consequence, in order to understand the skills these two children display, it is necessary to take into account the personal forces that each brings to this local setting. With his social inclinations, Mark uses his interpersonal skills as much as he uses his artistic skills. From Mark's perspective, the problems he faces at the art table include how to maintain and develop relationships with his peers, and the artistic skills he develops are linked directly to those interactions. In contrast, Kenny seems relatively uninterested in the social aspects of the art activity, and his skills are largely unconnected to the local setting. Because he is less likely to collaborate directly with peers, he can pursue his interests and use his skills without much interference from friends. For Kenny, the problems in drawing involve how to depict the figures and scenes of his favorite cartoons and movies.

## Conclusion

From a traditional perspective, it may seem that there is no cognition in this classroom. The focus has been on what a small group of children do in unstructured, spontaneous play. Nonetheless, in both settings the children find and solve a variety of problems. The problems they discover, the skills they use to address those problems, and the levels of success they achieve are shaped by the cultural, local, and personal forces at work in each situation. The observations at the sand table demonstrate that the cultural and local forces encourage the children to repeat a limited set of activities and to distribute their skills; and changes in the local forces contribute to changes in the products the children are capable of making. At the art table, the cultural and local forces have no such "global" effects on the boys' activities. Rather, they allow for independent activities, and as a result Mark's and Kenny's drawing skills are situated in different places: Mark's in social interactions with his friends, and Kenny's in the particular subjects in which he shows an interest.

### *Personal forces instead of personal properties*

While this view of cognition and intelligence suggests that personal forces are attributes that individuals carry with them from one setting to another, these forces are not independent properties located inside a person's head – they are not properties of the mind "solo." For one thing, the personal forces themselves are always already a reflection of the cultural and local forces in the settings where individuals have spent their time. Kenny's and Mark's strengths may have been evident very early in life; nonetheless, those strengths are also a reflection of the opportunities they have had to display and develop their predispositions and of the support their efforts have received.

In addition, the effects of these personal forces on behavior and development are always contingent on the cultural and local forces in particular situations. Thus, the cultural and local forces at the art table neither support Kenny in, nor discourage him from, displaying the same drawing skills and interests he shows at home; yet in another culture, in another classroom, or even at another time in this kindergarten, the cultural and local forces could change in ways that would affect the display and development of his skills and interests. Rather than allowing the children to draw anything they like, the teacher could require the children to learn how to draw particular subjects, or she could replace the crayons and markers with paints. If Kenny moved to another school or to another grade, he might find his opportunities to use his spatial skills in drawing and construction activities reduced by the demands of academic tasks.

### Applying the concentric model

Those who hold a traditional view have often supported their stance by arguing that intelligence tests have substantial predictive power; yet such tests can, at best, predict academic performances in school. By taking an expanded view of intelligence and examining the personal, local, and cultural forces in a particular situation, we may be able to get a better understanding of what people are likely to do and how they are likely to perform under a wide variety of conditions.

Instead of assuming that a person will display the same skills at roughly the same level in all situations, we can, with this expanded view, understand some of the variability in a person's performance. On the one hand, any analysis that focused solely on the skills that Mark displays on his own would predict that Mark cannot create particularly realistic pictures; such an analysis would fail to anticipate what Mark can do under common conditions in the classroom and would seriously underestimate his capacity to draw. On the other hand, with an understanding of the coalition of forces at work in Mark's art activity, one can predict that taking Mark out of this class-room might have a dramatic effect on both the subjects he draws and the skills he displays. In another classroom, one would predict that he would engage in art activities only about as often as the friends he met there. Further, the drawing skills he displays in the new setting may be closely related to those of his new classmates. If one knew the characteristics of the local setting to which Mark was moving – in particular if one knew whether Mark would be able to collaborate with other children and if one knew the interests and activities of those other children – one would have a good sense of what Mark might do when he arrived.

In contrast, if Kenny were in a different classroom with different peers – if the local setting were changed – it is likely that the change would not have a significant effect on his drawings. Kenny might well continue to draw pictures of Dracula, Nintendo characters, and other subjects that are his particular concerns. Knowing Kenny's interests and his activities at home would be more germane to predicting what he would do and how he would perform in the new situation.

While suggestive, the observations reported in this chapter must be bolstered by further investigations of children's skills and behavior in different settings. In particular, sytematic analyses of chil-dren's behavior over time as they move from one setting to another – from home to school, and from one grade to the next – may shed light on how personal, local, and cultural forces come together in the classroom.

### *Synchronizing forces in education*

Knowledge about personal, local, and cultural forces can also carry us beyond the sand play and drawing of these children to wider conclusions about how they learn and the conditions in which they might learn most effectively. Expanding our knowledge to include an understanding of the conditions in which people live and learn is par-ticularly critical, because personal, local, and cultural forces often push in different directions (see Ogbu, 1978, for related discussions).

The interests of an individual child may not match those of peers or meet the expectations of parents. A child may excel in activities that are not prized in a particular culture, or the materials available may call for abilities or interests a child does not possess. Although fortuitous "coincidences" of factors, in some cases, may contribute to the development of prodigies (Feldman, 1986) or to the achievements of eminent individuals (Gruber, 1980), mismatches can lead to educational difficulties and limit personal achievements (Granott & Gardner, in press).

For example, in the classroom described in this chapter, children are encouraged to initiate and carry out their own activities; independent children like Kenny may flourish in such a setting. Children like Mark, who are more interested in developing friendships than in pursuing activities of their own, may not take advantage of their other strengths or develop them to the extent that they could in a more structured setting. In addition, with its art table, sand table, and block and construction areas, this classroom demands drawing and building skills. As a consequence, those children who bring to the classroom the spatial skills and knowledge needed to draw Ninja Turtles and build tunnels have a better chance to do well than those who lack experience with these materials.

By monitoring the personal, local, and cultural forces at work in educational situations, we may begin to understand some of the activities in which a person is likely to engage; and we may gain some sense of the skills a person is likely to develop in the future even if we cannot tell exactly what he or she will be doing next. With this knowledge, parents and educators can develop programs and strategies that are responsive to the changing needs of individual children as well as to the changing circumstances in our societies.

### References

Barker, R. G., & Wright, H. F. (1954). *Midwest and its children: The psychological ecology of an American town.* Evanston, IL: Row, Peterson.

Bronfenbrenner, U. (1979). *The ecology of human development.* Cambridge, MA: Harvard University Press.

Collins, A., Brown, J. S., & Newman, S. E. (1989). Cognitive apprenticeship: Teaching the craft of reading, writing, and mathematics. In L. Resnick (Ed.), *Cognition and instruction: Issues and agendas* (pp. 453–94). Hillsdale, NJ: Erlbaum.

Feldman, D. (1986). *Nature's gambit: Child prodigies and the development of human potential.* New York: Basic Books.

Gardner, H. (1983). *Frames of mind.* New York: Basic Books.

(1989). *To open minds: Chinese clues to the dilemma of contemporary education.* New York: Basic Books.

(1990). Intelligence in seven steps. *New Horizons for Learning.*

Gearhart, M., & Newman, D. (1980). Learning to draw a picture: The social context of an individual activity. *Discourse Processes, 3,* 169–84.

Gibson, J. (1977). The theory of affordances. In R. Shaw & J. Bransford (Eds.), *Perceiving, acting, and knowing.* Hillsdale, NJ: Erlbaum.

Goodenough, F. (1926). *Draw-a-Man test.* New York: World Book.

Granott, N., & Gardner, H. (in press). Abilities in domains. In R. J. Sternberg & R. K. Wagner (Eds.), *Mind in context.* Cambridge University Press.

Gruber, H. (1980). "And the bush was not consumed:" The evolving systems approach to creativity. In S. Modgil & C. Modgil (Eds.), *Toward a theory of psychological development.* Windsor: NFER Press.

Heath, S. (1983). *Ways with words.* Cambridge University Press.

Kuschner, D. (1989). "Put your name on your painting, but . . . the blocks go back on the shelves." *Young Children, 45*(1), 49–56.

Lave, J. (1988). *Cognition in practice.* Cambridge University Press.

Lewin, K. (1951). *Field theory in social science: Selected theoretical papers.* Chicago: University of Chicago Press.

LeVine, S. (1979). *Mothers and wives: Gusii women of East Africa.* Chicago: University of Chicago Press.

Ogbu, J. (1978). *Minority education and caste: The American system in cross-cultural perspective.* New York: Academic Press.

Reed, R., & Csikszentmihalyi, M. (1983). The experience sampling method. In H. T. Reis (Ed.), *Naturalistic approaches to studying social interaction* (pp. 41–56). New Directions for Methodology of Social and Behavioral Science, Vol. 15. San Francisco: Jossey-Bass.

Scribner, S. (1984). Studying working intelligence. In B. Rogoff and J. Lave (Eds.), *Everyday cognition: It's development in social context.* Cambridge, MA: Harvard University Press.

Scribner, S., & Cole, M. (1981). *The psychology of literacy.* Cambridge, MA: Harvard University Press.

Stevenson, H. W., Lee, S. Y., & Stigler, J. W. (1986). Mathematics achievement of Chinese, Japanese, and American Children. *Science, 231:* 693–9.

Stodolsky, S. (1988). *The subject matters.* Chicago: University of Chicago Press.

Tobin, J. J., Wu, D. Y., & Davidson, D. H. (1989). *Preschool in three cultures.* New Haven, CN: Yale University Press.

Vygotsky, L. S. (1978). *Mind in society.* Cambridge, MA: Harvard University Press.

# 7 Distributed expertise in the classroom

*Ann L. Brown, Doris Ash, Martha Rutherford, Kathryn Nakagawa, Ann Gordon, and Joseph C. Campione*

It is commonly agreed that we are currently witnessing a resurgence of interest in situated cognition, for want of a better name (for a brief history, see Cole & Engeström, Chapter 1, this volume). A main tenet of this philosophy is that knowledge does not consist of static "furniture of the mind" (Hall, 1881); knowledge is situated in activity. Railing against the prevailing cognitive position that knowledge consists of representations in the mind, Lave (1988) further argues:

> The point is not so much that arrangements of knowledge in the head correspond in a complicated way to the world outside the head, but that they are socially organized in such a fashion as to be indivisible. "Cognition" observed in everyday practice is distributed – stretched over, not divided among – mind, body, activity and culturally organized settings (which include other actors). (p. 1)

Ways of knowing are deeply connected to the cultural artifacts of situations, artifacts that include tools and people. In this chapter we will indicate how an appreciation of the distributed nature of expertise influences, and is played out, in the design of our classrooms. To do so, we will give examples of distributed cognition in classrooms among students, teachers, computer tools, and other artifacts that frame their thinking (see also Brown, 1992).

In its new clothes, the concept of situated learning rests heavily on the notion of communities of practice (Bordieu, 1972). Lave and

The research reported in this chapter was supported by grants from the James S. McDonnell and Andrew W. Mellon Foundations, and by Evelyn Lois Corey research funds to the first three authors.

Wenger (1991) argue that participation in practice is the main activity through which learning occurs:

Conceiving of learning in terms of participation focuses attention on ways in which it is an evolving, continuously renewed set of relations. . . . Participation . . . can be neither fully internalized as knowledge structures nor fully externalized as instrumental artifacts or overarching activity structures. Participation is always based on situated negotiation and renegotiation of meaning in the world. This implies that understanding and experience are in constant interaction – indeed, are mutually constitutive. (pp. 49–52)

In this chapter we will examine grade school science classes as a community of practice, although J. S. Brown, Collins, and Duguid (1989) argue that this is just what schools typically are not. They argue that the professions, trades, and academic disciplines create cultures of practitioners into which novices are inducted during a long period of apprenticeship. Enculturation is time-consuming because it involves adopting the ways of knowing, cultural practices, discourse patterns, and belief systems of the discipline or trade in question.

J. S. Brown et al. (1989) make a distinction between authentic activity, somewhat loosely defined as the activity of actual practitioners of a craft, and the contrast class – schoolwork – that is to a large part inauthentic. This point was made some years ago by Cole and Bruner (1971), who pointed out the lack of continuity between school activities and both the cultures of childhood and legitimate adult occupations, as of course did Dewey (1902). In this chapter we will discuss what makes common school activities inauthentic and outline just what we feel *would* constitute authentic activity in, say, grade school.

It is clearly romantic to suggest, as do J. S. Brown et al., that students in public schools be enculturated into the cultures of mathematicians, historians, and literary critics. For a start, practitioners of these callings do not as a rule populate schools; teachers of these subjects may be consumers of the outputs of these disciplines, but they are rarely practitioners. History teachers are seldom historians. Practicing mathematicians infrequently teach high school, let alone grade school.

If it is not to apprentice children to the traditional academic disciplines, what is the purpose of schooling? Schools evolved to encourage a form of universal literacy that would enable graduates to be informed consumers, interpreters, and critics of science, history, economics, and literature. As Wineburg (1989) points out, the popularity of Stephen Jay Gould to millions of paleontologically untutored readers and of Barbara Tuchman to history buffs demonstrates that, to a certain degree, biology and history can be enjoyed by educated nonspecialists. He argues that "to write history (to be a historian) people may need to adopt the belief systems of historians and be conversant with their culture. But writing history and learning to appreciate it are different things." Even without an appreciation for daily life in grade school, the armchair philosopher must see the impracticality of suggesting that children be enculturated into the society of historians, biologists, mathematicians, and literary critics. This may be the desired state of first-rate graduate school education, but it is surely not a reasonable expectation for grade school. And while the point is well taken that many classroom rituals are divorced from the activities of scholars and professionals and even the spontaneous learning of childhood (Gardner, 1991), the question remains, What should constitute authentic activity in the classroom?

We argue that schools should be communities where students learn to learn. In this setting teachers should be models of intentional learning and self-motivated scholarship, both individual and collaborative (Brown, 1992; Brown & Campione, 1990; Scardamalia & Bereiter, 1991). If successful, graduates of such communities would be prepared as lifelong learners who have learned how to learn in many domains. We aim to produce a breed of "intelligent novices" (Brown, Bransford, Ferrara, & Campione, 1983), students who, although they may not possess the background knowledge needed in a new field, know how to go about gaining that knowledge. These learning experts would be better prepared to be inducted into the practitioner culture of their choosing; they would also have the background to select among several alternative practitioner cultures, rather than being tied to the one to which they were initially indentured, as in the case of traditional apprenticeships.

Ideally, in a community of learners, teachers and students serve as role models not only as "owners" of some aspects of domain knowledge, but also as acquirers, users, and extenders of knowledge in the sustained, ongoing process of understanding. Ideally, children are *apprentice learners*, learning how to think and reason in a variety of domains. By participating in the practices of scholarly research, they should be enculturated into the community of scholars during their 12 or more years of apprenticeship in school settings. Redesigning classrooms so that they can bolster this function is a primary aim of our research group (Brown, 1992). In our classroom interventions we try to create a community of discourse (Fish, 1980) where the participants are inducted into the rituals of academic and, more particularly, scientific discourse and activity (Brown & Campione, 1990, in press; Lempke, 1990; Michaels & O'Connor, in press).

In this chapter we will concentrate on how expertise is spread throughout the classroom and how such distributed expertise influences the community of discourse that provides the seeding ground for mutual appropriation. We begin with a discussion of the central theoretical concepts that guide our work and then proceed with a practical discussion of how to engineer communities of learning. We then discuss the roles of participants in the community (Brown & Campione, 1990, in press) and conclude with a discussion of what authentic school activity might be.

## Mutual appropriation and negotiation in a zone of proximal development

Theoretically, we conceive of the classroom as composed of zones of proximal development (Vygotsky, 1978) through which participants can navigate via different routes and at different rates (Brown & Reeve, 1987). A zone of proximal development can include people, adults and children, with various degrees of expertise, but it can also include artifacts such as books, videos, wall displays, scientific equipment, and a computer environment intended to support intentional learning (Campione, Brown, & Jay, 1992; Scardamalia & Bereiter, 1991). A zone of proximal development is the region of activity that learners can navigate with aid from a supporting context, including but not limited to people (Vygotsky, 1978). It defines the distance between current levels of comprehension and levels that can be accomplished in collaboration with people or powerful artifacts. The zone of proximal development embodies a concept of readiness to learn that emphasizes upper levels of competence. Furthermore, these upper boundaries are seen not as immutable but as constantly changing with the learner's increasing independent competence at successive levels.

In our classroom, researchers and teachers deliberately create zones of proximal development by seeding the environment with ideas and concepts that they value and by harvesting those that "take" in the community. But so too do the children. Participants in the classroom are free to appropriate vocabulary, ideas, methods, and so on that appear initially as part of the shared discourse and, by appropriation, transform these ideas via personal interpretation. Ideas that are part of the common discourse are not necessarily appropriated by all, or in the same manner by those who do. Because the appropriation of ideas and activities is multidirectional, we use the term "mutual appropriation" (Moschkovich, 1989; Newman, Griffin, & Cole, 1989; Schoenfeld, Smith, & Arcavi, in press).

It is useful to address the difference between the terms "internalization" and "appropriation," used to express the essential learning mechanism in Vygotskian theory. Rogoff (1990) uses the term "appropriation" as a substitute for "internalization" within a Vygotskian model of learning because internalization implies that individuals are separate from one another and learn by observing and then taking within themselves the results of that observation. The term "appropriation" is readily being used in place of "internalization" because of the widespread belief that use of the term "internalization" (1) merely renames a learning mechanism that is not understood and (2) implies that the fruits of learning, although initially gained in social interaction, somehow come to reside in individual minds.

The first question – whether the use of the term "internalization" really gets us farther along in addressing the time-honored problem of the actual mechanism of learning, that is, the Hoffding step (1892) – is addressed by Bereiter (1985) in his article on problematic learning and Fodor's (1980) learning paradox:

Following Vygotsky, . . . one might formulate the following explanation: Learning does indeed depend on the prior existence of more complex structures, but these more complex cognitive structures are situated in the culture, not the child.·. . . Through . . . shared activities the child internalizes the cognitive structures needed to carry on independently. Such an explanation, satisfying as it may appear, does not eliminate the learning paradox at all. The whole paradox hides in the word "internalizes." How does internalization take place? (p. 206)

To Rogoff (1990) and Newman et al. (1989), the concept of appropriation is seen as the answer to a prayer, in that they believe it solves the problem of Fodor's (1980) paradox and Bereiter's (1985) concept of problematic learning. Fodor also criticized Vygotsky's theory for not telling us where hypotheses come from, that is, for not unpacking the essential learning mechanism. We believe this critical question still remains unanswered, even with the change in terms (but see Newman et al., 1989).

The second, and more compelling, reason for switching to the term "appropriation" is that it is theoretically neutral with respect to the location of knowledge for those allergic to the notion of having anything inside the head. And theoretical disputes notwithstanding, we have found the concept of mutual appropriation operating within a zone of proximal development (ZPD) to have practical implications for how classrooms are orchestrated and observed. In their discussion of appropriation, Newman et al. (1989) emphasize that it is a two-way process:

> . . . the teacher reciprocally applies the process of appropriation in the instructional interactions. In constructing a ZPD for a particular task, the teacher incorporates children's actions into her own system of activity.
> *Just as the children do not have to know the full cultural analysis of a tool to begin using it, the teacher does not have to have a complete analysis of the children's understanding of the situation to start using their actions in the larger system.* The children's actions can function within two different understandings of the significance of the task: the child's and the teacher's. Both are constrained by sociohistorical understandings of the activity setting in which they are interacting. The fact that any action can always have more than one analysis makes cognitive change possible. Children can participate in an activity that is more complex than they can understand, producing "performance before competence," to use Cazden's (1981) phrase. While in the ZPD of the activity, the children's actions get interpreted within the system being constructed with the teacher. Thus the child is exposed to the teacher's understanding without necessarily being directly taught. (pp. 63–4)

The term "mutual appropriation" refers to the bidirectional nature of the appropriation process, one that should not be viewed as limited to the process by which the child (novice) learns from the adult (expert) via a static process of imitation, internalizing observed behaviors in an untransformed manner. Rather, learners of all ages and levels of expertise and interests seed the environment with ideas and knowledge that are appropriated by different learners at different rates, according to their needs and to the current state of the zones of proximal development in which they are engaged.

The third central concept that guides our thinking is that of mutual negotiation. Via emergent discourse genres and activity structures, meaning is constantly negotiated and renegotiated by members of the community. Speech activities involving increasingly scientific modes of thinking, such as conjecture, speculation, evidence, and proof, become part of the common voice of the community; conjecture and proof themselves are open to renegotiation in multiple ways (Bloor, 1991) as the elements that compose them, such as terms and definitions (O'Connor, 1991), are renegotiated continuously. Successful enculturation into the community leads participants to relinquish everyday versions of speech activities having to do with the physical and natural world and replace them with "discipline embedded special versions of the same activities" (O'Connor, 1991).

The core participant structures of our classrooms are essentially dialogic. Sometimes these activities are undertaken face to face in small or large group interactions; sometimes they are mediated via print or electronic mail; and at still other times they go underground and become part of the thought processes of individual members of the community (Vygotsky, 1978). Dialogues provide the format for novices to adopt the discourse structure, goals, values, and belief systems of scientific practice. Over time, the community of learners adopts a common voice and common knowledge base (Edwards & Mercer, 1987), a shared system of meaning, beliefs, and activity that is as often implicit as it is explicit.

The metaphor of a classroom supporting multiple, overlapping zones of proximal development that foster growth through mutual appropriation and negotiated meaning is the theoretical window through which we view the system of classroom activity and the community practices that arise within it. In the next section we will turn to the practical, and describe how we attempt to engineer daily activity so that classrooms can be transformed into learning communities.

### Engineering a community of learners

Over the past five years, we have been engaged in several attempts to design innovative classroom practices that would encourage students, teachers, and researchers to rethink the philosophy of learning that underlies their practices. In this section, we first delineate the basic classroom activity structures, then describe how we foster the classroom ethos that would permit intentional learning and distributed expertise. We discuss data from a variety of repetitions of our design experiments (Brown, 1992; Collins, in press), but in general the students are fifth- through seventh-graders from inner-city schools. In one representative sixth-grade class, 60% of the students were African Americans, 15% Asian, 12% Caucasian, 6% Pacific Islanders, and 7% other. Forty-two percent of the families of these children were recipients of Aid to Families with Dependent Children. The majority of the children can be described as academically at risk on the basis of standardized scores that paint an unduly pessimistic picture of their capabilities. It is important to note that the children in this classroom were emergent language learners in many ways. In addition to the fact that 87% were bilingual or bidialectical, all were being introduced to the discourse of science for the first time (Ochs, 1991; Rutherford, 1991).

### Main features of the classroom

*Collaborative learning.* Two forms of collaborative learning serve as repetitive structures in the classroom: reciprocal teaching (Palincsar & Brown, 1984) and the jigsaw method (Aronson, 1978).

*Reciprocal teaching* is a method of enhancing reading comprehension modeled after studies of Socratic or Inquiry teaching and theories about plausible reasoning, explanation, and analogy (Brown & Palincsar, 1989; Collins & Stevens, 1982). The procedure was designed to encourage the externalization of simple comprehension-monitoring activities and to provide a repetitive structure to bolster student discourse. An adult teacher and a group of students take turns leading a discussion, the leader beginning by *asking a question* and ending by *summarizing* the gist of what has been read. The group rereads and discusses possible problems of interpretation when necessary. Questioning provides the impetus for discussion. Summarizing at the end of a period of discussion helps students establish where they are in preparation for tackling a new segment of text. Attempts to *clarify* any comprehension problems that might arise occur opportunistically, and the leaders asks for *predictions* about future content. These four activities – questioning, clarifying, summarizing, and predicting – were selected to bolster the discussion because they are excellent comprehension-monitoring devices; for example, an inability to summarize what has been read indicates that understanding is not proceeding smoothly and remedial action is called for. The strategies also provide the repeatable structure necessary to get a discussion going, a structure that can be gradually eliminated when students are experienced in the discourse mode (Brown & Palincsar, 1989).

In the context of these reciprocal reading groups, students with various levels of skill and expertise can participate to the extent that they are able and benefit from the variety of expertise displayed by other members of the group. Reciprocal teaching was deliberately designed to evoke zones of proximal development within which novices could take on increasing responsibility for more expert roles. The group cooperation ensures mature performance, even if individual members of the group are not yet capable of full participation.

An important point about reciprocal teaching is that the authenticity of the target task (text comprehension) is maintained throughout; components are handled in the context of an authentic task, reading for meaning; skills are practiced in context. The aim of understanding the texts remains as undisturbed as possible, and the novice's role is made easier by the provision of expert scaffolding and a supportive social context that does a great deal of the cognitive work until the novice can take over more and more of the responsibility. The task, however, remains the same, the goal the same, the desired outcome the same. There is little room for confusion about the point of the activity. As we have argued before:

> The cooperative feature of the learning group in reciprocal teaching, where everyone is trying to arrive at consensus concerning meaning, relevance, and importance, is an ideal setting for novices to practice their emergent skills. All the responsibility for comprehending does not lie on their shoulders, only part of the work is theirs, and even if they falter when called on to be discussion leaders, the others, including the adult teacher, are there to keep the discussion going. The group shares the responsibility for thinking and thus reduces the anxiety associated with keeping the argument going singlehandedly. Because the group's efforts are externalized in the form of a discussion, novices can contribute what they are able and learn from the contributions of those more expert than they. It is in this sense, the reciprocal teaching dialogues create a zone of proximal development for their participants, each of whom

may share in the activity to the extent that he or she is able. Collaboratively, the group, with its variety of expertise, engagement, and goals, gets the job done; the text gets read and understood. (Brown & Palincsar, 1989, p. 415)

The *jigsaw method* of cooperative learning was adapted from Aronson (1978). Students are assigned part of a classroom topic to learn and subsequently to teach to others via reciprocal teaching. In our extrapolation of this method, the setting is an intact science classroom where students are responsible for doing collaborative research and sharing their expertise with their colleagues. In effect, the students are partially responsible for designing their own curriculum. Students are assigned curriculum themes (e.g., animal defense mechanisms, changing populations, food chains), each divided into five subtopics (e.g., for changing populations: extinct, endangered, artificial, assisted, and urbanized; for food chains: producing, consuming, recycling, distributing, and energy exchange). Students form five *research groups*, each assigned responsibility for one of the five subtopics. The research groups prepare teaching materials using state-of-the-art but inexpensive computer technology (Campione et al., 1992). Then, using the jigsaw method, the students regroup into *learning groups* in which each student is the expert in one subtopic, holding one-fifth of the information. Each fifth is combined with the remaining fifths to make a whole unit, hence "jigsaw." The expert on each subtopic is responsible for guiding reciprocal teaching learning seminars in his or her area. Thus, the choice of a learning leader is now based on expertise rather than random selection, as was the case in the original reciprocal teaching work. All children in a learning group are experts on one part of the material, teach it to others, and prepare questions for the test that all will take on the complete unit.

*The research cycle.* In a typical research cycle, lasting approximately 10 weeks, the classroom teacher or a visiting expert introduces a unit with a whole class discussion, a benchmark lesson (Minstrell, 1989) in which she elicits what the students already know about the topic and what they would like to find out. She also stresses the "big picture," the underlying theme of that unit and how the interrelated subtopics form a jigsaw; the complete story can be told only if each research group plays its part. Subsequent benchmark lessons are held opportunistically to stress the main theme and interconnectedness of the activities and to lead the students to higher levels of thinking. The students see that their studies are connected to larger global issues. Gradually, distributed expertise in the various groups of students is recognized. Students turn to a particular group for clarification of information that is seen to be within their domain. Faced with questions and information from nonexperts, the research teams upgrade, revise, and refine their research agendas.

The majority of time is spent in the research-and-teach part of the cycle. Here the students generate questions, a process that is under continual revision. They plan their research activities and gather information using books, videos, and their own field notes, all with the help of Browser (Campione et al., 1992), an electronic card catalog, developed for use on the Macintosh system, that enables children to find materials via cross-classification (e.g., "Find me all examples of insect mimicry in the rain forest"). Students also have access, via electronic mail, to experts in a wider community of learners, including biologists, computer experts, and staff at zoos, museums, and other sources.

At intervals during the research cycle, students break up into reciprocal teaching sessions to attempt to teach their evolving material to their peers. Fueled by questions from their peers that they cannot answer, they redirect their research and undertake revisions of a booklet covering their part of the information. Reciprocal teaching sessions are also scheduled opportunistically by the students themselves when a research group decides that a particular article is crucial for their argument and is difficult to understand. Reciprocal teaching thus becomes a form of self-initiated comprehension monitoring.

At the end of the unit, the students conduct full reciprocal teaching sessions in groups composed such that each child is an expert on one-fifth of the material. They teach their material to one another. Finally, the students as a whole class conduct a quiz game in preparation for a test covering all sections of the material. This test is composed of questions made up by the research teams on their material, supplemented by items generated by the teacher. A whole-class debriefing session follows the test, where students discuss not only "right" versus "wrong" answers but whether or not the questions were important, meaningful, or just plain fair. After this experience, the students revise their booklets and combine them into a single whole-class book on the entire unit, consisting of the five separate sections of the five research teams together with an overall introduction and discussion concentrating on the common theme and big picture to which all subunits contributed. This research cycle is then repeated with the next unit.

*The ethos of the classroom.* In order for these classrooms to be successful, it is imperative that a certain ethos be established early and maintained throughout. How this is done is difficult to describe and equally difficult to transmit to novice teachers except through demonstration, modeling, and guided feedback. Expert teachers claim to recognize "it" when they see it. But what is it?

We believe that the classroom climate that can foster a community of learners harbors four main qualities. First is an atmosphere of individual responsibility coupled with communal sharing. Students and teachers each have "ownership" of certain forms of expertise but no one has it all. Responsible members of the community share the expertise they have or take responsibility for finding out about needed knowledge. Through a variety of interactive formats, the group uncovers and delineates aspects of knowledge "possessed" by no one individual. The atmosphere of joint responsibility is critical for this enterprise.

Coupled with joint responsibility comes respect, respect among students, between students and school staff, and among all members of the extended community that includes experts available by electronic mail (as described later). Students' questions are taken seriously. Experts, be they children or adults, do not always know the answers; known-answer question-and-answering games (Heath, 1983; Mehan, 1979) have no home in this environment. Respect is earned by responsible participation in a genuine knowledge-building community (Scardamalia & Bereiter, 1991). When an atmosphere of respect and responsibility is operating in the classroom, it is manifested in several ways. One excellent example is turn taking. Compared with many excerpts of classroom dialogue, we see relatively little overlapping discourse. Students listen to one another.

Concomitant with this development is the emergence of children who become experts in social facilitation and dispute reconciliation. Consider this diplomatic statement from a student who, at the beginning of the intervention, was notorious for his arrogance and inability to admit to being wrong – or to listen:

At first I thought I agreed with S [that pandas are fat because they are indolent], except it really takes a lot of exertion to climb trees. It does. They must burn their energy climbing because remember we saw them in that laser disc . . . how the panda was climbing trees to get to the bamboo.

I'm sort of getting two pictures. First you're saying there's plenty of bamboo, and they sit around and munch it all day and then you say that their bamboo is dying off. Can you sort of set me straight?

This brings us to the third critical aspect of the classroom: A community of discourse (Fish, 1980) is established early in which constructive discussion, questioning, and criticism are the mode rather than the exception. Meaning is negotiated and renegotiated as members of the community develop and share expertise. The group comes to construct new understandings, developing a common mind and common voice (Wertsch, 1991).

The final aspect of these classrooms is that of ritual. Participation frameworks (Goodwin, 1987) are few and are practiced repeatedly so that students, and indeed observers, can tell immediately what format the class is operating under at any one period of time. One common way of organizing the classroom is to divide the students into three groups, those composing on computers, those conducting research via a variety of media, and those interacting with the classroom teacher in some way: editing manuscripts, discussing progress, or receiving some other form of teacher attention. Another repetitive frame is one in which the class is engaged in reciprocal teaching or jigsaw group activities, with approximately five research/learning groups in simultaneous sessions. Still another activity is one in which the classroom teacher or an outside expert conducts a benchmark lesson, introducing new items, stressing higher-order relationships, or encouraging the students to pool their expertise in a novel conceptualization of the topic.

The repetitive, indeed ritualistic, nature of these activities is an essential aspect of the classroom, for it enables children to make the transition from one participant structure (Erickson & Schultz, 1977) to another quickly and effortlessly. As soon as students recognize a participant structure, they understand the role expected of them. Thus, although there is room for discovery in these classrooms, they are highly structured to permit students and teachers to navigate between repetitive activities with as little effort as possible.

### Distributed expertise

In order to foster and capitalize on distributed expertise, certain classroom rituals are deliberately engineered for that effect while other opportunities arise serendipitously. As described before, the two major forms of collaborative learning, jigsaw and reciprocal teaching, are designed so that students will teach from strength. In addition to the two main teaching/learning activity structures, expertise is intentionally distributed through the practice of instructing only a few children in some aspect of knowledge – for example, when novel computer applications are introduced. Only one group receives instruction in the use of, say, a scanner that will enable them to copy pictures and text, including their own compositions, directly into their documents. It is the responsibility of each designated group to tutor all other students in the class in the use of a particular application. Students who have this responsibility behave differently from those who do not, repeating what the teacher says and attempting to perform each step before proceeding, a form of self-monitoring. It may take several repetitions of this selective teaching for students to take their responsibility seriously. They must realize that unless the scanner students share their newfound knowledge, members of their class will be denied expertise in the use of this tool. But by the same token, the scanner students are dependent on those who have privileged access to, say, MacDraw, in order to learn that application. In this way, an atmosphere of mutual dependency and trust is built up, with students recognizing shared responsibility for knowledge dissemination.

Expertise is distributed by design, but in addition variability in expertise arises naturally within these classrooms. We refer to this phenomenon as "majoring." Children are free to major in a variety of ways, free to learn and teach whatever they like within the confines of the selected topic. Children select topics of interest to be associated with: Some become resident experts on DDT and pesticides; some specialize in disease and contagion; some adopt a particular endangered species (pandas, otters, and whales being popular). Others become animal "trivial-pursuit" experts, amassing a body of knowledge about rare and unusual animals. Still others become environmental activists, collecting instances of outrages from magazines, television, and even newspapers, and demanding that the class write to Congress and complain. And still others become experts in graphics and desktop publishing and other aspects of the technology; for although all students are inducted into the basics of the computer environment, progression to the use of increasingly complex software is a matter of choice. Within the community of the classroom, these varieties of expertise are implicitly recognized, although not the subject of much talk. As the children are free to ask help of the adults or one another, help-seeking behavior reveals who is seen to own what "skills," what "piece" of the knowledge, and so on. Subcultures of expertise develop: who knows about Cricket or Powerpoint; who can help you back up files; who knows everything there is to know about the *Valdez* oil spill; and so on.

Another interesting phenomenon is the process by which this knowledge is disseminated. For example, consider the computer mavens. In one study, in order to whet the children's interest, we added software without telling them. A minority of the children enjoyed this game, eager to find out what the new icon in their desktop was. When they had learned how to use it (with expert help), they spread this information to a subset of other computer majors and to no one else. The members of this subcommunity were clearly recognized by both in-group members and the community at large, as witnessed by the depth of knowledge dissemination within the group and the pattern of help-seeking behavior by noncognoscenti.

Recognition of expertise was also reflected in the roles students assumed in the discussions. When an expert child made a statement, the class deferred to that child in both verbal and nonverbal ways. Status in the discussion did not reside in the individual child, however, as in the case of established leaders and followers, but was a transient phenomenon that depended on a child's perceived expertise within the domain of discourse. As the domain of discourse changed, so too did the students who received deferential treatment.

Table 7.1. *Changes in classroom philosophy*

| Role of | Traditional classroom | Intentional learning environment |
|---|---|---|
| Students | Passive recipients of incoming information | Students as researchers, teachers, and monitors of progress |
| Teachers | Didactic teaching | Guided discovery |
| | Classroom manager | Model of active inquiry |
| Content | Basic literacy curriculum, lower vs. higher skills | Thinking as basic literacy |
| | Content curriculum | Content curriculum |
| | Breadth | Depth |
| | Fragmented | Recurrent themes |
| | Fragmented | Explanatory coherence |
| | Fact retention | Understanding |
| Computers | Drill and practice | Tools for intentional reflection |
| | Programming | Learning and collaboration |
| Assessment | Fact retention | Knowledge discovery and utilization |
| | Traditional tests | Performance, projects, portfolio |

## Traditional classrooms versus communities of learners

The activity patterns in our classrooms contrast in striking ways with those in traditional classrooms. We present a few examples in Table 7.1. These contrasts should be viewed as ends of continua rather than dichotomous; as bald dichotomies they represent stereotypes.

Far from being passive recipients of incoming information, students take on the role of active researchers and teachers, monitoring their own progress and that of others when they adopt the role of constructive critics. Teachers, also, are no longer managers and didactic teachers, but models of active learning and guides to aid the students' learning. The content is intended as a "thinking curriculum" (Resnick, 1987), where depth of understanding and explanatory coherence are valued over breadth of coverage and fact retention. Computers are used as tools for communication and collaboration, but also as aids to reflective learning – students set their own learning goals and monitor their own progress (Brown & Campione, 1990;

Scardamalia & Bereiter, 1991). Finally, tests and assessments are on-line and dynamic, concentrating again on the understanding and use of knowledge rather than fact retention.

In the context of this chapter, it is important to note that the design of our classrooms is itself an excellent example of the influence of distributed expertise. A main tenet of the design experiment is that of a meaningful collaboration between teachers and researchers. We aim at the development of both teacher-researchers and researcher-teachers. Whereas some in our group have devoted the lion's share of their professional activities to theory and research on children's thinking and learning, others have specialized in biology or technology, and still others have been more concerned with the practical orchestration of learning in the classroom. No set of individuals has a complete set of answers, and the multiple and distributed pieces of expertise are equally valued. Discussions involving these groups – as with the discussions among students, between students and adults, and so on – provide a setting for mutual appropriation. The ideas that emerge in the discourse, and their implementation in the class-room, are dictated or owned by no individual group, but are substantially influenced by all. In this process, an instructional program emerges, and all the participants come away with appreciably altered understandings.

In this section, we will amplify this theme and consider five roles within the community of learners that contribute to an atmosphere of distributed expertise: those of the student, teacher, curriculum, technology, and assessment.

*The role of students.*    Students are asked to serve as teachers, editors, advisers, and mentors, making comments on one another's work and entering a network of learners with various degrees of expertise in the domain. In addition, rather than just reading about science, they are asked to do science through hands-on experiments, constructively criticizing the work of others, and seeing their work come to fruition in published forms. Students are encouraged to think of themselves as junior scientists, to the extent possible, rather than functioning only as consumers of others' science.

An essential part of the classroom is establishing a collaborative and cooperative atmosphere. Students are required to collaborate most directly in their research groups, but they also collaborate with other groups and with community members outside the classroom walls. In the course of doing research, students are bound to encounter information that would be helpful to other groups, and we encourage them to communicate those findings, verbally or electronically. Similarly, when students share their long-term projects in jigsaw, they are encouraged to provide feedback to one another, including both constructive criticism and suggestions about additional information sources.

*The role of teachers.* Although teachers and students view themselves as community members, the adult teacher is clearly first among equals, for she has a clear instructional goal. In many forms of cooperative learning, students are left to construct learning goals for themselves; the goals change over time as interests change, and groups sometimes concoct goals far different from those envisaged by the authorities (Barnes & Todd, 1977). In our classroom, the research direction of the group is not so democratic: The adult teacher's goal is clearly one of keeping the discussion focused on the content and seeing that enough discussion takes place to ensure a reasonable level of understanding.

Teachers are encouraged to hold goals for each research group, with the hope that the students will reach those goals through their own efforts. But if they do not, the teacher will invite the students to arrive at a mature understanding by whatever means she can, including, as a last resort, explicit instruction. Teachers and researchers construct goals for what they want each research group to accomplish. The jigsaw method is dependent on each group of students' understanding and conveying their material to others. It is imperative, for example, that the students responsible for photosynthesis understand this difficult concept that is a mainspring of the entire food chain unit. If students do not achieve robust understanding without aid, the teacher must engineer methods that ensure that understanding.

Teachers in the program are also made aware of common misconceptions that students may harbor concerning, for example, the nature of plants (Bell, 1985) or natural selection (Brumby, 1979). Armed with this information, teachers are better able to recognize the occurrence of misconceptions and fallacious reasoning so that they may then confront students with counterexamples or other challenges to their inchoate knowledge – for example, by having students who believe that plants suck up food through the soil conduct experiments on hydroponic gardening.

Clearly, we do not advocate untrammeled discovery learning (Brown, 1992). Although there is considerable evidence that didactic teaching leads to passive learning, by the same token unguided discovery can be dangerous too. Children "discovering" in our biology classrooms are quite adept at inventing scientific misconceptions. For example, they readily become Lamarckians, believing that acquired characteristics of individuals are passed on and that all things exist for a purpose. They overdetermine cause, thus blinding themselves to essential notions of randomness and spontaneity (the teleological stance: Keil, 1989; Mayr, 1988). Teachers are encouraged to see these common problems as fruitful errors, waystages on the route to mature understanding that they can manipulate and direct in useful ways.

But the role of the teacher in discovery learning classrooms is problematic. It is still largely uncharted. Invoking comfortable metaphors such as the teacher as coach does not tell us how and when the teacher should coach. We know that challenging students' assumptions, providing them with counterexamples to their own rules, and so on are good instructional activities; but how intrusive should the teacher be? When should she guide? When should she teach? When should she leave well enough alone? In short, how can the teacher foster discovery and at the same time furnish guidance?

We encourage our teachers to adopt the middle ground of *guided discovery,* but this role is difficult to maintain. Consider the position of a teacher who knows something the students do not. Here she is in the position of making a judgment about whether to intervene. She must decide whether the problem centers on an important principle or involves only a trivial error that she can let pass for now. Consider a teacher who does not know the answer, or one who may share the students' puzzlement or misconception. She is first required to recognize this fact (which she might not be able to do) and, after admitting puzzlement or confusion, find ways to remedy it – for example, by seeking help. This is not an easy role for many teachers; it demands competence and confidence. The connection to a wider community of learners and experts that electronic mail provides encourages classroom teachers to admit that they do not know and seek help, thereby modeling this important learning strategy for their students.

Guided learning is easier to talk about than do. It takes clinical judgment to know when to intervene. The successful teacher must continually engage in on-line diagnosis of student understanding. She must be sensitive to current overlapping zones of proximal development, where certain students are ripe for new learning. She must renegotiate zones of proximal development so that still other students might become ready for conceptual growth. She must appropriate and capitalize on emergent ideas and help refine them and link them to enduring themes. Determining the region of sensitivity to instruction (Wood, Bruner, & Ross, 1976) for the whole class, a subgroup, or an individual child, on-line and unaided, if it is not magic (Bandler & Grinder, 1975), is certainly a work of art. Guided discovery places a great deal of responsibility in the hands of the teacher, who must model, foster, and guide the "discovery" process into forms of disciplined inquiry that would not be reached without expert guidance (Brown, 1992; Bruner, 1969).

In addition to guiding a course through the curriculum content, the teacher should also be a role model for certain forms of inquiry activities. If students are apprentice learners, the teacher is the master craftsperson of learning whom they must emulate. In this role, the teacher models scientific inquiry through thought and real experiments. Children witness teachers learning, discovering, doing research, reading, writing, and using computers as tools for learning, rather than lecturing, managing, assigning work, and controlling the classroom exclusively.

The teacher's job is also to encourage habits of mind by which children are encouraged to adopt, extrapolate, and refine the underlying themes to which they are exposed. Bruner (1969) argues that education

should be an invitation to generalize, to extrapolate, to make a tentative intuitive leap, even to build a tentative theory. The leap from mere learning to using what one has learned in thinking is an essential step in the use of the mind. Indeed, plausible guessing, the use of the heuristic hunch, the best employment of necessarily insufficient evidence – these are the activities in which the child needs practice and guidance. They are among the great antidotes to passivity. (p. 124)

But again, this requires not untrammeled discovery learning, but the expert guidance of a gifted teacher.

*The role of the curriculum.*   The teacher's role is a complex one; she is constantly faced with seemingly conflicting responsibilities: She must see that curriculum content is "discovered," understood, and transmitted efficiently, and at the same time she must recognize and encourage students' independent majoring attempts. This brings us to the thorny question of the role of a set curriculum in discovery classrooms. True, it would be possible to allow the students to discover on their own, charting their own course of studies, exploring at will, but in order to be responsive to the course requirements of normal schools, we must set bounds on the curriculum to be covered.

In general our approach is to select enduring themes for discussion and to revisit them often, each time at an increasingly mature level of understanding. For example, in the biology classroom, we concentrate on interdependence and adaptation. In the environmental science classroom, themes might include balance, competition and cooperation, and predator–prey relations that are central to an understanding of ecosystems. In the health education classroom, an understanding of disease and contagion is central. Although we aim at depth over breadth in coverage, we decided against recourse to biochemical substrata with middle school children. Instead, the students are invited into the world of the nineteenth-century naturalist, where they read, do research, conduct experiments, participate in field trips, and engage in various forms of data collection and analysis around the central repeating themes.

In choosing our curriculum units we try to focus on a few "lithe and beautiful and immensely generative" ideas, to use Bruner's classic phrase (Bruner, 1969, p. 121). We believe that it is unreasonable to expect children to reinvent these ideas for themselves. Providing expert guidance, in the form of teachers, books, and other artifacts, is one of the prime responsibilities of schooling. Immensely generative ideas may be few, and the idea behind education is to point children in the right direction so that they might discover and rediscover these ideas continuously, so that on each encounter the theme will be recognized and students may deepen their understanding in a cyclical fashion (Bruner, 1969). Certain central themes are seeded early by the teacher and revisited often.

While seeding the environment with generative ideas, the teacher is also free to encourage the knowledge-majoring activities of individual children or groups of mavericks who choose to do even more specialized work than that invited by the curriculum topics shared by all. Because of these self-initiated tangents, no two classes cover exactly the same material, even though they are seeded by the same teacher talk and the same supports, including books, videos, and experiments. For example, one sixth-grade class devoted two weeks of research to uncovering the history and effects of DDT because DDT had been featured in a play they had enacted and in a passage they had been reading in reciprocal teaching sessions. The classroom teacher was not prepared for this departure; her first response was to urge them on to the next part of the curriculum that she had scheduled; but then she capitalized on their knowledge and interest in order to introduce the higher-level theme of systemic disruption in food webs using their DDT knowledge as a basis, a good example of mutual appropriation.

Similarly, in one sixth-grade class, certain children became deeply involved with cross-cutting themes that would form the basis of an understanding of such principles as metabolic rate, reproduction strategies, and hibernation as a survival strategy. A member of the group studying elephants became fixated on the amount of food consumed, first, by his animal, the elephant, and, subsequently, by other animals studied in the classroom, notably the panda and the sea otter. Although relatively small, the sea otter consumes vast quantities of food because, as the student wrote, "It doesn't have blubber, and living in a cold sea, it needs food for energy to keep warm." When an adult observer mentioned the similar case of the hummingbird's need for a great deal of food, this student caught on to something akin to the notion of metabolic rate, a concept he talked about in most subsequent discussions.

Two girls studying whales became interested in fertility rates and the fate of low birth weight babies. They discovered that one reason certain species of whales are endangered is that their reproduction rate has slowed dramatically. They also discovered that the peregrine falcon's inability to produce eggs with protective shells was a cause of endangerment. Talking to an adult observer, they asked about the fate of low birth weight babies, because "they don't have those little baby boxes [incubators] in the wild and can't feed them with tubes." They decided that low birth weight babies would be "the first to die" – "good prey for predators." Again, these students introduced the concept of declining fertility rates into the discussion, and it was taken up in the common discourse in two forms: simply as the notion of the number of babies a given species had and, more complexly, as the notion of reproductive strategies in general. The teacher appropriated the students' spontaneous interest in the common problems of endangered animals – amount of food eaten, amount of land required, number of young, and so on – and encouraged them to consider the deeper general principles of metabolic rate, and survival and reproductive strategies.

*The role of technology.*    Our classrooms have the support of sophisticated state-of-the-art technology, including computers and video materials. Although some have argued that technology has had, and will have, little impact on the way teachers teach (Cuban, 1986), others have argued that the availability of supportive computer environments could have a fundamental effect on learning and teaching in classrooms (Schank & Jona, 1991). Currently, computers are used in grade school primarily to replace teachers as managers of drill and practice or to teach children to program. But the problem with these activities is that most people do *not* use computers in this fashion – they use personal computers as just that, personal tools to aid learning. They use word processing and desktop publishing (including ready access to graphics and perhaps spreadsheets). They set up and access their knowledge files. They use electronic mail. We believe this is how grade school children should initially view computers – as invaluable tools for their own sustained learning: building up a portfolio, maintaining and revising their files, using graphics tools, and networking. We want them to harness technology as a means of enhancing their thinking – planning and revising their learning goals, monitoring and reflecting on their own progress as they construct personal knowledge files and share a communal database.

Although several extremely powerful computer environments have been developed (see particularly CSILE, Scardamalia & Bereiter, 1991), we chose to work with commercially produced and stable software available to any school and capable of running on relatively inexpensive hardware (for details see Campione et al., 1992). This computer environment was designed to (1) simplify student access to research materials, including books, magazines, videotapes, and videodiscs; (2) support writing, illustrating, and revising texts; (3) allow for data storage and management; and (4) facilitate communication within and beyond the classroom.

We will discuss two aspects of the computer environment critical to a discussion of distributed expertise: (1) computer activities that facilitate thinking and (2) computer activities that help shape thought.

1. *Facilitating thinking.* We will limit our attention to two features of the environment that encourage the kinds of thinking we wish to facilitate in the classroom. These involve two applications, QuickMail and Browser.

Our students make use of a commercially available, child-friendly electronic mail package called "QuickMail." With QuickMail, students can send messages electronically to members of the classroom, to their teacher, and to mentors at the university and elsewhere in the community. Communication does not rely on the memorization of elaborate codes or typing efficiency; to make contact with another individual or group, the child needs only to "click" on an icon visually depicting the target – for example, a picture of a peer or adult, or a token of a group (e.g., a dolphin for the Dolphins). In addition, the system is customized by the design of special forms that facilitate specific interactions – for example, a "permission to publish" form that students use when they wish to publish in the system or a "junior scientist to senior scientist" message form. It also provides a simple way for students to enclose within their messages documents created with other applications.

The use of QuickMail was rapidly established only in classrooms where the teacher provided support and encouragement and, most important, modeled the use of the application herself. It was also rapidly established as part of classroom practice when there was a clear purpose for the activity, one such purpose being the necessity to communicate with community members outside the classroom.

QuickMail use was only sporadic if the classroom teacher did not use it herself, or when communication was restricted to those within the same four walls. Indeed, why would one QuickMail a query to a peer sitting five feet away?

In one successful QuickMail classroom, the teacher (MR) modeled the use of computers on a daily basis, spending a minimum of one hour a day using the computers in the classroom, communicating through QuickMail, or doing miscellaneous writing or planning tasks (ranging from organizing a kickball game to preparing homework assignments). As she put it, "They see me using the computer all the time." MR's attitude toward both her own and her students' use of computers was extremely positive, and there was a strong sense in the classroom of the teacher enthusiastically *joining* with the students in the use of the computers. MR overtly encouraged and supported student use. She talked explicitly and often about the computer as a tool that can make many different activities easier. She explained:

I really want the kids to see that they're . . . using the computer like they would use a pencil. Only it's more high tech, so it does some things nicely that they would otherwise have to do using a more laborious process. . . . It's simply ways to make what you already are going to do easier . . . so you can go about the business of learning what you want to learn. . . . And I really don't want them to think that I couldn't do this unless I had a computer, but because I have a computer, I can do that much more.

MR also had early and consistent recourse to the use of QuickMail herself, corresponding with the students concerning their written projects, assignments, and often their personal life. She also corresponded with fellow members of the research team at Berkeley in the presence of students, thereby modeling the transmission of queries and comments and the receipt of replies. Students readily began communicating with one another and the university staff, due in good part to this modeling and encouragement. As a result the students used electronic mail as a routine part of classroom life.

QuickMail became another forum for creating zones of proximal development involving students and the community at large. For example, consider the following exchange between a graduate student (MJ) with a biology background and a group of students (Da 4 Girlz). The interaction was initiated by the students, who asked about the status of hibernation for incarcerated bears:

Our major questions are (WHAT HAPPENS TO THE BEARS THAT LIVE IN THE ZOO IF THEY CAN'T HIBERNATE?). DA [the science teacher] said that they don't need to hibernate because they are fed every day. But she said that was only a thought so I am asking you to please help us by giving us all you know and all you can find.

The graduate student responded with some information; admitting that he didn't really know the answer, he suggested a hypothesis and provided a phone number the group could call to find out more information on their own. Throughout the interchange, the graduate student systematically seeded three pieces of information critical for an understanding of hibernation: the availability of resources, longevity, and warm- versus cold-bloodedness:

You probably think about hibernating in the same way as you think about sleeping, but they aren't the same. Bears hibernate in response to the weather conditions and the availability of food. If the conditions are reasonably fair (not too cold) and food is available the bear probably won't hibernate. I don't know, but I hypothesize that during the times when bears would usually hibernate, bears in captivity are probably a bit slower, still showing signs of their tendency to hibernate at that time of the year.

How could you find out if my hypothesis is true? (Hint: Knowland Park Zoo, 632-9523)

The topic is then dropped by the group but taken up by one group member (AM) who is "majoring" in hibernation and wishes to know about hibernation patterns in insects. She inquires of the network in general:

I was wondering if you can find out an answer to this question. The question is does insects hibernate? The reason why we ask that is because MR [classroom teacher] read a book named Once There was A Tree. And in it, it said something about the insects slept in the bark of the tree when winter came, then when spring came they got up and did what they usually do till winter comes then they start all over again.

Receiving no response, the student then addresses the graduate student directly about the topic. As a gesture of good faith, she begins by offering some facts of her own before asking for information:

Bears hibernate because what ever they eat is gone during the winter (like berries) and they can't eat so that's what hibernation is for. It is for them to get away from starvation. So what does truantula's eat? Can they always get their food? If they can't get their food would they have to hibernate or die? Could we ask somebody that knows about insects?

The graduate student responds with another prompt to encourage the student to take the initiative and contact experts, this time at the San Francisco Zoo, pointing out that the contact person there is ready and willing to help. On receiving yet another request for information from the persistent AM, the graduate student re-enters the fray. Following a lengthy paragraph on the reproduction and survival strategies of insects, he continues with a series of questions intended to push the student to further and further depths of inquiry, a typical strategy of guides in a zone of proximal development. In this communication, he introduces the notion of longevity, prompting AM to consider the fact that if an insect lives only one season, hibernation would not have much survival value for the species!

So you ask . . . what does this have to do with your questions about hibernation? Consider the difference between the life style of your typical mammal and that of the typical insect. Why is hibernation important to some mammals? Why might hibernation not be a successful strategy for most insects? Some insects, such as tarantulas, live for 10 or more years. Do you think that they might hibernate? How might their life style be different from that of other insects?

Resisting this lead, the student again adopts the easier path of asking for direct information. "I'm not really sure if a tarantula hibernates. What do you think?" to which the graduate student again responds with some critical information about warm-bloodedness:

I'm really not sure either. I do know that insects are cold blooded, which means that they don't have a constant body temperature. This means that they depend on warmth from the sun or other objects in order to become active (move around and hunt). This happens pretty much every day. As the sun sets, it gets cold and cold-blooded animals slow down. But hibernation is something that happens over a greater period of time (over a year rather than a day). Where do you think we could find out more about this question?

The interaction continued for several days. The graduate student has seeded the zone of proximal development with three critical pieces of information during this exchange. AM picks up on two of these features (availability of resources and longevity), although she never understands warm-bloodedness. QuickMail has exciting possibilities as a medium for sustaining and expanding zones of proximal development and is an essential feature of our learning environment, freeing teachers from the burden of being sole guardians of knowledge and allowing the community to extend beyond the classroom walls.

QuickMail is also used frequently as a private means of discussing personal dilemmas, both among students and between students and the classroom teacher. Less often such personal queries arise in discourse with outside experts. Buried in a series of legitimate questions about biological issues, a student asks a researcher: "I also wanted to know how you came about making your career about science do you really like science or do you have to know someone special to get into the field of science?" The response, again tactfully buried in legitimate science discourse, was:

I just got interested in science when I was in grade school, and decided that was what I was going to try to do when I grew up, and it worked! To answer one of your questions, you don't have to know anyone to get into science, you just have to have an interest in it and the motivation to work hard to get good at it. Actually, I didn't know any scientists when I was young, and no one in my family had ever gone to University before I did. Since you are working with the University now, you know more scientists than I did.

QuickMail is an indispensable extension of the learning community outside the classroom walls, and not just in terms of content-specific expertise.

*2. Shaping thought.* The second application, "Browser," enhances and organizes shared thinking. We designed Browser (written in HyperCard 2.0) for several reasons. First, it allows filing of, and searching through, documents by topics (e.g., animal defense mechanisms) and themes (e.g., camouflage, mimicry). Browser is a hierarchical system featuring three main windows, one providing a list of topics, a second the themes associated with each topic, and the third a list of resources. Opening the resources window results in a list of all the titles available. Use of the themes and topics windows pares down that list considerably. For example, if a student opens the topics window and highlights animal defense mechanisms, the resources display is reduced to all entries having to do with that topic. If the themes window is also opened, and camouflage selected, the list of entries is further reduced to those satisfying both constraints. Thus, to use Browser effectively, students must specify in some detail what information they need; that is, they must pose their research question sharply. This is not a skill entering students possess. Their initial uses of Browser consist almost exclusively of opening the resources window and scanning the set of titles in an attempt to find something that may be relevant. It is only with prompting and practice that they come to understand the need for specifying their research needs in sufficient detail to organize and restrict their search. In this way, Browser is one of several aspects of the environment that lead students to appreciate the need for, and practice, formulating specific questions.

Given a topic and theme, Browser generates a list of titles and indicates the media type (text, magazine, videotape, or videodisc) of each entry. If a specific selection is stored on the file server, the student can call it up directly. Browser also allows students to expand the system by generating their own themes and topics and by writing their own summaries and comments on new selections. We begin by providing examples of summaries for some of the basic entries, but after the students become familiar with the system, they generate and discuss their own summaries and comments. Furthermore, when students choose to publish their own work, they are required to generate key words, in the form of general topics and subthemes, and to provide a summary. Over time, the library becomes progressively more annotated by the students themselves, with their entries providing us with important data concerning their ability to cross-classify and summarize and indicate what they see as significant. Because of student authoring, no two classes generate the same Browser.

We emphasize again that the very act of using Browser serves as a scaffold to certain forms of thought processes such as hierarchical organization and double classification. In this way aspects of the computer environment shape as well as augment the shared knowledge base of the class. We first noticed the way in which increasing competence with the software affected the organization of thought in an earlier experiment when the children had access to only HyperCard and Microsoft Word (Brown & Campione, 1990). Limited exposure to HyperCard was not successful. The method of organization was not transparent to children, and it encouraged some well-known bad research and writing habits of children this age, such as the copy–delete strategy whereby students merely copy sections from a text, deleting what they regard as uninformative (Brown & Day, 1983). Once a card was filled, that was the end of that thought. The idea that a thought could extend for more than one card was never entertained. And the organization structure of the cards was such that it initially precluded the emergence of sophisticated text structures. Each card contained all that was known, for example, about a particular animal; and texts consisted of the random linking together of a set of independent cards. The complex linking features of the software were never exploited successfully. An optimistic child described organization in HyperCard as being "like a collage," but more representative was the comment, "Ms. S, I don't have a HyperCard mind."

Although the virtues of HyperCard were not readily transparent to the majority of the children, the file folder system of the regular Macintosh interface was iconically powerful. In order to find their notes on, for example, the crested rat, students had to know that this animal provided an example of an animal defense mechanism, under which topic they needed to enter the file on mimicry, and to know that it was necessary to refer to the file on visual mimicry, and only then would they find the animal in question, one that visually mimics a skunk to defend itself. Forced to organize information into files within files within files, the children regularly practiced the use of hierarchical organization. These search activities involving hierarchical organization were appropriated for use in writing. Student-generated texts progressed from having no discernible organizational structure to having quite sophisticated hierarchies (Campione et al., 1992). Hierarchical search activities, practiced over a long period of time, reinforced hierarchical organizational structure, and such practices transformed the organization of writing samples. In this case the zone of proximal development included students and machines, rather than exclusively people. Certain interactions with technology can powerfully shape thought.

*The role of assessment.* The final feature of our design experiments centers on the equally thorny problem of assessment. How does one maintain standards of accountability – to students, teachers, and parents, to school officials who are responsible for the students' progress, and to fellow scientists – while at the same time keeping the social contract with students, who are encouraged to view themselves as co-equal participants in a community of sharing? This is a difficult tightrope to walk, and our approach has been to be honest with the children and to allow them to participate in the assessment process as much as possible.

In addition to fairly traditional tests, we feature a variety of dynamic assessments (Campione, 1989; Campione & Brown, 1990) of the students' developing knowledge. Dynamic assessment methods present children with problems just one step beyond their existing competence and then provide help as needed for them to reach independent mastery. Again, competence is fostered in social interactions before individual mastery is expected. The degree of aid needed, both to learn new principles and to apply them, is carefully calibrated and measured. The required amount of aid provides a much better index of students' future learning trajectories in a domain than do static pretests. In particular, the ease with which students apply, or transfer, principles they have learned is regarded as an indication of their understanding of those principles; and this transfer performance is the most sensitive index of a student's readiness to proceed within a particular domain (Brown, Campione, Webber, & McGilly, 1992).

The dynamic assessment procedure is based on the same loosely interpreted Vygotskian theory that provided the underpinning for the development of reciprocal teaching. As can be seen in Table 7.2, both are based on the same type of learning theory but differ in their primary goals – assessing a student's level of understanding or enhancing that level. The primary difference rests in the nature and timing of the adult (expert) aid. In assessment, aid is metered out only as needed, permitting students to demonstrate independent competence when they can and permitting adults to gauge the extent of that competence. In the reciprocal teaching mode, help is given opportunistically as a result of the teacher's on-line diagnosis of need. Common to this theoretical approach to both diagnosis and instruction is the central notion of supportive contexts for learning. Four main principles are involved in the design of the dynamic assessments: (1) Understanding procedures rather than just speed and accuracy are the focus of assessment and instruction. (2) Expert guidance is used to reveal as well as promote independent competence. (3) Microgenetic analysis permits estimates of learning as it actually occurs over time. (4) Proleptic teaching (Stone & Wertsch, 1984) is involved in both assessment and instruction, for both aim at one stage beyond current performance, in anticipation of levels of competence not yet achieved individually but possible within supportive learning environments.

Table 7.2. *Assessment and instruction in a zone of proximal development*

| Main similarities |
| --- |
| Based (loosely) on Vygotsky's learning theory |
| Guided collaboration with expert feedback |
| Strategy modeling by experts (apprenticeship model) |
| Externalization of mental events via discussion formats |
| On-line assessment of novice status |
| Help given, responsive to student needs |
| Aimed at problem solving at the level of metacognition |
| Understanding measured by transfer, flexible use of knowledge |

| Main differences | |
| --- | --- |
| Dynamic assessment | Reciprocal teaching |
| Goal: Individual assessment | Goal: Collaborative learning |
| Test: Knowledge and strategies | Teach: Knowledge and strategies |
| Aid: Standardized hints | Aid: Opportunistic |
| Hints: Hard to easy to measure student need | Hints: Easy to hard to scaffold student progress |

As just one concrete example of this approach, we will describe a clinical interview designed to uncover students' biological knowledge. (For a discussion of dynamic assessment of emergent computer expertise, see Campione et al., 1992.) The students regarded participation in this interview as privileged one-on-one time with a visiting expert. At some level, of course, the students must have known it was a test, but the classroom ethos, involving the gaining and sharing of expertise, was such that the children enjoyed the chance to act as consultants and to discuss difficult concepts with the interviewer (DA; see Ash, 1991, for more details).

In the clinical interview, a series of key questions is raised concerning, for example, the food chain or adaptation. First, the interviewer elicits basic expository information. If the student cannot answer adequately, the interviewer provides hints and examples as necessary to test the student's readiness to learn the concept. If the student seems knowledgeable, the experimenter might question the student's understanding by introducing *counterexamples* to the student's beliefs (Is a mushroom a plant? What about yeast?), and again if appropriate, she might ask the student to engage in *thought experiments* that demand novel uses of the information. For example, when a student has sorted pictures of animals into herbivores and carnivores, and provided a good description of the categories, she may be asked, "What would happen on the African plain if there were no gazelles or other meat for cheetahs to eat? Could they eat grain?" Students previously judged knowledgeable on the basis of their expository information can be surprisingly uncertain about this, suggesting that cheetahs could eat grain under certain circumstances, although they would not live happily. Some even entertain a critical-period hypothesis – that the cheetah could change if it were forced to eat grain from infancy, but once it reached adolescence, it would be too set in its ways to change. Only a few invoke notions of form and function, such as properties of the digestive tract, to support the assertion that cheetahs could not change. These extension activities of thought experiments and counterexamples are far more revealing of the current state of students' knowledge than their first unchallenged answers, which often provide an overly optimistic picture of their knowledge.

Consider the following excerpts from John, a sixth-grader. During the pretest interview, John mentioned speed, body size, mouth size, and tearing teeth as functional physical characteristics of carnivores. He seemed to have the carnivore–herbivore distinction down pat. But when presented with the cheetah thought experiment, he mused: " . . . Well, I mean if people can, like, are vegetarians, I mean I think a cheetah could change."

This is a good example of a common reasoning strategy: personification as analogy (Carey, 1985; Hatano & Inagaki, 1987). When asked how this might happen, he said:

Well . . . just to switch off, . . . but um, it would be easier for them to change on to plants than it would be for me; if I had been eating meat . . . because there would still be meat around for me to eat, but for them there wouldn't be . . . so if they wanted to survive, they're going to have to eat grass.

When asked if it would be easier for a baby cheetah to eat grass, he responded:

Well, if it was a baby, it would be easier because it could eat it . . . it would be right there, it would just have to walk a little bit to get it . . . but I think it would be easier . . . but then if it happens for a long time, then the animals come back, [the gazelles return], then it probably would have lost its speed, because they wouldn't have to run. . . . Yeah, and they'd get used to the grass and not care about the animals, because along the line they would forget.

During the posttest clinical interview six months later, when asked the same question, John makes complex analogies to the cow's intestinal system, arguing that herbivore digestive tracts are more complicated than those of carnivores. By knowing an animal's diet, he argues, he would be able to predict its digestive tract length and how long digestion might take, and vice versa.

This time, when confronted with a variant of the cheetah thought experiment, John responded:

No . . . no, their digestive system isn't good enough . . . it's too uncomplicated to digest grasses and also their teeth wouldn't be able to chew, so then the grass would overpopulate . . . and the cheetah dies.

When asked if baby cheetahs could survive by eating grass, John asserted that they would probably be the first to die.

These responses are in distinct contrast to those given to the same questions during the pretest. John has abandoned personification (Hatano & Inagaki, 1987) as an explanation ("Humans can do it so cheetahs can too") and replaced it with a form–function justification. Thrown a novel twist on the old question – whether deer might be able to eat meat if there were no longer grass, the newly confident John favored the interviewer with a broad smile and said: "Nice try . . . the digestive tract of the deer is too complicated and also the teeth wouldn't be able to grind meat."

Another example of the rich picture that can be drawn from dynamic assessment and thought experiments comes from Katy, a sophisticated seventh-grader who gave a textbook-perfect description of photosynthesis that would in traditional tests certainly be taken as an indication that she fully understood the basic mechanisms. She was then asked, "What would happen if there were no sunlight?" Katy's response never included the critical information that since plants make food with the sun's energy, a serious reduction in the availability of sunlight would disrupt the entire food chain. Instead she concentrates on light to see with:

That would kill off the plants, beetles, and . . . um . . . nocturnal things would be OK. The dayturnal things . . . snakes, rabbits, hares . . . would be all right, they could be nocturnal. But the dayturnal things would need sunlight to see . . . couldn't find their food in the dark and would eventually starve to death. Hawks would also die out, but owls are nocturnal . . . would be able to see at night and . . . um . . . raccoons would probably be near the top of the food chain.

Katy clearly had not understood the basic place of photosynthesis as the mainspring of life. She could repeat back the mechanisms and form food chains when directly asked, but she could not yet reason flexibly with her newfound knowledge.

Using these thought experiments, we can track the development not only of the retention of knowledge, but also of how fragile or robust that knowledge is and how flexibly it can be applied. The philosophy of negotiation and appropriation within a zone of proximal development is just as apparent in our assessment procedures as in our classroom practices. Indeed, these clinical assessments are collaborative learning experiences in their own right. As such, the line between assessment and instruction becomes increasingly blurred, intentionally so (Campione, 1989).

### Authentic school activity

We began this chapter by raising the question: What constitutes authentic activity in the early years of schooling? We argued that it is surely impractical to suggest that grade schools at least could become apprenticeship sites for inducting children into the community practices of mathematicians or historians. Most of the children who take part in our environmental science classrooms are not intending to become biologists or environmental scientists, and it is not intended that they should. But if they develop into individuals able to evaluate scientific information critically and to learn about new developments in science, then we would be more than satisfied. In regard to the continuity between school and authentic practice, we believe the best we can do is to avoid obvious discontinuity with the cultures of practicing scientists. To this end, we introduce students to the world of working scientists through visits and electronic mail, and we immerse them in the discourse structures of inquiry, conjecture, evidence, and proof. Furthermore, we encourage them to invent real and thought experiments that they share with the community at large via publications, seminars, and science fairs. Some of the best examples of continuity between grade school practices and disciplinary-based discourse modes come from work in grade school mathematics (Lampert, 1986; O'Connor, 1991), examples we try to emulate in grade school science. We want students to be practicing members of a science community to the extent possible; hence, the metaphor of the nineteenth-century naturalist guides our activities.

Although we attempt to avoid obvious discontinuity in activities between grade school science and legitimate scientific practice to the degree that we are able (the children have no biochemical knowledge), we believe that the true apprenticeship in schools is to a community of scholars. Although many authentic adult activities are disciplinary-bound, there are domain-independent learning activities that do allow the intelligent novices more ready access to a new domain and the subsequent freedom to select a community of practice of their choosing (Brown et al., 1983).

A common translation of the notion of cognitive apprenticeships is that students be apprenticed to the community practice of, say, mathematics (Collins, Brown, & Newman, 1989). But a more compelling argument is to take the title seriously and think in terms of "thinking" or "learning" apprenticeships. We believe that "thinking apprenticeships" should be the authentic activity of grade school life, although we recognize that this position is controversial. During their tenure in school, young children should ideally be absorbed into a community of research practice where they gradually come to adopt the ways of knowing, cultural practice, discourse patterns, and belief systems of scholars. We know that we have made progress toward this goal when a leading scholar in the field, looking at videotapes of our students, exclaims, "But they look just like us; it looks like a graduate seminar." Schools should provide a breeding ground for young scholars where they can be prepared for a career as lifelong intentional learners.

The central theoretical ideas underpinning our classroom design experiments (Brown, 1992; Collins, in press) are those of mutual appropriation and negotiation within multiple overlapping zones of proximal development. Life in our science classrooms involves situated negotiation and renegotiation of ideas, terms, definitions, and so on (O'Connor, 1991), so that something like a common voice (Wertsch, 1991) and a common knowledge base (Edwards & Mercer, 1987) emerge over time. This common voice evolves continuously via "situated negotiation and renegotiation of meaning" (Lave & Wenger, 1991). Participants in the community are free to appropriate "ideas in the air" and transform these ideas via personal interpretation and incorporation. Within the same classroom, participants pass in and out in multiple zones of proximal development as they appropriate ideas and ways of knowing that are ripe for harvesting. Although a common voice emerges, individuals develop ownership of separate parts of that common knowledge through a process of majoring, the intentional focusing on aspects of the system that a learner decides to specialize in. Distributed expertise is a central facet in authentic communities of scientific practice – hence the need to share knowledge among scientists via papers, conferences, electronic mail, and other means. This distributed expertise is no less desirable for grade school classrooms, when authentic learning is the name of the game, than it is for practicing scientists. The idea that all children of a certain age in the same grade should acquire the same body of knowledge at the same time, an essential assumption underlying mass assessment, is one of the reasons that contemporary school activities are to a large part inauthentic.

### Conclusion

In this chapter we have described our attempt to foster communities of learning in the classroom, practices we believe are the legitimate activities of an institution that ideally came into being to promote learning. Central to these learning activities is the display of distributed expertise. Ideas and concepts migrate throughout the community via mutual appropriation and negotiation. Some ideas and ways of knowing become part of common knowledge. Other forms of knowledge and knowing remain the special reserve of those who choose to major in a particular form of expertise. Expertise is shared and distributed within the community by design and by happenstance. The classroom is designed to foster zones of proximal development that are continually the subject of negotiation and renegotiation among its citizens. Through their participation in increasingly more mature forums of scholarly research, students are enculturated into the community practice of scholars. When they work, and they do not always work, our classrooms encourage the development of a community of discourse pervaded by knowledge seeking and inquiry processes. Expertise of one form or another is spread throughout and beyond the classroom, and this emergent expertise influences the discourse that provides the seeding ground for the mutual negotiation and appropriation activities of its members.

## References

Aronson, E. (1978). *The jigsaw classroom.* Beverly Hills, CA: Sage.
Ash, D. (1991). *A new guided assessment of biological understanding.* Unpublished manuscript, University of California, Berkeley.
Bandler, R., & Grinder, J. (1975). *The structure of magic.* Palo Alto, CA: Science & Behavior Books.
Barnes, D., & Todd, F. (1977). *Communication and learning in small groups.* London: Routledge & Kegan Paul.
Bell, B. (1985). Students' beliefs about plant nutrition: What are they? *Journal of Biological Education, 19,* 213–18.
Bereiter, C. (1985). Toward a solution of the learning paradox. *Review of Educational Research, 55,* 201–26.
Bloor, D. (1991). *Knowledge and social imagery.* Chicago: University of Chicago Press.
Bordieu, P. (1972). *Outline to a theory of practice.* Cambridge University Press.
Brown, A. L. (1992). Design experiments: Theoretical and methodological challenges in creating complex interventions in classroom settings. *Journal of the Learning Sciences, 2*(2), 141–78.
Brown, A. L., Bransford, J. D., Ferrara, R. A., & Campione, J. C. (1983). Learning, remembering, and understanding. In J. H. Flavell & E. M. Markman (Eds.), *Handbook of child psychology* (4th ed.), *Vol. 3: Cognitive development* (pp. 77–166). New York: Wiley.
Brown, A. L., & Campione, J. C. (1990). Communities of learning and thinking, or A context by any other name. *Human Development, 21,* 108–26.
(in press). Restructuring grade school learning environments to promote scientific literacy. In *Restructuring learning: Analysis and proceedings of the annual conference of the Council of Chief State School Officers.* San Diego, CA: Harcourt Brace Jovanovich.
Brown, A. L., Campione, J. C., Webber, L. S., & McGilly, K. (1992). Interactive learning environments: A new look at assessment and instruction. In B. R. Gifford & M. C. O'Connor (Eds.), *Changing assessments: Alternative views of aptitude, achievement and instruction* (pp. 121–211). Boston: Kluwer.
Brown, A. L., & Day, J. D. (1983). Macrorules for summarizing texts: The development of expertise. *Journal of Verbal Learning and Verbal Behavior, 22*(1), 1–14.
Brown, A. L., & Palincsar, A. S. (1989). Guided, cooperative learning and individual knowledge acquisition. In L. B. Resnick (Ed.), *Knowing, learning, and*

*instruction: Essays in honor of Robert Glaser* (pp. 393–451). Hillsdale, NJ: Erlbaum.

Brown, A. L., & Reeve, R. A. (1987). Bandwidths of competence: The role of supportive contexts in learning and development. In L. S. Liben (Ed.), *Development and learning: Conflict or congruence?* (pp. 173–223). Hillsdale, NJ: Erlbaum.

Brown, J. S., Collins, A., & Duguid, P. (1989). Situated cognition and the culture of learning. *Educational Researcher, 18,* 32–42.

Brumby, M. (1979). Problems in learning the concept of natural selection. *Journal of Biological Education, 13,* 119–22.

Bruner, J. S. (1969). *On knowing: Essays for the left hand.* Cambridge, MA: Harvard University Press.

Campione, J. C. (1989). Assisted assessment: A taxonomy of approaches and an outline of strengths and weaknesses. *Journal of Learning Disabilities, 22,* 151–65.

Campione, J. C., & Brown, A. L. (1990). Guided learning and transfer. In N. Frederiksen, R. Glaser, A. Lesgold, & M. Shafto (Eds.), *Diagnostic monitoring of skill and knowledge acquisition* (pp. 141–72). Hillsdale, NJ: Erlbaum.

Campione, J. C., Brown, A. L., & Jay, M. (1992). Computers in a community of learners. In E. DeCorte, M. Linn, H. Mandl, & L. Verschaffel (Eds.), *Computer-based learning environments and problem solving* (NATO ASI Series F: Computer and Systems Sciences), Vol. 84, pp. 163–92. Berlin: Springer.

Carey, S. (1985). *Conceptual change in childhood.* Cambridge, MA: MIT Press.

Cazden, C. (1981). Performance before competence: Assistance to child discourse in the zone of proximal development. *Quarterly Newsletter of the Laboratory of Comparative Human Cognition, 3,* 5–8.

Cole, M., & Bruner, J. S. (1971). Cultural differences and inferences about psychological processes. *American Psychologist, 26,* 867–76.

Collins, A. (in press). Toward a design science of education. In E. Scanlon & T. O'Shea (Eds.), *New directions in educational technology.* New York: Springer.

Collins, A., Brown, J. S., & Newman, S. (1989). Cognitive apprenticeship: Teaching the crafts of reading, writing and mathematics. In L. B. Resnick (Ed.), *Knowing, learning, and instruction: Essays in honor of Robert Glaser* (pp. 453–94). Hillsdale, NJ: Erlbaum.

Collins, A., & Stevens, A. (1982). Goals and strategies of inquiry teachers. In R. Glaser (Ed.), *Advances in instructional psychology* (Vol. 2, pp. 65–119). Hillsdale, NJ: Erlbaum.

Cuban, L. (1986). *Teachers and machines: The classroom of technology since 1920.* New York: Teachers College Press.

Dewey, J. (1902). *The child and the curriculum.* Chicago: University of Chicago Press.

Edwards, P., & Mercer, N. (1987). *Common knowledge.* London: Open University Press.

Erickson, F., & Schultz, J. (1977). When is a context? Some issues and methods on the analysis of social competence. *Quarterly Newsletter of the Institute for Comparative Human Development, 1,* 5–10.

Fish, S. (1980). *Is there a text in this class? The authority of interpretive communities.* Cambridge, MA: Harvard University Press.

Fodor, J. (1980). On the impossibility of acquiring "more powerful" structures. In M. Rattelli-Palmarini (Ed.), *Language and learning: The debate between Jean Piaget and Noam Chomsky* (pp. 142–62). Cambridge, MA: Harvard University Press.

Gardner, H. (1991). *The unschooled mind.* New York: Basic Books.

Goodwin, C. (1987, June). *Participation frameworks in children's argument.* Paper presented at the International Interdisciplinary Conference on Child Research. University of Trondheim, Norway.

Hall, G. S. (1881). The contents of children's minds. *Princeton Review, 11,* 249–72.

Hatano, G., & Inagaki, K. (1987). Everyday biology and school biology: How do they interact? *Newsletter of the Laboratory of Comparative Human Cognition, 9,* 120–8.

Heath, S. B. (1983). *Ways with words.* Cambridge University Press.

Hoffding, H. (1892). *Outlines of psychology* (M. E. Lowndes, Trans.). London: Macmillan Press.

Keil, F. (1989). On the development of biologically specific beliefs: The case for inheritance. *Child Development, 60,* 637–48.

Lampert, M. (1986). Knowing, doing, and teaching multiplication. *Cognition and Instruction, 3*(4), 305–42.

Lave, J. (1988). *Cognition in practice: Mind, mathematics and culture in everyday life.* Cambridge University Press.

Lave, J., & Wenger, E. (1991). *Situated learning: Legitimate peripheral participation.* Cambridge University Press.

Lempke, J. L. (1990). *Talking science.* Norwood, NJ: Ablex.

Mayr, E. (1988). *Toward a new philosophy of biology.* Cambridge, MA: Harvard University Press.

Mehan, H. (1979). *Learning lessons: Social organization in the classroom.* Cambridge, MA: Harvard University Press.

Michaels, S., & O'Connor, M. C. (in press). Literacy as reasoning within multiple discourses. In *Restructuring learning: Analysis and proceedings of the annual conference of the Council of Chief State School Officers.* San Diego, CA: Harcourt Brace Jovanovich.

Minstrell, J. A. (1989). Teaching science for understanding. In L. B. Resnick & L. E. Klopfer (Eds.), *Toward the thinking curriculum: Current cognitive research* (pp. 129–49). The Association for Supervision and Curriculum Development.

Moschkovich, J. (1989, April). *Constructing a problem space through appropriation: A case study of tutoring during computer exploration.* Paper presented at the meetings of the American Educational Research Association, San Francisco.

Newman, D., Griffin, P., & Cole, M. (1989). *The construction zone.* Cambridge University Press.

Ochs, E. (1991). Indexicality and socialization. In J. W. Stigler, R. A. Shweder, & G. Herdt (Eds.), *Cultural psychology: Essays on comparative human development* (pp. 287–308). Cambridge University Press.

O'Connor, M. C. (1991). *Negotiated defining: Speech activities and mathematical litera-cies.* Unpublished manuscript, Boston University.

Palincsar, A. S., & Brown, A. L. (1984). Reciprocal teaching of comprehension-fostering and monitoring activities. *Cognition and Instruction, 1*(2), 117–75.

Resnick, L. B. (1987). *Education and learning to think.* Washington, DC: National Academy Press.

Rogoff, B. (1990). *Apprenticeship in thinking.* Oxford: Oxford University Press.

Rutherford, M. (1991). *Second language learning in a "community of learners" classroom.* Unpublished manuscript, University of California, Berkeley.

Scardamalia, M., & Bereiter, C. (1991). Higher levels of agency for children in knowledge building: A challenge for the design of new knowledge media. *Journal of the Learning Sciences, 1,* 37–68.

Schank, R. C., & Jona, M. Y. (1991). Empowering the student: New perspectives on the design of teaching systems. *Journal of the Learning Sciences, 1,* 7–36.

Schoenfeld, A., Smith, J., & Arcavi, A. (in press). Learning: The microgenetic analysis of one student's evolving understanding of a complex subject matter domain. In R. Glaser (Ed.), *Advances in instructional psychology* (Vol. 4). Hillsdale, NJ: Erlbaum.

Stone, C. A., & Wertsch, J. V. (1984). A social interactional analysis of learning disabilities remediation. *Journal of Learning Disabilities, 17,* 194–9.

Vygotsky, L. S. (1978). *Mind in society: The development of higher psychological processes* (M. Cole, V. John-Steiner, S. Scribner, & E. Souberman, Eds. and Trans.). Cambridge, MA: Harvard University Press.

Wertsch, J. V. (1991). *Voices in the mind.* Cambridge University Press.

Wineburg, S. (1989). A response to Brown, Collins and Duguid. *Educational Researcher, 18,* 44–8.

Wood, D., Bruner, J., & Ross, G. (1976). The role of tutoring in problem solving. *Journal of Child Psychology and Psychiatry, 17,* 89–100.

# 8 On the distribution of cognition: some reflections

*Raymond S. Nickerson*

A discussant of a book composed of chapters by many authors can work toward any of several objectives: summarization, clarification, amplification, reconciliation, analysis, or critique from a particular perspective. My objective in the following comments is both modest in comparison with these possibilities and opportunistic. It is modest in that the comments do not serve a specific theoretical agenda and are not made in the hope of changing anyone's mind about any burning theoretical issues. It is opportunistic in that I selectively focus on several points or themes that struck me as especially interesting, for whatever reasons. I make no effort to review or critique the chapters in a comprehensive way.

I take my cue from Pea's observation in Chapter 2 that the idea of distributed intelligence is not a theory of mind or of anything else so much as it is a "heuristic framework for raising and addressing theoretical and empirical questions." I believe it serves that purpose quite well. The idea of intelligence (knowledge, cognition) being distributed in a group, or in artifacts, customs, and situations, is in my view an interesting one not so much because of any questions it might answer as because of the many it raises.

I found the foregoing chapters thought-provoking indeed. Reading them set me to thinking about a variety of questions. What is new in the new look at cognition? What is insightful and revealing? On the assumption that the concept of distributed cognition and the ideas associated with it represent a genuinely new point of view, what follows? What are the implications for education?

I am grateful to David Perkins and Gavriel Salomon for helpful comments on a draft of this chapter.

229

How should we think about shared knowledge? How does it relate to what is in the minds of those who are said to share it? What do we mean when we say that a specific collection of people (political party, fraternal organization, scientific field, religious denomination, professional organization, nation) knows, believes, decides, . . . ? Could a statement that a group knows $X$ mean anything more than that some or most members of that group know $X$? And how do we characterize what an individual knows?

I hope I shall be excused for sharing, in what follows, some of the directions in which the ideas I encountered in the preceding chapters prompted me to go, despite the fact that I seldom succeeded in arriving at very firm conclusions. One takes journeys not just to reach destinations, but to enjoy the trips.

## What is new?

As I read and thought about these chapters, I often found myself asking whether some assertion was an old observation expressed in new words, a genuinely useful new way of thinking about an old concept, a new insight, a profundity, common sense, or something totally outside my ken. I was a little surprised at the frequency with which I could not decide among the alternatives.

Cole and Engeström note in Chapter 1 that the idea that the content and process of thinking are distributed among individuals as well as packed within them is not new in psychology, although there appears to be renewed interest in it. They point to variations on this theme in the writings of Wundt, Munsterberg, the Soviet cultural-historical psychologists Leont'ev, Luria, and Vygotsky, and the anthropologists White and Geertz. These investigators recognized the importance to human psychology of cognitive resources that are to be found not in a single individual's head but in the sociocultural surround; in books and other communication media; in tools, including language, through which people interact with other people and the environment; in other people and in the legacies of previous generations; in specialization and the division of labor; in the rules by which we live; and elsewhere.

Such historical precedents notwithstanding, it seems clear that interest in the social, situational, and cultural aspects of cognition is greater within mainstream cognitive and educational psychology now than it was until fairly recently. It would be surprising, given the level of attention these aspects of cognition are receiving, if new ideas did not emerge. What is disappointing is the fact, and I believe this is the point that Cole and Engeström make, that so often ideas that have been in the literature for some time are not recognized as such. Most of us pay less attention than we should to anything written more than a very few years ago, and consequently we fail to recognize when ideas that are genuinely new to us have run through other minds in the past.

Just as the question of what is new gives me trouble as I read about distributed cognition, so does the question of what is insightful or especially revealing. Much of what is being said, or at least what I think is being said, sounds much like common sense and is not really debatable. Not only do we all recognize that knowledge is distributed in society, but we have a practical, if partial, understanding of how it is distributed. We know enough to call the plumber and not the pharmacist when the sink is plugged.

Does anyone doubt that the same people act differently in different situations, that people are influenced by the social and cultural contexts in which they live, that what one can do depends to a large degree on the tools and materials at one's disposal, that there are countless useful tools in the world including many that simplify cognitive tasks, that what skills people develop depends in part on the kinds of artifacts they must use, that it is easier to do certain things in some environments than in others, that two heads are (sometimes) better than one, that specialization of function within groups is often useful, that it is a waste of time and effort to keep some types of information in one's head . . . ?

I am not trying to make the point that there is nothing profound in the new look, or that observations that appear to be commonsensical – once made – cannot be insightful; nor do I want to argue that observations like those above are not worth making. As Stanislav Ulam (1976, p. 303) once put it, "Sometimes obvious things have to be repeated over and over before they are realized." I am simply confessing to not being able to tell from reading, in all cases, whether something is being presented as a discovery or as a reminder of what we all know.

### On the distribution of knowledge in a group

At one level the idea of knowledge being distributed in a group is intuitively compelling – who can doubt that a collection of people houses a store of knowledge that differs from, and in some sense exceeds, that housed by any single member of the group? But what it could mean for a group to know something is anything but clear. And how to represent what a group knows and to relate that to what the individual members of the group know is a complex matter that has not been adequately addressed.

Clearly the collective knowledge of a group must be greater (or at least not less) than the knowledge of any of its members. The group composed of A and B knows what A knows *and* what B knows, and unless A's knowledge is identical to B's, or what either A or B knows is a proper subset of what the other knows, what they know in combination must be greater than what either of them knows individually. Even if one of them knows much less than the other, as long as the less knowledgeable person knows *something* the other does not, their combined knowledge must exceed what even the more knowledgeable individual knows alone. So much seems obvious.

But is it? Reflection raises some doubts. The argument appears to require the assumption that knowledge combines only additively. Consider the extreme case in which A and B each knows only one "fact." A knows that a platypus is a mammal; B knows that it is not. Would we say, in this case, that what they know in combination exceeds what each of them knows individually? One might object that this is not an acceptable example, because at least one of the individuals does not "know" a fact but only thinks he does. But this raises the question of what it means to know something, and that is a thorny question indeed.

Defining knowledge as "true beliefs" does not solve the problem, because people differ with respect to what they will accept as evidence of truth, and all human knowledge is uncertain to some degree. Any definition of knowledge that is sufficiently liberal to admit the possibility of people possessing it is likely also to leave open the possibility of the knowledge of individuals combining in less than totally additive ways.

But let us ignore the problem of deciding what it means for an individual to know something and assume, for the moment, that to know $X$ is to hold the true belief that $X$. It is still not clear what we are saying when we say that knowledge is distributed over a group. Are we saying that the group, as an entity, knows something? And if we are saying that a group, as such, knows $X$, what might that mean? That one or more members of the group know $X$? Suppose that one member of the group knows $X$ while all the other members believe not-$X$; would we say that the group knows $X$?

When we say that the group knows $X$ and $Y$, even though no single member of the group knows $X$ and $Y$, are we saying that at least one person in the group knows $X$ and at least one other knows $Y$? Suppose those members who know $X$ believe not-$Y$ and those who know $Y$ believe not-$X$; would we say that the group, as such, knows $X$ and $Y$? Should we say that a group knows $X$ only if a majority of the group's members knows $X$? If we do this, we leave open the possibility of the group knowing less than some of its members.

An individual who knows explicitly $A$ and *if $A$ then $B$* knows implicitly – assuming logical competence – $B$. But if one member of a group knows $A$ (but not *if $A$ then $B$*) while another knows *if $A$ then $B$* (but not $A$), should we say that the group implicitly knows $B$?

Should we conceive of the group as having metaknowledge, as we conceive of individuals as having metaknowledge? What then would it mean to say that a group knows $X$ and knows that it knows $X$? Or that it thinks it knows $X$, although not-$X$ is true? Or what would it mean to say that the group believes $X$ to be true but is not sure?

However we answer these questions, it seems to me that our conception of what it means for a group to know something must differ in very substantive ways from our conception of what it means for an individual to know something. I wonder if the difference is not sufficiently great to warrant using different words to represent the two situations.

If we were able – and we are not – to represent the knowledge of a single individual in such a way as to do justice to its richness and breadth, its various degrees of specifity and certainty, its mix of explicitly and implicitly included facts and beliefs, its inconsistencies and contradictions, and its understanding, more or less, of countless concepts, principles, relationships, and processes, it would be a complex representation indeed. One can only vaguely imagine how one would go about combining the representations of individual knowledge bases to derive a representation of the aggregate knowledge base of a group. Clearly, any representation that came close to capturing the complexity of the situation would include much more than a listing of all the true beliefs – on any definition – contained in one or more of the individual representations.

### Diminishing returns

One of the paths down which my thoughts were prompted to wander by the idea of knowledge distributed over a group brought me to the question of how to think about gains to be obtained, in terms of the knowledge available for application to a problem, from increasing the size of a problem-solving group.

Suppose we characterize the knowledge of an individual in terms of the number of facts that individual knows, and ignore, for the purpose of this exercise, all the obvious objections to such a simpleminded characterization. Suppose further that every individual knows the same number of facts, say $n$, and that *each* of any two individuals picked at random knows $pn$ facts that the other one does not know and that $(1 - p)n$ facts are known by both of them in common. (Obviously, $p < 1$.)

On these assumptions, when two people pool their knowledge, the combined knowledge base consists of the sum of their individual stores, $2n$, less what they know in common, $(1 - p)n$; so the number of different facts in the combined store is $2n - (1 - p)n = (1 + p)n$. Another way to think about the combined store is as the sum of the $2pn$ facts that exist in one or the other unique individual stores and the $(1 - p)n$ that are common to both, which gives $2pn + (1 - p)n = (1 + p)n$.

If we add a third person to the group, by our assumptions Person 3 has $(1 - p)n$ facts in common with Person 1 and $(1 - p)n$ in common with Person 2, but not precisely the same facts in both cases. Assuming a random distribution of facts among the members of our population, we would expect that Person 3 would have $p(1 - p)n$ facts in common with Person 1 alone, $p(1 - p)n$ with Person 2 alone,

$(1 - p)^2 n$ in common with both, and $p^2 n$ in common with neither. More generally, all three people in our group would have $p^2 n$ unique facts, any two would have $p(1 - p)n$ in common only to the two of them, and all three would share $(1 - p)^2 n$. Inasmuch as there are three individuals, three pairs, and only one triple, the total knowledge of the group would be $3p^2 n + 3p(1 - p)n + (1 - p)^2 n$, or $(1 + p + p^2)n$. This makes intuitive sense: A one-person group has $n$ facts, a second person brings $pn$ *new* facts, and a third person brings $p^2 n$ additional new facts.

Generalizing this formula, we have, letting $T_m$ represent the total knowledge of a group of $m$ members, each of whom knows $n$ facts, and $\binom{m}{k}$ the number of combinations of $m$ things taken $k$ at a time

$$T_m = n \sum_{k=1}^{m} \binom{m}{k} p^{m-k} (1 - p)^{k-1}$$

The $k$th term of the expansion of this equation divided by the combinatorial factor $\binom{m}{k}$ gives the number of facts that a random subset of $k$ members of a group of size $m$ share uniquely, which is to say the number of facts that all the members of that subset and only the members of that subset have. If we wish to know only the value of $T_m$ and have no interest in how facts are distributed over subsets of the group, we can use the simpler formula

$$T_m = n \sum_{k=1}^{m} p^{k-1}$$

Consider a group of two members and $p = .5$. Each member of the group knows $.5n$ facts that the other does not know, and the members also have $.5n$ facts in common. Their combined knowledge base of $(1 + p)n$, or $1.5n$, facts is half again as large as that of either one of them alone. Suppose that we now add to the group Person 3, who, by our assumptions, has $.5n$ facts in common with Person 1 and $.5n$ in common with Person 2, but not precisely the same facts in both cases. Assuming a random distribution of facts among the members of our population, we would expect that Person 3 would have $p(1 - p)n$, or $.25n$, facts in common with Person 1 alone, $.25n$, in common with Person 2 alone, $(1 - p)^2 n$, or $.25n$, in common with both, and $p^2 n$, or $.25n$. in common with neither.

More generally, the distribution of knowledge over the three-person group is as follows: The group, as a whole, has $1.75n$ facts, $.25n$ of which are in the individual knowledge bases of all three members of the group, $.75n$ are in the knowledge bases of precisely two of the members ($.25n$ in both 1 and 2, $.25n$ in 1 and 3, and $.25n$ in 2 and 3), and $.75n$ are in the knowledge base of only a single member (each member has $.25n$ unique facts). In other words, any single member of the group knows $.25n$ facts that no one else in the group knows; any random pair of members also knows $.25n$ facts uniquely; and the entire group of three shares $.25n$ facts. Thus, if $n = 100$, each of the members of the group has 25 unique facts, each pair shares 25 facts, 25 facts are known by all three, and the combined knowledge base contains 175 facts.

The addition of Person 3 to the original two-person group added $.25n$ *new* facts to the corporate knowledge base, which grew from $1.5n$ to $1.75n$ facts by virtue of this enlargement. With further increases in the size of the group, the number of facts in the corporate knowledge base would grow, but by progressively smaller amounts. Specifically, given $p = .5$, the amount of new knowledge acquired diminishes by half with each additional member. It follows that the total amount of knowledge the group can ever acquire, no matter how large it gets, is $2n$ facts, or twice what is stored in any individual member's head.

The way in which knowledge is distributed over the group also changes as the group grows. The amount that all members of the group hold in common diminishes by half (again, given $p = .5$) with the addition of each new member, approaching 0 at the same rate that $T$ approaches its maximum. In general, the amount that any $k$ members have *uniquely* in common – knowledge that all $k$ members have and nobody else has – also diminishes by half with each new member.

Of course, the assumption that any two people in a group have half of their knowledge in common is arbitrary, but it raises an interesting question: How much (what percentage) of what each of two randomly chosen normal adults from the same culture knows are they likely both to know? What would be a reasonable guess? Mine, strictly from the vantage point of my armchair, is that it is relatively large – much larger than 50 percent. I suspect that it is very easy to underestimate how much of the knowledge any two people have they have in com-

Table 8.1. *Total number of different facts (as multiples of n) in knowledge base of group of m members, assuming that each of any random two members has pn facts the other does not have and that they have (1 − p)n facts in common*

| | | | m | |
|---|---|---|---|---|
| $p$ | 2 | 4 | 8 | 16 |
| .2 | 1.20 | 1.248 | 1.249 | 1.249 |
| .5 | 1.50 | 1.875 | 1.992 | 1.999 |
| .8 | 1.80 | 2.952 | 4.092 | 4.859 |

mon, in part because it is easy to underestimate the size of the commonsense knowledge base of both and in part because the differences are more salient than the likenesses. The situation is analogous to that of comparing dogs and cats; we are likely to focus on their differences, but I believe that reflection would convince most of us that their similarities are far more numerous. (Imagine comparing dogs and cats with sand dollars.)

This argument loses some force when one considers knowledge with respect to special domains (gardening, computer programming, ancient Egyptian hieroglyphics). One might expect the knowledge that each of two experts in different domains has that the other does not have to be greater on average than the knowledge that each of two random people (who are not domain experts) has that the other does not have, although we may easily underestimate the size of the common knowledge store and its importance to communication even in this case. If we consider *only* domain-specific knowledge, then we might convince ourselves that the percentage of experts' knowledge in their domains of expertise that is not shared with people who are not experts in those domains is quite high.

In any case, the assumption regarding common knowledge is easily changed. Table 8.1 shows the consequences of setting it at .2, .5, and .8 for groups of size 2, 4, 8, and 16. The reader may wish to work it out for some other percentages. (Recall that $p$ represents the proportion of the facts known by *each* of any two individuals picked at random that are known by that individual uniquely, while $1 - p$ represents the proportion known by both of them in common.) If $p$ is small ($1 - p$ is large), $T$ asymptotes very quickly and at a number not much greater than $n$. With $p = .2$, for example, the total knowledge in the corporate knowledge base never exceeds the knowledge in any single head by more than 25%. With $p = .8$, the total knowledge of a 16-person group is about 5 times as great as that of a single member and is still increasing modestly with each addition.

It is not surprising that the larger the group, the less that is gained by adding a new member. Perhaps it is not surprising that the larger the group, the less that is gained by increasing it by a fixed proportion, say by doubling it. What may be somewhat surprising, however, is how fast the knowledge base reaches asymptote when $p$ is .5 or smaller. According to this model, very little new knowledge is gained in those cases by adding new members to even a rather small group.

## What is wrong with this model?

This model is a grossly oversimplified representation of the way the corporate knowledge of a group might grow with increases in the group's size. Is there anything to be learned from it all the same? Does it prompt any interesting conjectures or hypotheses?

Probably the most glaring shortcoming of the model is the characterization of what one knows in terms of the number of facts stored in one's head. Everyone will recognize the inappropriateness of such a view. But how *should* we characterize what an individual knows? Or what a group knows? Or what a society or culture knows? This, I believe, is an extraordinarily difficult question, and one that we do not have the vaguest idea how to begin to answer.

It seems to me that human knowledge has two particularly striking characteristics. One is its fragmentary nature and the other is the fact that so much of it is implicit. I remember fragments of incidents but seldom, if ever, can recall one in its entirety. What I know about history, or chemistry, or economics, or any other subject is fragmentary in the extreme. When I say that I am familiar with a song, I usually mean I recognize it when I hear it and might be able to hum or whistle segments of it or approximations thereof. When I claim to know the meaning of a particular word, I mean that I believe I understand what it is intended to signify when I encounter it in context or that I would be able to use it more or less appropriately; I do not mean that I could give all the definitions of the word that one would find in the dictionary or exhaustively describe its various uses. To know individuals means typically something like being able to recognize them on sight, feeling free to call them by name, and knowing a few things about them – but certainly not all there is to know.

No less apparent than the fragmentary nature of knowledge (at least my own) is the fact that so much of what we know, we know only implicitly. I know, for example, that Zachary Taylor had a mother and father, both of whom lived beyond puberty. I know that they were oxygen-dependent, that they never rode in an airplane, and that they are both now dead. You know these things too, although it is doubtful whether either you or I ever learned them explicitly; chances are we never even thought of them before. But we have no trouble inferring these bits of knowledge and countless others equally useful or trifling from what is stored explicitly in our minds. One might argue, as Goldman (1986) has done, that one cannot believe something until one consciously has the thought, but even if one accepts that argument, one is left with the fact that what is (easily) inferable from what one explicitly knows (or believes) is available for use in contexts that will provoke the necessary inferences and therefore should be counted as part of the knowledge on which one can draw, consulting nothing other than one's head.

These observations do not help us much with the question of how to characterize what – or how much – a person or group knows. I make them simply to lend credence to the claim that this is a very difficult problem and, I hope, to gain some sympathy for the argument that, given the current state of our understanding of what it means to know something, characterizing the knowledge of individuals or groups in terms of the "number of facts" they possess is not that much worse than other manageable possibilities that come to mind. Any characterization that we are likely to come up with should be taken with a large grain of salt. This one has the virtue of conceptual simplicity and serves as a useful point of departure for discussing several other questions relating to the distribution of knowledge over a group.

### The emergence of knowledge

An assumption underlying the simple distribution-of-knowledge model that I have described is that there are no interactions among the knowledge bases of the individuals comprising the group. An alternative model might recognize the possibility that the knowledge of a group could be greater than the union of the knowledge of the individual members. One can imagine a variety ways in which this could be the case. One might, for example, make a distinction between stored facts and accessible facts – the latter being a subset of the former – and assume that the amount of knowledge that individuals can access from their own stores depends to some degree on the kinds of stimulation they get from people with whom they interact. From this vantage point, one might expect the knowledge that can be accessed from individual stores would be greater when those individuals function in interactive groups than when they work alone.

There is also the possibility that new knowledge may be inferred from two or more knowledge bases in combination that could not be inferred from any one of them alone. Consider again the case of two members of a group each of whom knows a different one of two facts (e.g., *A* and *if A then B*) that, in combination, provide the basis for inferring a new fact (*B*). As long as the two facts reside in different knowledge bases that do not communicate, the inference cannot be made, but when the knowledge bases come together it can. More generally, what can be inferred from a set of logically related facts is likely to increase with the number of facts in the set.

Finally, new knowledge in the form of insights and discoveries may be produced as a consequence of interactions among the members of a group, and in this way too a corporate knowledge store could come to include facts not contained originally in any of the individual stores, or even by implication in all of them combined. We do not understand this process, but we do not understand what provokes "original" ideas – where such ideas come from – in any case.

My point is not that new knowledge is generated in these ways as a consequence of the interactions among the members of a group but that it conceivably could be. Whether it is, in fact, is an empirical question for research. The general question of whether groups engaging in problem solving and other intellectually demanding tasks typically display corporate capabilities that seem to be more than the union of the capabilities of all of their members has been a long-standing research focus in social psychology. I do not know the literature well enough to say whether there is a consensus as to the answer.

## Social implications of the distribution of knowledge

What would society be like if everybody knew precisely what everybody else knew? One can only speculate, of course, but some consequences of such a condition are fairly obvious. Clearly the world – at least the world of people – would be a dull place. Our interest in one another as individuals surely stems in part from the fact that we know enough in common to communicate, but also in part from our differences, cognitive as well as other kinds. If we all had precisely the same knowledge, we would not be able to inform one another, to learn from one another, or to surprise one another. If Thomas (1979, p. 71) is right that, apart from language, it is our "insatiable, uncontrollable drive to learn things and then to exchange the information with others" that distinguishes us as human beings from all other creatures on earth, having all our knowledge in common would not be compatible, in principle, with one of the most distinctively human of our qualities.

From a practical point of view, the fact that we do not all have the same knowledge is what makes knowledge-based professions and knowledge industries possible. Knowledge is a marketable commodity precisely to the degree that it is useful and not everyone has it. Physicians, engineers, lawyers, pharmacists, mechanics are paid at least as much for what they know as for what they do; or to make the same point another way, they can do what they do only because they know what they know. If everybody had the same knowledge as they, their services would be in considerably less demand.

A clear illustration of the empowerment that comes with expertise is given in this book by Brown and her colleagues in Chapter 7. They describe an experimental study in which each of the students in a middle school class was assigned to two small groups, a research group and a learning group. Each research group studied a subset of the topics from an ecology curriculum; all of the students in a given research group studied the same material simultaneously. The learning groups were constituted so as to include one student from each of the research groups; thus, each member of a learning group had studied a different subset of the topics the class was attempting to cover. One might think of each learning group as a collection of experts on different aspects of the domain of interest or, in terms of the focus of this book, as a distributed-knowledge base. The experts' task was to teach the other members of their learning groups the part of the curriculum they had covered in their research groups.

What especially caught my attention in the reporting of the results of this experiment was the description of the "culture of expertise" that grew up spontaneously in the class. Students developed and pursued different specific interests, became specialists as it were, and, as a consequence, were able to serve as special-knowledge resources for the class as a whole. This is a thought-provoking observation, illustrating, as it does, the fact that knowing something very well – better than anyone else around – puts one in a position to contribute something to the group that no one else can contribute. Society recognizes the value of unique knowledge in a variety of ways. With respect to job opportunities, awareness of the importance of being very knowledgeable with respect to – being very good at – *something* is seen, of course, in the pervasive interest in specialization.

The principle applies beyond the workplace. Being uniquely, or even unusually, knowledgeable about something makes one an "authority," and being an authority on $X$ is being an authority, no matter what $X$ is. Like any other principle, this one can be carried to an unreasonable extreme, and we have the stereotypical specialist who knows all there is to know about some excessively narrow subject and nothing about anything else. This, in my view, is a result that the educational system should attempt to avoid. I believe that the students who are best served by the system are those who emerge with a nontrivial amount of knowledge about many things and truly extensive knowledge about one or a few – a Jack of all trades and master of (at least) one.

## The distribution of intelligence over artifacts and situations

As I type these words, I am aware that not only the mechanics of getting my thoughts on paper but the thought process itself is affected by the nature of the tools I am using and especially their considerable word-processing capabilities. I suspect that most people who use a word-processing system in more than a casual way will acknowledge that such use most likely has an effect on their writing that goes beyond increasing the speed with which ideas can be put into print. Brown et al. note that the hierarchical organization of material that the Macintosh interface provides was reflected in the writing of their grade school subjects, and they surmise that the word-processing tool they used encouraged them to develop hierarchical structures and improved the quality of their writing.

There are many other tools in use today – computer-aided design systems, process schedulers, statistical analysis packages, simulation models, musical composition aids, programs for manipulating symbolic mathematics – that provide invaluable assistance to people engaged in cognitively demanding tasks and that undoubtedly influence the nature of the outcome qualitatively in other ways. Cognitive tools, or tools that augment human intellect, have been a subject of great interest among computer technologists for at least 30 years (Engelbart, 1963; Licklider, 1960), and they are everywhere increasingly in evidence today.

Pea (Chapter 2) notes that many of the electronic tools that are now appearing on the market – jogger pulse meters, automatic street locators, currency exchange calculators – have been designed for the purpose of automating the solving of problems of common interest. Such tools, he suggests, carry patterns of previous reasoning and can be used with little or no awareness of the struggle that went into developing them. He and other contributers make the point also that even much simpler tools than those that have been spawned by the computer industry, as well as artifacts more generally, can facilitate cognitive aspects of the tasks for which they are employed. They note that the environments in which we live are full of artifacts that we use constantly, sometimes relatively automatically, to reduce the amount of mental effort we have to expend to accomplish specific goals. Cole and Engeström use the term "artifact-mediated activity" to convey the general notion.

I find these observations very compelling. Unquestionably, many of the activities in which we engage would be impossible without the artifacts that mediate them. Representing thoughts on paper would not be possible without the paper, some implement that can be used to make marks on it, a language, and a scheme for representing visually the thoughts that can be expressed within it. But this does not, in my view, diminish the importance of the traditional idea of intelligence as a property of the individual. I may say that the intelligence needed to solve a particular problem is distributed over human problem solvers and the tools and situational factors without which they would be unable to reach solutions. But if I do, I will want to distinguish, in some way, the intelligence that the human being brings to a situation from that which resides in the tools and the situation itself. And I shall certainly be led to wonder about intelligence of the first kind when I notice that one individual solves a problem whereas another, in the same situation and with the same tools at hand, does not.

I do not mean to deny by these remarks that artifacts can be given abilities that are cognitive or cognitive-like, because I believe they can, although I am far from persuaded that a machine knowing $X$ and John Doe knowing $X$ amount to the same thing. In this regard, and a propos the comments in the preceding section regarding social consequences of the distribution of knowledge, it is interesting to speculate on what the consequences might be if the researchers and technologists who are working on the development of computer-based expert systems ever are successful in building systems that can provide truly expert consultation to the general public on matters for which we currently pay professionals for their advice. Who will want to be a medical diagnostician when the world is populated with machines that are demonstrably more reliable than human experts in figuring out the causes of physical ailments and prescribing effective treatments, and that will do so at nominal cost?

I am not suggesting that success in the development of truly expert systems in specific domains, should such success occur, will leave no cognitive work for human beings to do. But I do mean to suggest that the existence and wide availability of such systems could change significantly the economic implications of the way domain-specific knowledge is distributed among specialists and redefine the purposes that human experts can best serve. It could also affect our views about what constitutes a good general education; about the kinds of knowledge a well-informed citizenry should possess; about the roles that people, machines, and people–machine combinations can play in the performance of intellectually demanding tasks, and about how knowledge is best stored for future access and use.

Although the current intellectual abilities of machines have often been overstated and expected near-future accomplishments of artificial intelligence have sometimes been expressed in hyperbolic terms, there can be little doubt that machines are acquiring more and more capabilities of a cognitive sort. It seems to me inevitable that, in *some* sense of "knowledgeable," machines will become more knowledgeable than people in many areas. How machine knowledge will differ from human knowledge and how it can best be used to complement human knowledge to humane ends are extremely important questions for research and reflection. Knowledge is going to be distributed in quite different ways in the future than it has been in the past, and I do not think we have a very clear understanding of the implications of this fact.

## Knowledge accumulation

Several contributors to this volume refer to the fact that cultures accumulate knowledge over time and that, as a consequence, new knowledge that is acquired by one generation becomes available to succeeding ones. Or said the other way around, every generation inherits the accumulated knowledge of all preceding generations.

This is possible, in part, because of the uniquely human trick of representing information with symbols that can be recorded on relatively permanent media. Also, as Pea points out, much of what is learned by one generation is passed on to succeeding generations in the form of artifacts, conventions, and practices. The history of toolmaking is a treasury of examples of how discoveries of new and ever more effective ways to facilitate the realization of desired objectives have been preserved for posterity in tangible form.

Any generation that refused to avail itself of this munificent inheritance – were that possible – would pay a dear price indeed. It seems to me that in emphasizing the effectiveness of discovery learning – as many educational researchers do, and rightfully, I think – it is essential not to lose sight of the fact that not everything we need to know can be discovered anew by every learner and not to discount, even implicitly, the enormous advantage that being able to appropriate for ourselves knowledge that others have discovered gives us as a species and as individuals. Discovery learning is good and useful as far as it goes, but it does not go far enough.

The fact that the knowledge developed by science is cumulative also makes clear the role of culture in perpetuating the scientific enterprise and ensuring the continuing cumulative nature of its discoveries. Scientific advances are the products of the times in which they are made as well as of the individual scientists who generally are credited with making them. Most scientific work is focused very sharply on ideas that are prevalent among scientific communities at the time, and their exploration makes use of the instruments and techniques that are then available. Even the major new directions in thinking that Kuhn (1970) has described as paradigm shifts, and Kuhn and others (e.g., Boorstin, 1985; Cohen, 1985) have more commonly referred to as revolutions, are constrained by the knowledge, investigative techniques, and attitudes prevailing among scientists of the day.

Einstein's theory of relativity could not have been advanced in the sixteenth century, or probably even in the eighteenth. It could have been advanced without Einstein in the twentieth. Whether it would have been, at least in the precise form in which he expressed it, is a question to which we will never know the answer, thanks to the fact that Einstein happened to appear on the scene when he did. This is not to deny the brilliance of Einstein's work, but simply to note that the theoretical advances for which we remember him were as much products of the work and theorizing on which he built as of his own thinking. Einstein explicitly acknowledged the impossibility of conceiving the theory of relativity without the benefit of the discoveries of the great men of physics that had preceded him (Holton, 1981).

Cohen (1985), who has written extensively on what constitutes revolution in science, describes the continuity of scientific progress the following way:

In science, absolute newness tends not to be a defining feature of revolutions. Most (if not all) revolutions exhibit features of continuity so that even the most radical ideas in science prove again and again to be mere transformations of existing traditional ideas. . . . This is so characteristic a feature of science that some scientists, such as Albert Einstein, have ended up by conceiving their own work to exhibit evolution rather than revolution; a radical transformation and restructuring of what is known or believed rather than the invention of something new.

It is important to recognize that what Cohen describes is the rule and not the exception. Discoveries or theoretical advances in science that are completely new and unanticipated by the work of any of the predecessors of the scientists who make them are extremely rare, if they occur at all. Copernicus, Newton, Darwin, Mendeleev were giants who revolutionized thinking about some aspect of the world, but none of them did it in a vacuum. What could be more different from the theory of Ptolemy than that of Copernicus? Yet Boorstin (1985), in his masterful and engaging history of discovery, described Copernicus's debt to Ptolemy this way: "The modern advance to Copernicus' heliocentric system would be hard to imagine if the geocentric system had not been there for revision. Copernicus would not change the shape of the system, he simply changed the location of the bodies" (p. 295).

### Individual versus corporate goals

A topic that Cole and Engeström mention that I would like to comment on is the division of labor and the desirability, after Leont'ev, of distinguishing between individual goal-directed actions and collective activity. We hear much today about the problem in industry of workers whose jobs are so narrowly focused that they cannot identify with, and consequently take no pride in, or responsibility for the quality of, their product as a whole. In recent years various industries have attempted to address this problem by giving individual workers more scope, by making small teams responsible for the beginning-to-end assembly of products that will bear their stamp of approval when completed, and in a variety of other ways.

The distinction between individual goal-directed actions and collective activity is an important one relative to the problems of industrial productivity and product quality. Whenever the goals of a corporation and those of the corporation's employees are incompatible, the corporation's performance suffers. Members of a corporate entity are not likely to work for the good of that body unless they believe it to be in their individual best interest to do so. This fact has been characterized by Hardin (1968) as the "tragedy of the commons."

It is important to note that in order for individual goal-directed actions to further the goals of a corporation to which an individual belongs, it is not necessary that the individual's goals be identical with those of the corporation. It is not essential, in other words, for individuals to adopt the corporation's goals for their own. What is necessary is that the relationship between the individual's goals and those of the corporation be such that when individuals work to achieve their own goals they will in fact, albeit perhaps incidentally from their point of view, be furthering the goals of the corporation as well. Any corporation that does not recognize this fundamental fact is bound to have problems with productivity and quality control. Trying to convince employees to put out extra effort for the benefit of the company is futile unless they see how that effort furthers their own goals.

A question that arises from the distinction between individual goal-directed actions and collective activity – whether the collective is a corporation or other multiperson entity – is whether the collective activity should be thought of as anything more than the totality of the individual actions. This is another variant of the old and much-debated question of whether the whole is more than the sum of its parts. It is expedient to speak of the behavior of corporations, of political parties, of government agencies, of civic groups, of nations. Is this just a convenient way of referring to the totality of the behaviors of the individuals who comprise these groups, or do we mean to impute to such entities action possibilities that are somehow more than the composite of the actions of their members?

David Perkins (personal communication) has reminded me that, at least from a legal point of view, corporations, towns, nations, and various other collective entities are not equated with the individuals that comprise them. A corporation, for example, is bound by its contracts, not the individuals within it; the individuals may change but the contractual obligations remain with the corporate entity. I suspect it is useful to think of groups as being more than the sum of the individuals that comprise them in a psychological sense as well. Individuals whose knowledge and skills are complementary should be able to accomplish things in collaboration that they could not do working as individuals. The psychology of groups is a topic that has received a great deal of attention; the current interest in distributed cognition may bring some new questions and perspectives to this area of research.

### Personal, local, and cultural contributions to cognition

Hatch and Gardner (Chapter 6) argue that terms such as "cognition" and "intelligence" should be sufficiently broadly defined to include the conditions under which problems are discovered and solved and within which skills are developed. They identify three kinds of forces – personal, local, and cultural – that can contribute both to what people do and to what they are capable of doing in the classroom. From this it follows, they suggest, that it makes no sense to consider specific skills an individual may or may not have without taking into account the conditions that allow those skills to be expressed.

Personal forces are the attributes and experiences of individuals that they carry with them from one local situation to another. Local forces include "resources and people who directly affect the behavior of an individual within a specific 'local' setting" such as the home, the classroom, or the workplace. Local forces also include the tools and materials with which people express their skills. "At the local level, intelligence cannot be separated from the particular conditions in which it is used. Problem-solving behaviors that are effective in one local setting may not apply or may not be produced in others." Cultural forces include schooling, child-rearing practices, language practices, and other "institutions, practices, and beliefs that transcend particular settings and affect a large number of people."

These different forces are seen as interdependent and not isolable, although their relative influence may differ from individual to individual and may shift for an individual over time. A very important point is that "personal, local and cultural forces often push in different directions," and the development of a child's potential can be severely constrained when the child excels, or has the ability to excel, in activities not valued by the culture in which the child is raised.

Hatch and Gardner devote most of their chapter to a discussion of how the three forces influenced the classroom activities of four kindergartners during "free play" over a period of several months. They describe, clearly and convincingly, many ways in which the behavior of the children was enabled or constrained by the conditions prevailing at the activity sites where the behavior took place, and how the behavior changed in response to changes in those conditions.

They note, for example, how the addition of water at a sand table altered the activities at that site.

The distinction among interdependent forces affecting cognition seems to me useful and intuitively reasonable. I find it easy to believe both in their existence and in their importance in helping determine what skills can be learned and how they can be displayed. And Hatch and Gardner's account of the activities of the children in their study is a compelling illustration of situational constraints on behavior. I balk, however, at the observation that the children's skills were "literally embedded in the sand." Hatch and Gardner argue that "if skills are simply contained in children's heads, the emergence of a limited set of activities and the sharing of skills at the sand table is difficult to explain."

An alternative way of looking at the situation, it seems to me, is to consider the children's skills to be contained in their heads (and hands) and the constraints on how those skills can be expressed to be embedded in the sand. To say that the skills themselves are embedded in the sand seems unhelpful. I would argue, as before, that if one wants to say that some cognitive capability is distributed over people and situations, one is likely to find it essential or at least convenient to make a distinction between what the individual brings to the situation and what the situation provides; referring to both with the same term can be confusing.

### Funds of knowledge in households and classrooms

Moll, Tapia, and Whitmore (Chapter 5) present case-study data to illustrate (1) that the behavior of household members must be understood in relation to the broad historical and economic contexts in which the households are embedded that tend to constrain and shape, although not completely determine, that behavior, and (2) that the social arrangement of a classroom helps determine how and why students acquire knowledge.

Households and classrooms are seen as "culturally mediated systems of knowledge." "Funds of knowledge" is put forth as a key concept in understanding the dynamics of both situations. With respect to households, this term refers to the reservoir of knowledge and other resources that households contribute to and from which they draw through the social networks in which the households exist and by which they are interconnected. A propos the general theme of this book, it is important to note that funds of knowledge are distributed throughout the networks and not collected in central repositories. The knowledge that is contained in these funds is of a practical sort: how to find housing and jobs, how to get better buys on goods and services, and how to deal with government agencies and other institutions.

In illustrating the applicability of the funds-of-knowledge concept to the classroom, Moll, Tapia, and Whitmore describe the interactions among the members of a third-grade literature study group within a bilingual classroom that is part of a magnet school. The children in this study group had quite different home situations and cultural backgrounds (specific background information is given for three of them). Members of the group read the same books and then discussed them in class. The applicability of the funds-of-knowledge concept is seen in this context in the way children shared in their classroom discussions knowledge they had acquired as a consequence of their home and cultural backgrounds, and the operation of social factors in classroom learning is revealed in the various roles that children (and teachers) play in providing cognitive resources to one another.

Home and school are surely among the most significant factors shaping the cognitive development of children, and their influence is exerted concurrently and continuously over many of a child's formative years. It seems highly unlikely that we can understand the role of either of these factors completely without considering the role of the other and of the ways in which they interact. Studying households and classrooms simultaneously, as Moll, Tapia, and Whitmore have done, seems to me an eminently good idea.

## Apprenticeship in learning and scholarship

As an alternative to the idea that schools should attempt to usher students into the culture of mathematicians, historians, and literary critics, Brown et al. (Chapter 7) argue that they should strive to be communities of learning and self-motivated scholarship. The goal with respect to students, in their view, should be to give them the ability – and presumably the desire – to continue to learn after leaving school and for the remainder of their lives. Teachers, they suggest, should be, first and foremost, competent learners, not only "owners of domain knowledge" but "acquirers, users, and extenders of knowledge in the sustained, ongoing process of learning." Students then would be able to serve apprenticeships in learning and scholarship, which is the kind of apprenticeship opportunity schools should provide.

I find this view very compatible with my own belief that schools have a responsibility to attempt to ensure that students leave with a considerable amount of domain knowledge, the capacity and disposition to think, and the ability and desire to continue to learn (Nickerson, 1988). None of the contributers to this book, I suspect, would be likely to take exception to the idea that schools should attempt to produce people who can think and learn. There might be some differences of opinion, however, as to how much emphasis should be placed on the teaching/learning of domain knowledge.

I can only state my own belief that domain knowledge is as deserving of emphasis as are thinking and learning, though not more so. With respect to these objectives, I see education as a three-legged stool; remove any one of its legs and the whole thing falls over. The acquisition of domain knowledge is what can make education an exciting quest; without it, thinking is vacuous and learning would seem to have no point. Of course, teaching domain knowledge as disconnected facts to be memorized but not thought about is not education, but everyone agrees on that.

### Knowing more than is in one's head

Perkins (Chapter 3) proposes a way of viewing learning that considers not only what students retain in their heads but what they store in notebooks or other memory repositories. What is learned "lingers not just in the mind of the learner, but in the arrangement of the surround [the immediate physical and social resources outside of the person] as well, and it is just as genuinely learning for all that."

I like this view, with certain qualifications that I believe are consistent with what Perkins has said. When I read a book that is relevant to some topic about which I am thinking, or perhaps writing, I mark sections that I find particularly thought-provoking and that I may want to reread and ponder or use at a later time. (I buy books I want to read carefully – rather than borrow them from the library – because I find it almost impossible to read without a pen in hand.) I make no effort to commit the substance of these sections to memory, or even necessarily to remember where they are located.

Having finished a book, I may be able to recall a few specific points that I found particularly interesting or useful. Of far greater importance to me, however, is the fact that I usually have a definite opinion as to whether I am going to want to return to the book at an opportune time, and I know that if I do so the sections that I found most interesting will be relatively easy to access. Now, have I *learned* what is in the marked sections of my books? If you asked me to tell you what they are, I could do so only in a tiny fraction of the cases. But they have affected my thinking, and they will be familiar when I reread them; and I consider them to be among the most important of the intellectual resources on which I intend to draw.

Many writers have the habit of jotting down ideas, often in incomplete and rough form, when they occur to them and filing them away for possible future reference. Some students of writing think this is a commendable habit (Howard & Barton, 1986). I suspect it is not uncommon for one to recall that one has written something on a particular topic sometime in the past, *not* recall precisely *what* one wrote, and yet feel fairly confident that it would be useful for a current purpose, if only it could be found. Presumably well-organized people have less difficulty than the rest of us in locating such notes when they are needed, and for them, at least, they constitute a valuable resource for cognitive work.

In this case it does not seem strange to think of one's notes as part of one's cognitive property inasmuch as they are the products of one's mind; however, because people may not be able to reconstruct ideas that they have articulated in the past, the situation is not unlike the one described by Perkins in which the notes in question are those produced by a student in the course of studying a particular subject. In neither case is the fact that one once wrote something down good evidence that it still exists "in one's mind."

Whether one's notes, marked-up books, and other information repositories are appropriately thought of as extensions of one's memory should depend, it seems to me, on how readily one can access the information in them when it is needed. If I have written some notes on a topic of interest but can neither find them nor recall what is in them – or, worse yet, do not even recall that they exist – they are useless to me and add nothing to what is in my head; however, if I know where the notes I have written are, or at least how to go about finding them, and I remember enough about their contents to know when it makes sense to retrieve them, they are an intellectual asset with the capacity to remind me of what I once thought and might want to think again. I am inclined to view them as at least as much a part of what I know, or think I know, as some of the stuff that may be in my head, but harder to retrieve. Perkins says essentially this, I think, in asserting that the functional criterion should be the information's accessibility, not its location.

### Information accessibility

Surely everyone will agree that sometimes it is important to have information immediately available in one's head and sometimes it is not. If I had to look up in the dictionary the meaning of most of the words I need to get this chapter written, I would be in bad shape; but I do not feel remiss in not having memorized a table of logarithms in order to have such information available in my head even though it has proved to be useful on occasion.

I suspect there is a law of memory according to which we tend to store information in our heads that we need relatively frequently and that is relatively difficult to access from an external store or to infer. Stated slightly differently, we are the more likely to commit something to memory the more important it is to us and the greater the effort involved in accessing it from other repositories. This is a very imprecise law, but plausible as a general principle, I think.

I memorize a few telephone numbers that I use fairly often, but am content to consult the phone directory for the vast majority of those I use only occasionally. It is, of course, no more difficult to look up one phone number than another, but by memorizing those numbers I use most often, I save myself a little trouble many times over. One might argue that the memorization of the frequently used numbers is not a matter of an intentional strategy but automatically occurs simply as a consequence of their frequent use. I believe that is true, modulo two caveats. First, frequent use, if it is to be invoked as a cause of commitment to memory, must involve more than "frequent exposure to." Frequent exposure to something does not suffice to ensure that what one is exposed to will necessarily be remembered in any detail (Nickerson & Adams, 1980). When making a phone call, one really must pay attention to the number one is dialing, at least for a short time, in order to complete the call. One need never pay attention to the details on the face of a coin in order to use it for the intended purpose, and consequently, despite frequent exposure to coins, we remember their details quite poorly.

Second, the "law," as stated, makes no reference to intention; it simply states a dependency of what is stored in memory on frequency of need and difficulty of access from places other than memory. I do believe the general principle makes sense, however, when applied to what we intentionally commit to memory as well as to what gets deposited there automatically. I am much more likely to put effort into storing information I expect to use frequently, especially if it is hard to get from some readily accessible source when it is needed, than into trying to remember what I expect to use very seldom or what is always available from some handy place other than my head. I have not made a great effort to memorize the twenty-odd birthdates in my immediate family of parents, children, children's spouses, and grandchildren because my wife knows them cold. It seems a waste of my limited resources to store birthdates that she has so readily at hand and is willing to make available to me; I do make a point, however, to rely on myself to remember hers.

This simple principle may go some distance in accounting for the types of information or knowledge people have built into tools and other artifacts over the centuries. I have a small collection of antique woodworking tools and, because of this interest, attend antique tool auctions from time to time. Two things have struck me about what I see there: the enormous variety of designs – one can look at hundreds of old planes without seeing precisely the same thing twice – and the fact that the vast majority of implements fall into a few categories representing the most common operations that had to be performed in woodworking – measuring, cutting, shaping, pounding, drilling, smoothing. Occasionally a tool turns up that no one can identify. One can be sure that it was used to do something that seldom had to be done; any frequently required operation spawned an amazingly wide assortment of implements with which that operation could be performed.

### Information access and education

The idea that, for practical purposes, what is important about information is that it be accessible when one needs it, and not whether it happens to be stored in one's head or in some other convenient place, has a number of important implications for education. I will mention what I see as the most obvious one, namely the implication that students must learn to use information resources effectively. Such resources include indexes, atlases, reference books, calculators, computers, schedules and timetables, and electronic information services of various sorts.

One can imagine a course built around the theme "finding information" or, better yet, instruction distributed throughout the curriculum that gives students guided experience in using an extensive range of tools to find specific items of information that may be useful for academic purposes or in everyday life or that may simply be of intellectual interest. The emphasis should not be on finding particular items of information specified by the teacher but on learning to use information-finding tools, resources, and strategies that will be effective in helping one find needed or desired information in one's postschool life. It may be that schools do explicitly teach students how to use information-finding tools; it is hard to believe that they do not. Yet not much attention is paid to this topic in the literature, so one assumes that it is not a high-priority focus. I do not remember ever being told, during my own school experience, what an index is, let alone how to use one effectively.

What I have said about information-finding tools applies as well, I believe, to external memory aids. Students need to know, for example, how to take notes, how to represent and organize information so it will be easy to access and use at a future time, how to construct a database tailored to their individual needs and interests. One wonders how many schools make some effort to teach students how to take notes, as opposed to encouraging them to take them and leaving them to learn how to do so on their own.

Memory aids span a very considerable range with respect to complexity and power. When I enlist my finger and a piece of string to help my head do something that I am not willing to trust it to do by itself, I am using a very simple memory aid the effectiveness of which has been proved many times. At the other end of the spectrum are a variety of computer-based tools that make possible the representation of information in multidimensional structures that we do not yet know how to exploit very well. The question of how to organize information to facilitate future reference is taking on new significance with the emergence of such tools. I believe that students who learn to use these tools effectively, and others like them that will continue to appear, are acquiring knowledge and skills that will serve them well in the future.

I have argued elsewhere (Nickerson, 1986) that one of the most exciting aspects of the revolutionary developments in information technology (computer and communication technologies in combination) that we have been witnessing and that are still going on is the prospect of making information of all kinds much more readily available to anyone who has a need or desire for it. The print technology that was developed in Europe beginning in the fifteenth century increased the accessibility of information to the average person manyfold and resulted in knowledge becoming distributed far more widely than it had been distributed before that time. No one can doubt that this was a major causal factor in the momentous changes that occurred during the Renaissance period and, in particular, in the explosion of new knowledge that came with the emergence of modern science and the empowerment of scholarship of all types.

What is happening in information technology holds the promise, in my view, of effecting another very substantial increase in information accessibility that could have consequences at least as dramatic as those resulting from the development of the capability of making inexpensive books. By "accessibility" here, I mean more than simply the electronic equivalent of transporting one to the Library of Congress and depositing one inside the door. I mean ready "cognitive access" to the information one needs when one needs it, represented in a form in which one can understand and use it. This kind of access does not yet exist, at least on any broad scale, but the technologies from which it could emerge do, and realization of it is one of the major challenges and opportunities that information technologists have today. The years ahead will see the development of increasingly powerful tools for finding, representing, and using information; people who learn to use such tools effectively will have at their disposal a much more comprehensive distributed-knowledge system than those who do not.

One might ask at this point: If information does indeed become much more accessible in the future than it is now, will learning still be necessary? If answers to questions can be obtained much more readily through new information resources, will it be so important to have knowledge in one's head? I believe the answer is unequivocally yes. I believe this for several reasons, but it will suffice to mention one. The asking of questions, except of the most superficial kind, is a knowledge-based activity. Only someone who knows quite a bit about biology is going to ask what is new in the sequencing of bases in the DNA molecule. And even if one were able to ask the question, say because one got it from someone else already formed, without some knowledge of the subject one would not understand the answer.

In general, the more one knows, the more useful a powerful information-finding resource is likely to be. This does not mean that such resources will be of no use to people who are not well informed to begin with; it means only that people who are well informed will be able to use them at a different level than will those who are not. Fortunately, such resources should facilitate learning; they should make it considerably easier for one to acquire the knowledge that is needed to function as an expert.

### Seeing what one looks for

Early in Chapter 4, Salomon makes what strikes me as an especially important point. To structure a discussion of whether we can afford to leave conceptions of individuals' cognitions out of a theory of distributed cognition, he raises four questions: "(a) How distributed are people's cognitions in daily life? (b) Are there cognitions that cannot be distributed and thus, by their very nature, are in the individual's territory? (c) Can we make do in our theoretical formulations without reference to individuals' mental representations? (d) Can the development of joint distributed systems be accounted for satisfactorily without consideration of how the individual partners develop?"

The important point that Salomon makes is that these questions cannot be answered empirically but that the answers one accepts, as *a priori* assumptions, determine the kinds of research questions one will ask.

The view that the thinking and experimentation of scientists as a group are far more influenced by presuppositions and *a priori* perspectives than is generally recognized has been advanced by a number of historians of science, notably Kuhn (1970), Holton (1973), and Popper (1962/1981). Popper, for example, argues that the widely held belief that science can begin with pure observations uninfluenced by any theory is absurd. All observation, he contends, is selective and is made from the vantage point of a particular frame of reference. What scientists see depends a great deal on what they are looking for.

Salomon, if I understand him correctly, is applying essentially this argument to the problem of doing research on the relative importance of individuals' and distributed cognition: What one learns depends on what kinds of situations one investigates, and what kinds of situations one investigates is determined, to no small degree, by one's presuppositions about where one will find something of interest if one looks. Applied broadly, this argument can help account for many of the theoretical debates in psychology (but not only there) that occupy some collection of researchers for a time and then gradually disappear, unresolved, into the archives.

### Either–or versus both–and

We seem to be creatures of extremes. We persist in seeing everything in either–or terms. In education, we contrast discovery learning with rote memorization, exploration with instruction, knowledge construction with information assimilation, domain knowledge with the ability to think, and we talk as though the student, the teacher, the system – whoever is in a position to make choices – must always choose one or the other. There is little middle ground, little recognition of the possibility that an effective educational process should include more than one mode or objective of learning or teaching. The theme of this book relates to another distinction – in this case between individual and distributed cognition – that seems to invite such dichotomous treatment.

Fortunately, in my view, several contributors argue against seeing this distinction in either–or terms. Salomon begins his chapter on a cautionary note with the observation that, while the idea of distributed cognition is novel and provocative, it can be carried too far. The concern he expresses is that the new look, in its emphasis on situational, social, and cultural variables, has gone to the extreme of removing the individual from the picture altogether. He goes on to make a case for viewing individual and distributed cognitions as interacting and mutually supportive aspects of cognitive performance and learning, and argues that neither aspect can be understood without consideration of how it relates to the other. In discussing each of the questions he raises, Salomon gives reasons why individuals' cognition must be taken into account in any adequate theory of distributed cognition.

In a similar spirit, Moll, Tapia, and Whitmore emphasize that recognizing the importance of the "mediational role of social relations" for an understanding of human activity does not require denying that the interests and activities of the individual are also critical to thinking and learning. It is not a question, they argue, of either "person-solo" or "person-plus," but rather a matter of recognizing the inseparability of persons and their social worlds. Hatch and Gardner, while stressing the interdependence and nonisolability of personal, local, and cultural forces contributing to cognition, also recognize the importance of each of them.

The plea in all of these cases, as I see it, is for recognition of the legitimacy of both the idea of distributed cognition and that of the individual mind. This is a plea, if I have it right, that deserves, in my view, a positive response. There can be little doubt of the importance of cultural, social, and situational variables as determinants of cognitive performance. Nor can we fail to acknowledge that what people can do on cognitively demanding tasks is influenced greatly by the nature of the tools and artifacts at their disposal. Probably it is not possible to understand an individual's behavior without understanding the context – goals, tools, other participants – in which it occurs. But it does not follow that what individuals bring, in their heads, to the problems on which they work is of no consequence, or that there are no questions worth asking about the cognitive capabilities that individuals possess.

## References

Boorstin, D. J. (1985). *The discoverers: A history of man's search to know his world and himself.* New York: Vintage Books.

Cohen, I. B. (1985). *Revolution in science.* Cambridge, MA: Harvard University Press.

Engelbart, D. C. (1963). A conceptual framework for the augmentation of man's intellect. In P. W. Howerton & D. C. Weeks (Eds.), *Vistas in information handling* (Vol. 1, pp. 1–29). Washington, DC: Spartan Books.

Goldman, A. I. (1986). *Epistemology and cognition.* Cambridge, MA: Harvard University Press.

Hardin, G. (1968). The tragedy of the commons. *Science, 162,* 1243–8.

Holton, G. (1973). *Thematic origins of scientific thought.* Cambridge, MA: Harvard University Press.

(1981). Einstein's search for the Weltbild. *Proceedings of the American Philosophical Society, 125,* 1–15.

Howard, V. A., & Barton, J. H. (1986). *Thinking on paper.* New York: Morrow.

Kuhn, T. S. (1970). *The structure of scientific revolutions* (2d ed.). Chicago: University of Chicago Press.

Licklider, J. C. R. (1960). Man–computer symbiosis. *Institute of Radio Engineers Transactions on Human Factors Electronics, HFE-1,* 4–11.

Nickerson, R. S. (1986). *Using computers: Human factors in information systems.* Cambridge, MA: MIT Press.

(1988). Technology in education in 2020: Thinking about the not-distant future. In R. S. Nickerson & P. P. Zodhiates (Eds.), *Technology in education: Looking toward 2020* (pp. 1–9). Hillsdale, NJ: Erlbaum.

Nickerson, R. S., & Adams, M. J. (1980). Long-term memory for a common object. *Cognitive Psychology, 11,* 287–307.

Popper, K. (1981). The myth of inductive hypothesis generation. In R. D. Tweney, M. E. Doherty, & C. R. Mynatt (Eds.), *On Scientific thinking* (pp. 72–6). New York: Columbia University Press. (Originally published 1962.)

Thomas, L. (1979). *The medusa and the snail: More notes of a biology watcher.* New York: Viking Press.

Ulam, S. (1976). *Adventures of a mathematician.* New York: Scribner.

# Index

access framework, 91–3
accessibility
  commentary on, 254–8
  dependence of learning on, 90
  framework for, 90–3
  information technology in, 256–8
  trade-off with understanding, 74–6, 90
accessible facts, 240
accommodation, 106
accountability, 217
accumulated knowledge, 245–7
action constraints, 48
action mediators, and intelligence, 49
activity system
  as basic unit of analysis, 8–9, 49n1
  compartmental organization effect, 33
  design in, 80–1
  developmental role, 79
  and distributed intelligence, 49–51
  expansive cycles, 40–2
  externalization–internalization, 40–1
  institutionalization of, 8–9
  means–ends adaptations, 50–1
  in mediational triangle, 7–8
  outer-directedness, 159
  in reading acquisition, 24–30
  reciprocal influences, 122–8
  workplace setting, transition, 30–42
Adams, M. J., 255
affordances, 51–4
  in artwork, classroom, 180
  in classroom learning, 176–7
  and concentric model of intelligence, 169, 176
  definition, 51

and distributed intelligence, 51–4, 169
  in inscriptional systems, 62
Agre, P., 54n3
Alexander, C., 80
algebra equations, 62–3
Allen, C., 55
Allen, S., 61
Altman, I., 120, 121, 122, 134
Amanti, C., 160
amplification of intellect, 81, 89
analogy, and reciprocal teaching, 195
analytic approach, 77–8
anchored instruction, 66
Anderson, R. C., 22
ANOVA model, 127
anthropology
  contribution of, 12–13
  and Mexican household study, 139
applied psychology, 3
apprentice learners, 190–1
apprenticing
  authentic activity in, 189, 222–3
  commentary on, 251–2
  in community of learners, 190–1, 251–2
  and intentional learning, 223
  in problem solving, 67, 69
appropriation, *see* mutual appropriation
Arcavi, A., 192
architects, 80
arithmetic skills, 100
Arney, W. R., 31
Aronson, E., 195, 197
artifact mediation
  affordances in, 51–4
  in classroom, 188–225

263

Printed in the United States
26292LVS00004B/1-18

9 780521 574235